CORTICAL VISUAL IMPAIRMENT

An Approach to Assessment and Intervention

Christine Roman-Lantzy

American Foundation for the Blind

Printed in the United States of America

2008 reprint

Library of Congress Cataloging-in-Publication Data

Roman-Lantzy, Christine, 1951-
Cortical visual impairment : an approach to assessment and intervention / Christine Roman-Lantzy.
    p. cm.
    Includes bibliographical references and index.
    ISBN 978-0-89128-829-9 (pbk. : alk. paper) — ISBN 978-0-89128-830-5 (ascii disk) 1. Children with visual disabilities—Education. 2. Children with visual disabilities—Rehabilitation. 3. Children with visual disabilities—Services for—United States. I. Title.

HV1626.R67 2007
362.4'18—dc22   2007021828

Color Photo Credits: Christine Roman-Lantzy: Photos 1, 2, 3, 4, 6, 7, 8, 9, 11, 12, 13, 14, 15, 17, 20, 21, 22, 24; Wance Kwan, Photos 10, 16, 19, 23, 25. Photo 5: Hidden Pictures® "Feeding Time," by Chuck Galey, February 2006. Used by permission of Highlights for Children, Inc., Columbus, Ohio. Copyrighted material. Adaptations in Photo 18 by John Costello, Boston Children's Hospital. Picture Communication Symbols © 1981–2007, Mayer-Johnson LLC. All Rights Reserved Worldwide. Used with permission.

The American Foundation for the Blind—the organization to which Helen Keller devoted her life—is a national nonprofit devoted to expanding the possibilities for people with vision loss.

Dedication

If the journey is more important than the destination, I can say that writing this book has been quite a trip. I must thank some people who provided aid and nourishment along the way. First, I thank my husband, Alan Lantzy for never letting me give up and for helping me navigate from the beginning to the end of this adventure. Thanks, too, for the tremendous support relating to the medical causes of CVI. You are my compass.

Thanks to my children who are the reason I am most proud. Zak and Hillary, I thank you for all the conversations about my work and specifically this book. You helped me find clarity and encouraged me to keep the destination in sight. Erin and Josh, you, too, listened to talk of what after a while must have seemed like a phantom book. Thanks Hillary and Erin for the clerical help that came when I needed your presence more than the typing.

I also want to thank the parents of the children I have been privileged to work with. You are the reason I do this work. I cannot imagine what it is like to walk in your shoes but I deeply respect the places you visit on your own, more difficult journey. If my work with you has provided some small degree of hope or help, then my efforts have been a success.

Contents

Foreword

Cortical Visual Impairment: An Approach to Assessment and Intervention, by Christine Roman-Lantzy, is a historic first in the literature of the field of blindness and visual impairment. This long-awaited publication spells out in detail a thoughtful, structured, and sequenced approach to interventive work with children diagnosed with cortical visual impairment (CVI). Heretofore, the diagnosis of CVI—in fact, the name of the condition, assessment techniques, and interventions to address it—has been framed in controversy from the very first time that a child's visual problems were identified with the visual pathways and processing centers of the brain rather than with the ocular structures of the eye. In the past, children experiencing this condition have often been excluded from the caseloads of professionals in the blindness field because they were seen as children with brain damage and left to those professionals trained to work with neurological impairments. Unfortunately, as in so many similar situations—the case of children who are deaf-blind, for example—these children have fallen through the cracks of the special education system, being ignored both by teachers of children with visual impairments and by those working with children with brain damage. Once again, however, our field has stepped forward to include rather than exclude children from services provided by professionals expert in serving students who are blind or visually impaired. The controversy is far from over, and accepting that vision is not a fixed entity but rather a capacity in the brain that can be developed remains an issue for many.

The primary contributing factor to the incidence of CVI in developed countries, such as the United States, is the survival of very low birth weight babies born prematurely, attributable to medical advances in areas such as neonatology. Medical success has resulted in growing numbers of neurologically affected infants and children. At this time the leading cause of blindness in young children, as noted by the American Printing House for the Blind, keeper of a national census of young blind and visually impaired children in this country, is CVI.

Published data and systematic documentation relating to CVI and its effects have been relatively sparse to this date, and intervention strategies have been varied and lacking in a systematic structure. In the present publication, for the first time, ten visual behaviors or characteristics relating to CVI are explained in detail, in an organized and logical way, and offered as the backbone for an assessment process. Guiding principles for program planning and intervention—precision, intentionality, reciprocity, expectation for change, and attention to the total environment—are also explained.

CVI is discussed as a condition in which improvement in vision is not only possible but likely. A major point made by Dr. Roman-Lantzy is that the intervener should always question what might have changed in the environment to understand a student's apparently inconsistent visual behavior, rather than what might have changed in the child. Other important aspects of intervention are the necessity of waiting for a response in the presence of latency in visual responses and the need for specialized and controlled sensory inputs. The process of learning to use vision is in many respects different for most children with CVI than it is for children with ocular impairments, and professionals working with children with CVI will find many invaluable insights in the following pages.

Parents of children with CVI have called on educators and other professionals to take action on behalf of their children, demanding a sense of urgency and advocating for early intervention. Because of the plasticity of the brain and its development, timing is of the essence—the earlier the better—for the receipt of educational and other services.

Those of us concerned about the education of children with visual and other impairments know that the educational team typically consists of parents, classroom teachers, teachers of students with visual impairments, occupational and physical therapists, and orientation and mobility instructors. This critical team approach is successful if everyone is in agreement about the level of functional vision the student has acquired and the appropriate intervention strategies to be used. This book addresses the issues inherent in team collaboration, pointing out the need to use observation, to chart behaviors in order to document the presence or absence of CVI-related characteristics, and to identify which characteristics are affecting the student's ability to use vision.

Dr. Roman-Lantzy has developed a number of helpful processes and charts to support this work, such as the CVI Range, which can be used to determine the child's level of functional vision and the overall impact of CVI; the CVI Resolution Chart, which can be used to record data collected and to serve as a way to map progress and monitor effects of CVI; and the IFSP/IEP Intervention Planning Worksheet, which enables the team to share information and act with consistency when implementing interventions.

The consistent, ongoing data collection not only serves the child with CVI but also allows professionals in the field of blindness and visual impairment to gain a better understanding of the characteristics related to CVI and the effectiveness of intervention strategies over time. This approach will support the development of a new base of information on the causes of CVI and interventions that are effective when working with this condition.

I consider *Cortical Visual Impairment: An Approach to Assessment and Intervention*, the work of Dr. Roman-Lantzy, to be a landmark piece of literature in that it is pragmatically based on experience and for the first time puts consistent, concrete tools in the hands of educational team members. It is time to put away our differences, including the controversy over designations such as cortical or cerebral visual impairment. We need to get on to the more important work of educating children. This book facilitates the achievement of that critical goal.

Susan Jay Spungin, Ed.D.
Vice President of International Programs
American Foundation for the Blind
Treasurer, World Blind Union

Preface

Increasingly in recent years, practitioners have encountered children who do not function visually even though there is no obvious damage to their eyes or their visual mechanisms. Although the visual behavior of such children is clearly the result of some malfunction somewhere in their visual systems, there seem to be some among professionals who serve visually impaired children who feel that children with this condition, commonly called cortical or cerebral visual impairment (CVI), "are not our responsibility."

Amidst this discussion, one hears the echoes of past arguments brought on either by advances in training and learning options or by the appearance of new and more complex disabilities. There was resistance to having school programs take on responsibility for teaching orientation and mobility. Some felt that teaching the use of low vision devices went beyond the traditional role of teachers of visually impaired students. The arrival of the "rubella population," with their multiple disabilities and special needs, resulted in a major shift in the responsibilities of vision professionals. All of these adjustments to meet the needs of children with visual impairments by members of our profession were, perhaps, heralded by the early and daring commitment of blindness-related programs to serve children who were hearing impaired as well as visually impaired.

The presentation by Christine Roman-Lantzy of methods of serving children with cortical visual impairment is right at home within this tradition of broadening our focus to meet the expanding needs and numbers of children with visual impairments. As medical advances continue to provide the gift of life to children who would previously not have survived their traumatic births, we will continue to find increasing numbers of such children whose brain functioning rather than eye damage inhibits or precludes normal vision. Building on the work of Dr. James Jan and his colleagues, Dr. Roman-Lantzy provides practical suggestions within the tradition of education of visually impaired individuals for assessing and improving the visual functioning of children with CVI. Although some among us will resist still another seeming expansion of the role of teachers of visually impaired students, most will recognize the present book as a much-needed aid in helping them effectively work with the children with CVI who are already on their caseloads and support them in using and improving the vision they have.

Moving our thinking forward as it relates to children with CVI is both the focus and the outcome of the publication of *Cortical Visual Impairment: An Approach to Assessment and Intervention*, by Dr. Christine Roman-Lantzy.

This effort is in keeping with the tradition of which we all are a part.

Richard L. Welsh, Ph.D.
President (retired)
Pittsburgh Vision Services
Pittsburgh, Pennsylvania

Acknowledgments

This book represents the work of one and the support of many.

Jim Jan's articles published in the *Journal of Visual Impairment & Blindness* created an "ah-ha" moment that launched my own work in cortical visual impairment (CVI). Without Dr. Jan's insights I imagine I would still be scratching my head about how to be effective with this unique group of students. I truly cannot thank him enough.

Thank you to the American Foundation for the Blind and AFB Press, particularly Natalie Hilzen who guided me from the initial conceptual stages to the final individual words on each page. Ellen Bilofsky, I so appreciate your efforts and your insights in the editorial process. Whenever I asked either of you if this book was harder than others to complete, you always had the good sense to tell me no.

I wish to acknowledge the members of the CVI Mentor and CVI Advisor Projects for providing me with the honor of teaching the materials that are presented in this book. You are and will continue to serve as invaluable resources to the eight states in which you work. Your dedication to learning and using my materials has, I hope, helped improve the visual function and quality of life for the students you teach. Thanks to Diane Kelly and Sandy Newcomb for sharing the list of CVI activities used in this book.

Tracy Evans Luiselli, I thank you for your leadership in our CVI Advisor sessions but even more for your encouragement and passion for our shared beliefs regarding the importance of the children we serve. I look forward to ongoing professional collaboration and personal friendship.

Thank you to the parents who provided permission for family photos to be used in the book. Your unfailing generosity in sharing your stories and your children with me has furthered my knowledge and has filled my heart.

Thank you, Susan Spungin and Rick Welsh, for providing introductory comments that help set the stage for the text. I am honored to have your perspectives.

Thank you to Alan Lantzy, David Hubel, and Gordon Dutton, for permission to use images, technical information, conversations, and clarifications of medical details.

I also acknowledge and thank the members of the Western Pennsylvania Hospital's Pediatric VIEW Program. I am fortunate to have a place to continue to develop my skills, learn from families, and gather data.

Finally, I must acknowledge my dear friends who have encouraged me through my professional ventures and supported me through my life adventures.

My Introduction to CVI

Mary Smith, a seasoned teacher of children with visual impairments, has a caseload of 17 children who range in age from 2 years to 19 years. Her students have a variety of educational needs. Mary has 3 students who are braille readers. She sees them on a daily basis and spends the greatest portion of her time with them. Mary's other visually impaired students include several who use enlarged print, auditory materials, or specialized technology. Mary also has 5 students who are in special education classrooms and are considered to have severe or profound educational needs.

When consulting with the classroom teacher of her students with severe or profound needs, Mary is asked to take a look at Joe, a new student who spends most of his class time staring at the overhead lights. Joe has a history of premature birth and has cerebral palsy and frequent seizures. He has a tracheostomy and uses a feeding tube. The complex records in his file include an ophthalmologist's report that indicates that Joe's eyes are normal and healthy. Despite the ophthalmologist's statement, Joe's mother and his teacher feel that something must be wrong with his vision—Joe doesn't seem to see, and he never looks into faces.

Once permissions are in place, Mary conducts a functional vision evaluation but is unable to get Joe to attend consistently to her testing materials. Mary agrees that Joe behaves as though he is visually impaired, but because he has a normal eye exam she can only conclude that perhaps Joe is too cognitively impaired to show an interest in his environment.

This vignette describes a situation not unlike those encountered by this author and perhaps many of my colleagues. When I was a young teacher of students with visual impairments in the mid-1970s, I had a mixed caseload of students whose abilities ranged from gifted to severely and profoundly mentally impaired. My braille-reading and low vision academic students required daily instruction, for which I felt adequately prepared. I loved the challenge and knew how to teach and advocate for these children. However, when I set foot in a residential setting for students with severe and profound special needs, I felt less like a professional armed with a college degree and training in visual impairment and more as though I were lost at sea.

Once on board in this school-like setting, I encountered children who could not walk or talk and a number of children who behaved as though they could not see. It was permissible at that time to share files, and I was handed inches-thick medical files, in which I searched for the magical vision-related words that would determine a student's eligibility for my caseload. Frankly, I wasn't entirely sure that I wanted to find the diagnoses that would mean I had the responsibility to teach these children. Most of the students with severe and profound needs referred to me did not have documented ocular visual impairments, but I agreed with the classroom teachers that they certainly acted as though they could not see. Later I learned that this kind of visual impairment is termed *cortical visual impairment* (CVI). I agreed to stay on, but I was concerned about whether my input would be of any value. Clearly I was there to learn more than to teach.

Soon I was won over by the amazing dedication of the special educators who chose to work with these children and their complex circumstances. I was won over, too, by the parents, who desperately wanted their children to learn. Most of all, I was won over by the students themselves, who worked so hard to do the simplest things . . . things that my own children at home would learn without conscious thought or effort. Therefore, since the mid-1970s I have been trying little by little to understand the unusual visual world of students with CVI. The journey has been long and certainly has not been smooth, but over these many years I have developed a framework that helps me to be a more effective teacher in this challenging field.

A WORK IN PROGRESS

The material I offer in this text is presented not as data derived from scientific experimentation, but as a set of methods that have improved my ability to assess and intervene appropriately. The materials represent a work in progress; they have changed and will continue to be adjusted as my experience and understanding increase. I have shared them with other professionals who have indicated that the methods and material described in this book have also provided them with a

framework in which to understand the visual functioning of their students and a process to improve it.

The CVI Range and CVI Resolution Charts that I developed are based on two foundations. The first is information from the work of Dr. James Jan and his colleagues in British Columbia. Dr. Jan began to define the set of unique behaviors exhibited by children that helped to differentiate CVI from ocular forms of visual impairment. The second is my own application of this information in working with children. As I tried to understand my students' behavior and to intervene to support their growth and development, a set of educational principles began to evolve.

All the materials described in this book are based on years of practice and the subsequent refinement of tools that I thought would help me be more accurate in my ability to assess and to provide effective interventions for the children with whom I have worked. For that reason, the materials in this book are uniquely mine. The first CVI Range was a simple checklist of behaviors, but over the course of years it has changed many times, based on my increased knowledge and experience. As I have already indicated, it is a work in progress and will most likely continue to be revised and refined in the future. A summary of the material and an overview is outlined in the sidebar, "CVI: Guiding Principles."

I have used versions of these materials with students all over the United States and in several other countries. My initial questions about these students began in 1973, before the term CVI was even used. At that time, I worked in an institutional setting with 35 children who had multiple disabilities. They did not have eye reports that qualified them to receive services as visually impaired students, but it seemed clear that they were not able to see. Since those early years I have worked with at least a thousand other children with CVI in

The following concepts may be used as an overview to the content of this book. Each of the principles will be described in greater detail in the chapters that follow.

1. CVI is best identified and diagnosed by
   - a normal eye exam or an eye exam that reveals an eye condition that cannot explain the profound lack of functional vision
   - a medical history that includes neurological problems
   - the presence of unique visual and behavioral characteristics

2. The unique visual and behavioral characteristics of CVI include
   - distinct color preferences
   - attraction to movement
   - visual latency
   - visual field preferences
   - difficulties with visual and environmental complexity
   - light-gazing or nonpurposeful gaze
   - difficulties with distance viewing
   - absent or atypical visual reflex responses
   - difficulties with visual novelty
   - absence of visually guided reach

3. In infants with CVI:
   - Visual function improves or declines but rarely remains static.
   - Vision can be rehabilitated with permanent increased function during the critical window of visual plasticity in the period of infancy.
   - Progress and permanency of visual function depends upon neurostability and environmental support.

4. In older students with CVI:
   - It is unknown when plasticity regarding the development of vision ends; therefore, progress in visual function should be expected, although the rate may be slower when the child is beyond the critical period of visual plasticity in infancy.
   - Adaptations must be designed on the basis of assessed needs.
   - Interventions should be integrated into daily routines.
   - "Vision stimulation" as an end goal should be avoided.

5. CVI may coexist with ocular forms of visual impairment.
   - Optic nerve atrophy, optic nerve hypoplasia, optic nerve dysplasia, and strabismus are the ocular conditions most commonly associated with CVI.
   - Eye specialists may diagnose only the ocular form of visual impairment even when both ocular and cortical visual impairments are present.

6. Functional vision assessment for students with CVI has a specialized protocol.

7. Interventions for children with CVI must emerge from assessed needs.

8. Environments for children with CVI must be adapted.
   - Adaptations must consider visual complexity.
   - Adaptations must consider auditory complexity.
   - Adaptations must be embedded as part of the daily routine rather than a stand-alone "treatment."

public schools, private schools, schools for blind students, home settings, workshops, and through the Western Pennsylvania Hospital's Pediatric VIEW (Vision Information and Evaluation at West Penn Hospital) Program in Pittsburgh and in its neonatal follow-up program. These children have spanned all ages, from preterm infants through age 21, and have exhibited all levels of cognitive function, from gifted to profound degrees of cognitive impairment. They have included children with CVI but with no additional disabilities, as well as those with a variety of motor, health, emotional, and social issues. The children with whom I have worked also include individuals born with CVI as well as those who developed CVI as a result of acquired brain trauma.

MULTISTATE MENTOR TRAINING PROGRAMS

At the time of this writing, the latest version of the CVI Range, an educational functional vision assessment for students birth to age 21, is being used in special mentor-training programs in eight states. These projects are the result of grants written through the Deaf-Blind Programs of these states and are funded under Section 307.11 of the Individuals with Disabilities Education Act. Their purpose is to create a pool of highly trained individuals who can function in the long term as resources to their individual states. There are two different five-year CVI training programs in progress, both scheduled for completion in 2008; each is a multistate program involving four states. One is the CVI Mentor Project for the states of Delaware, Maryland, Vermont, and West Virginia, with 24 professionals participating. The second is the CVI Advisor Program, involving 22 professionals from the states of Connecticut, Maine, Massachusetts, and New Hampshire. The professionals include teachers

of visually impaired students with visual impairment, orientation and mobility (O&M) specialists, specialists in deaf-blindness, early interventionists, special educators, state deaf-blind coordinators, physical therapists, occupational therapists, a teacher of hearing-impaired students, and family/parent specialists. The professionals work directly and in consultation with several hundred children with CVI and their families.

The preliminary results from the projects are encouraging. Although the training will not be complete until 2008, inter-rater reliability is currently above 90 percent; specifically, using the CVI Range, inter-rater reliability is approximately 94 percent. Other outcomes include increased understanding of CVI, increased confidence in working with students with CVI, and increased levels of functional vision among children, as measured by the CVI Range.

The training goals are multifaceted. Professionals will ultimately demonstrate competence in understanding the basic principles of CVI, demonstrate skill in functional vision assessment using the CVI Range, demonstrate skill in designing and implementing specialized interventions, and provide consultation and support to families and educational teams who support students with CVI. Additional goals include improving the level of confidence among the mentors in relation to CVI and establishing inter-rater reliability at or above 95 percent agreement.

Although my educational approach to working with students with CVI is unique, the foundation for this method is not unknown. My work is based primarily on the studies of Dr. James Jan and his colleagues, and I thank Dr. Jan, Dr. Maryke Groenveld, and Dr. Gordon Dutton. I also thank my husband, Dr. Alan Lantzy, a neonatologist and chair of the Department of Pediatrics of Western Pennsylvania Hospital. I have been able to see a little farther because I have stood on their shoulders.

1

Cortical Visual Impairment: An Overview

Cortical visual impairment (CVI), also referred to as cerebral visual impairment, is a term used to describe visual impairment that occurs because of brain damage (Huo et al., 1999). CVI differs from ocular forms of visual impairment in that the interference in visual function exists not in the structures of the eye or optic nerve, but in the visual processing centers and visual pathways of the brain (Jan & Groenveld, 1993). CVI is a term that may be used to describe a condition when a child or adult is visually unresponsive but has a normal eye examination or an eye exam that cannot explain the individual's significant lack of visual function; he or she may have an abnormal MRI (magnetic resonance imaging) or CAT (computed axial tomography) scan that shows damage to parts of the brain such as the visual cortex or optic radiations.

Although the term *cortical visual impairment* will be used throughout this book, it is important to recognize that experts do not agree whether cortical visual impairment, cerebral visual impairment, neurological visual impair-

ment, brain damage–related visual impairment, or some other term will ultimately be chosen as the most appropriate description of visual dysfunction stemming from damage to the visual centers of the brain. According to Gordon N. Dutton (personal communication, May 10, 2006) and James Jan (personal communication, May 11, 2006), at this time, the term *cortical visual impairment* is more commonly used in North America, while *cerebral visual impairment* is generally used in Europe. There is currently a lack of consensus about the conditions and causes encompassed by these terms.

VISION AND THE BRAIN: A HISTORICAL PERSPECTIVE

Although vision or sight, as a sense, is primarily associated with the eyes, in reality, vision is the product of a complex system of which the eyes are only one part. Essentially, the eyes are the receptors of incoming visual stimuli, and the visual systems of the brain interpret the information being received (Ward, 1996). So much of vision is attributable to the processing of visual information that it has been estimated that over 40 percent of the brain is devoted to visual function (Dutton, 2006). When this process is disrupted, the visual systems of the brain do not consistently interpret or understand what the eyes see.

Although our understanding of the brain's role in vision has received increasing attention in recent decades, the belief that the brain had areas regulating visual function existed as early as the 17th century (Hoyt, 2002). Historic figures including Sir Isaac Newton and Rene Descartes undertook studies related to this topic. However, it was not until the beginning of the 19th century that numerous researchers believed that vision was regulated by specified portions of the cerebral cortex. In the second half of the 19th century, David Ferrier and Hermann Munk decisively concluded that the occipital cortex is the primary center for visual functions (Hoyt, 2002). Many neurologists became convinced that seeing and understanding were two separate functions, and that patients with brain damage in certain parts of their brain became blind, while others with damage in other areas were able to see but were not able to label or identify what they were seeing. Munk specifically called this condition *mind-blindness*; Sigmund Freud later described the same phenomenon as *agnosia*.

In the 20th century, the English neurologist Gordon Holmes studied damage to the occipital cortex in wounded World War I veterans. Holmes and fellow researcher Grainger Stewart published numerous papers describing vision losses caused by lesions in the brain. They analyzed visual field deficits in men who sustained injuries in the posterior visual cortex and discovered that areas of damage in this part of the brain resulted in permanent scotomas, or blind spots, in the visual field (Hoyt, 2002).

The term *cortical blindness* emerged in the early 20th century to describe the temporary or permanent loss of vision in adults who experienced severe episodes of oxygen deficiency, or hypoxia, circulatory or inflammatory disease, or traumatic injury (Hoyt, 2002). Cortical blindness was defined as a bilateral loss of vision in the presence of an otherwise normal eye exam (Hoyt, 2002). Although children who suffered brain trauma undoubtedly exhibited visual disability before the late 20th century, damage to the brain was not consistently recognized as a significant cause of visual impairment in children until the mid-1980s.

However, the diagnosis of "cortical blindness" that is applied to adults who become adventitiously blind because of damage to both hemispheres of the brain does not seem appropriate in describing the visual dysfunction found in children who have damage to the visual centers of the brain. This is because in children, some degree of vision is almost always present and there is an expected prognosis of continued improvement in visual recovery (Groenveld, Jan & Leader, 1990).

The remarkable plasticity of the brain and its ability to recover from significant injury to the visual centers of the brain was documented by the Nobel Prize–winning researchers Hubel and Wiesel (1970), who studied what occurs in the central nervous system visual pathways as the result of abnormalities in the eye and, therefore, subsequent abnormal inputs to the brain. They were successful in tapping the signals from the nerve cells in various layers of the visual cortex, showing that visual cortical cells specialize in respect to interpreting specific components of the retinal image.

Thanks to the work of Hubel and Wiesel and that of others, much is now known about the brain's role in vision. The occipital lobes of the cerebral cortex at the back of the brain are primarily concerned with vision; the visual messages from the eye traveling along the optic nerve pathway in the form of electrical signals are routed to this location (see Figure 1.1). Images are reconstructed and "seen" in this area, as details of the visual scene are broken down and analyzed by millions of cells responsible for independently handling such elements as color, detail, and movement. Images are sent on to the temporal and parietal lobes of the brain. In the parietal lobe, the images are integrated with other sensory input so an intelligent interpretation can be made (Atkinson, 1984; Dutton, 2006). Visual cortical cells are strictly organized; the cortex analyzes each aspect of an image in an orderly sequence; and there is a precise and organized way in which specific visual functions are separated and processed by specific cortical areas. Essentially, each nerve cell stimulated is responsible for a particular detail of a figure.

THE CRITICAL PERIOD IN VISUAL DEVELOPMENT

As part of their work, Hubel and Wiesel were able to demonstrate that the ability of cortical cells to interpret impulse messages from the retina develops in infancy and that even relatively short periods of light and pattern deprivation can result in permanently impaired vision. Essentially, the development of vision is dependent upon an intact ocular system—the eye and its related structures—and also upon exposure to stimuli in the environment. The visual deprivation studies of Hubel and Weisel showed that when kittens were deprived of visual input during a critical period of visual development, vision was permanently affected. Specific visual functions are activated by corresponding experiences. That is, the ability to see movement develops through experiences

FIGURE 1.1   *Visual Pathways and the Brain*

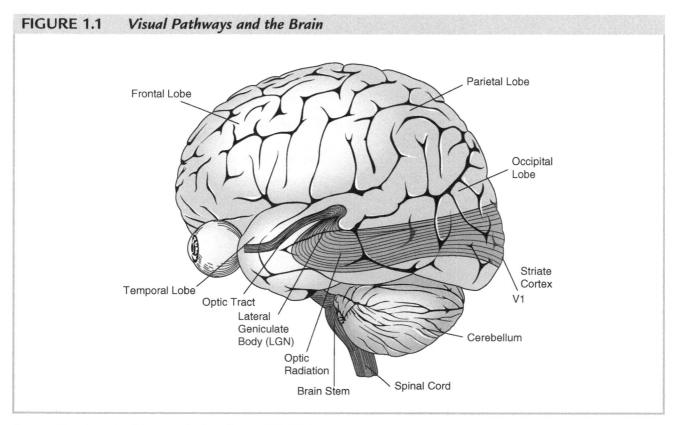

Source: Reprinted with permission from SKI-HI Institute, Logan, UT.

in which a child looks at the movements of people, crib mobiles, and manual gestures. The ability to see patterns requires exposure to objects with patterned surfaces—and so on.

For Hubel and Wiesel (1970), the period of plasticity for visual development is most pronounced in infancy, and in human infants the brain is believed to be most plastic between birth and age 3 years. Studies by Norcia and Tyler (1985) and Orel-Bixler (1989) describe the critical phases for the development of acute vision as occurring in an early period from birth to 10 months of age and a later period of slower development from 10 months to nearly 10 years. According to Atkinson (1984), however, human visual development is largely complete by 6 months of age. Although consensus regarding the specific time frame surrounding the period of plasticity does not yet exist, many theorists agree that the greatest opportunity for vision development occurs early in life and that there is a finite amount of time available to expose children to appropriate visual inputs that will stimulate the development of visual functioning in an optimal way.

Based on these findings, it is important to recognize that, to improve their visual functioning, children who sustain serious brain injury in infancy or early childhood may be able to "tap into" the critical period of visual plasticity when visual function is being developed. This period provides a window of opportunity for neuronal activity responsible for vision to be routed from the damaged areas of the visual pathways and primary visual cortex to other areas of the brain responsible for visual functions (Tychsen, 2001). Even if the window of plasticity for visual development remains open for as long as 10 years of age, the most opportune time for meaningful stimulation in all likelihood occurs in early infancy. For this reason, infants with brain injury should be screened as early as possible for potential vision difficulties associated with CVI.

IMPORTANCE OF EARLY INTERVENTION

All too often, parents report that when eye care or medical professionals examine their infant who demonstrates atypical "seeing" behaviors, they are advised that the child's eyes are normal. Many families report being given comments such as: "Children with brain injuries sometimes act this way," "There is no treatment for your child's vision," "The eyes are fine, we just don't know how well he understands what he sees," "She is blind and there is nothing that can be done," and "There's no harm in waiting, sometimes children grow out of this vision delay." Remarks like these reflect the confusion surrounding CVI. And there are, in fact, understandable reasons for this confusion. The eyes of children with CVI frequently appear to function normally. In children who have CVI, the visual systems of the brain do not consistently understand or interpret what the eye sees, and, depending on the extent and severity of damage to the brain, visual function can be affected in a wide variety of ways. Many ophthalmologists and other medical practitioners concerned with the measurement of visual acuity may not identify the presence of CVI in a child whose eyes are normal or who has an ocular condition that does not explain the profound loss of visual function. Many early interventionists may not regard a child with a normal ocular system as eligible for vision-related services.

Nevertheless, in light of the research on critical periods of development, there may, in fact, be harm done—or at a minimum, opportunities that are lost—when appropriate vision-related interventions fail to be initiated during the window of visual plasticity in infancy. Hubel and Wiesel stated in 1970 that "Innate mechanisms endow the visual system with highly specific connections, but visual experience early in life is necessary for their maintenance and full development" (p. 78). If the quality or quantity of visual input are impeded during this critical period, the impact on future visual development may in some cases be irreversible. As Banks and Dannemiller observed, "The presence of ocular or cortical abnormalities early in life causes permanent deficits in various capabilities. . . . This susceptibility of infants to visual abnormalities means that early diagnosis and treatment are required" (1987, p. 232). Thus, delay in identifying children with CVI may result in lost opportunities that might otherwise have facilitated long-term visual improvements. Farel and Hooper (1995) describe how experience can affect whether the visual cortex develops normal patterns of connections and conclude that, "Training is effective during a circumscribed (critical) period of development. For the visual system, this period is during the equivalent of infancy" (p. 5).

Despite the fact that most children with CVI show improvement in their visual functioning, it is a matter of concern that because of confusion about the nature of CVI, many children may not have the opportunity to profit from early diagnosis and appropriate intervention during the critical period of visual development (Jan, Groenveld, Sykanda & Hoyt, 1987). In recent years, there has been widespread recognition of the importance of early intervention—the identification of children's special needs, the accurate assessment of those needs, and the provision of appropriate intervention on the basis of that assessment—to support growth and development. For children with CVI, prompt identification, careful assessment, and planned intervention can facilitate visual functioning and, with it, the ability of the child to develop, learn, and read. With specific, systematic, targeted interventions, such as those described later in this book, children diagnosed with CVI can make significant and steady progress in their use of vision.

INCIDENCE OF CVI

As already indicated, in the past 20 years debate has occurred among medical professionals about the nature of CVI. Educators of students with visual impairments also have discussed the appropriateness and efficacy of providing specialized instruction to children whose visual differences arise in the visual pathways and processing centers of the brain, rather than in the ocular structures of the eye. CVI may not always be viewed in every quarter as a "legitimate" form of visual impairment, particularly by some eye care specialists who document normal eye examinations in children with CVI, and by some vision educators whose training primarily centered on the needs of children with ocular visual impairments. Despite these questions, however, CVI is recognized today as the primary cause of visual impairment in children in so-called first world countries in which advanced medical interventions are available to infants and children (Skoczenski & Good, 2004), and it is likely to remain so for the foreseeable future.

Children who once died as a result of prematurity or brain injury are now surviving in greater numbers. In 1963, Patrick Bouvier Kennedy, newborn son of John and Jacqueline Kennedy, died from complications of prematurity. President Kennedy's son was born at 34 to 35 weeks' gestation, and infants of that gestational age now survive at rates greater than 95 percent in the United States. According to Als (1999) more than 95 percent of infants born 8 to 12 weeks premature will survive if cared for in a neonatal intensive-care unit. Neonatologists, pediatric neurologists, and other pediatric practitioners who specialize in caring for infants or children with brain injury have made significant advances in the survivability of critically ill and premature children. Many more children now survive, but the total number of children with significant disabilities has also increased. Decreased mortality has not resulted in decreased morbidity. Younger and more fragile infants and children have a greater risk of neurodevelopmental impairment. There is an important relationship between advances in medicine and numbers of neurologically affected surviving individuals, a relationship resulting in greater numbers of infants and children with CVI. As Dutton has observed, "It is estimated that over 40 percent of the brain is devoted to visual function, so it is not surprising that a large proportion of children with damage to the brain have visual problems" (2006, p. 4).

A REVOLUTION IN VISION EDUCATION

In many ways the increasing incidence of CVI among children may prompt a kind of revolution in the field of vision education. Revolutions bring about change but not without struggle. In the 18th century, Valentin Haüy created a revolution with his belief that people who were blind would be able to learn if specialized teaching methods and educational materials were used. He helped establish the first formal school for the blind in Paris, France, and dissolved much of the stigma that was previously associated with blind individuals in society. Today the notion that people who are blind can learn is taken for granted.

In the 1960s, Natalie Barraga also caused vision educators to struggle as they slowly moved away from the long-held principles of sight saving toward the application of her revolutionary research that indicated vision was not a fixed entity but a capacity that can be developed. Barraga's principles of visual efficiency required educators to reconsider previous beliefs, teaching methods, and educational materials; she is now recognized as one of the seminal figures in the field of low vision. Where once students with low vision were blindfolded and placed in dimly lit classrooms in the belief that their vision needed to be preserved, they are now taught in classrooms in which proper lighting, high-contrast materials, and the use of low vision devices and systematic reading approaches with print media are recognized as standard practice.

Similarly, the increased incidence of CVI among children may spur both a broadened understanding and a revolutionary reevaluation of accepted beliefs and practices. Students who are visually impaired because of brain differences rather than pathologies or structural problems of the eye pose challenges yet to be resolved. The fields of medicine and special education have not identified a body of best practices for assessment and intervention for children and students with CVI. Educators, medical professionals, and early interventionists have begun to engage in a continuing dialogue (see, for example, Dennison & Lueck, 2006). The issues being discussed include the definitions of CVI, appropriate terminology, diagnostic criteria, directions for research, and evidence-based interventions and educational practices. In the face of the complexities of CVI, it is likely that for the present, more questions than answers will emerge.

2

Medical and Other Causes of Cortical Visual Impairment

Cortical visual impairment (CVI) is now the most common cause of visual impairment in children in the United States, and its increasing incidence is a matter of international concern as well. Many aspects of this complex condition are puzzling. Because CVI is attributable to damage, injury, or insult to the brain, rather than to abnormalities of the eye, professionals in the field of blindness and visual impairment working with children who experience CVI may need to become familiar with a new vocabulary, conceptual framework, and intervention landscape. This chapter provides an introduction to the range of medical profiles and backgrounds of children who may exhibit visual responses and behaviors associated with CVI.

Because CVI is frequently seen in children who were born prematurely, have neurological disorders, or have acquired brain injury, it is helpful for practitioners to know the causes and conditions that may give rise to CVI. When the presence of this challenging condition is suspected, or the cause of a child's visual diffi-

culties is sought, attempts to diagnose or identify the reason behind those difficulties need to include a review of medical and other records, which may reveal some of the conditions described in this chapter. Professionals may therefore find it useful to become familiar with these conditions and the terms that are commonly used to describe them, as outlined in the sections that follow.

As explained in Chapter 1, the causes of CVI can generally be thought of as conditions that affect the visual pathways or visual processing centers of the brain (Jan & Groenveld, 1993) (see Figure 2.1). According to Skoczenski and Good (2004), CVI is "a condition in which children have reduced visual acuity as a result of damage to posterior visual pathways." They further state that "in most cases, the eyes of such children are structurally normal, yet they have diminished visual capacity."

The most common conditions associated with a diagnosis of CVI are asphyxia, perinatal hypoxic-ischemic encephalopathy, intraventricular hemorrhage, periventricular leukomalacia,

FIGURE 2.1   *The Visual Cortex*

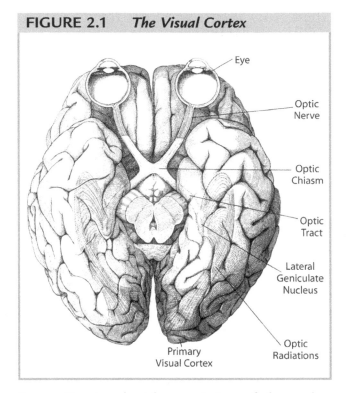

Source: Reprinted with permission of the author from David H. Hubel, *Eye, Brain, and Vision,* Scientific American Library Series No. 22 (New York: Scientific American Library, 1988), p. 61.

cerebral vascular accident, central nervous system infection, structural abnormalities, and trauma (Huo, Burden, Hoyt & Good, 1999; Teplin, 1995; Jan & Groenveld, 1993). Described another way, these causes include oxygen deficiency in the brain during or after birth; cerebral hemorrhage; shunt malfunction in children with hydrocephalus; hypoglycemia; meningitis; encephalitis; malformation of the brain during prenatal development; intrauterine infections; head injury; epilepsy; or cerebral tumor. In addition, children with CVI commonly have other neurological problems associated with damage to the brain, such as cerebral palsy, cognitive impairment, seizure disorders, microcephaly (abnormally small head), hearing loss, memory dysfunction, and hyper or hyposensitivity to sensory stimulation (Dennison, 2003).

CONGENITAL AND PERINATAL CAUSES OF CVI

Asphyxia and Perinatal Hypoxic-Ischemic Encephalopathy

Brian was born at 40 weeks' gestation. His mother had gestational diabetes. Even though his prenatal testing indicated a typically sized infant, Brian weighed over 10 pounds at birth. Because of his unexpected size he became lodged in the birth canal and suffered subsequent asphyxia. Despite appropriate measures to resuscitate Brian, he had very low muscle tone and was unable to breathe on his own. After 15 minutes, Brian finally gasped his first breath. Brian had seizures in the neonatal period and after three weeks in the neonatal intensive care unit, he went home on phenobarbital and with a feeding tube. Although Brian's initial hospital imaging studies were normal, when he was discharged he demonstrated the visual behaviors characteristic of CVI.

The fundamental requirements of the brain are glucose and oxygen. When the brain is deprived of one of these elements, the potential for long-term brain dysfunction exists. Asphyxia is a lack of oxygen or excess of carbon dioxide. It occurs when less than normal levels of oxygen are delivered to the cells of the body and when subsequent carbon dioxide and acid levels become higher than normal (Rivken, 1997). Too little oxygen, or *hypoxia*, disrupts the autoregulation of the major blood supply of the brain, creating too little blood flow, or *ischemia*. The extent of damage from asphyxia depends on both the severity and duration of the episode (Rivkin, 1997). If the period of oxygen deprivation is short, the body may recover without long-term effects. If deprivation of oxygen to the brain is severe, however, cellular death is the result; the effects may include organ damage, cerebral palsy, seizures, hearing loss, and CVI (Batshaw & Perret, 1992). Causes of acute asphyxia can include but are not limited to placenta previa (placenta covering the cervix), placental abruption (separation of the placenta from the wall of the uterus), ruptured uterus, prolapsed umbilical cord, severe shoulder dystocia (when a baby's shoulders become stuck during delivery after the head has emerged), twin-to-twin transfusion, maternal diabetes, maternal infection, multiple gestation, and precipitous labor (Good et al., 1996). (Asphyxia can also be a cause of CVI perinatally or later in life.)

Hypoxic-ischemic encephalopathy (HIE) can result from asphyxia and is a term used to describe abnormal neurological function resulting from low blood flow to the brain (Polin, Yoder & Burg, 2001). The combination of *hypoxia* and *ischemia* results in irritation of the brain, *encephalopathy*. Not all cases of asphyxia result in HIE, but HIE frequently results from asphyxia. Many children who have HIE will experience motor problems including cerebral palsy, seizure disorder, developmental delay, hearing disorder, and CVI (Polin et al., 2001).

Intraventricular Hemorrhage

Janet was born at 27 weeks' gestation. She had many of the typical complications of prematurity including respiratory distress syndrome, episodes of apnea (suspension of breathing) and bradycardia (slow heart rate), stage II retinopathy of prematurity, and elevated levels of bilirubin (a substance that causes jaundice when it accumulates in the blood). On day 6 of life, a routine ultrasound of her brain showed a bilateral grade III intraventricular hemorrhage. Subsequent ultrasounds showed that she developed hydrocephalus as a secondary complication of her large bleed. Janet was discharged from the hospital on her 80th day of life, two days after a ventriculo-peritoneal shunt was surgically inserted to relieve intracranial pressure. At 15 months

Janet was first evaluated because of her parents' concerns that Janet wasn't looking at them. The evaluation revealed that Janet had the characteristics typical of CVI.

Intraventricular hemorrhage (IVH) is bleeding that occurs in the germinal matrix and/or ventricles and surrounding tissues of the brain. The germinal matrix is a region of the brain outside the ventricles that functions as the incubator for brain cell production (Volpe, 1987; see Figure 2.2). The germinal matrix in premature infants contains abundant blood vessels. These blood vessels become less prominent as the infant matures, and by term, or normal delivery time, at 40 weeks' gestation, the work of the germinal matrix is essentially complete (DeReuck, 1984). In the premature infant the tiny blood vessels of the germinal matrix are especially fragile and sensitive to changes in blood flow. Events that cause either too little or too much blood flow to this vulnerable area may result in bleeding in or around the germinal matrix (Vaucher, 1988). Degree of prematurity is associated with both increased incidence and severity of IVH (Ment, Duncan & Ehrenkranz, 1987). The least mature infants

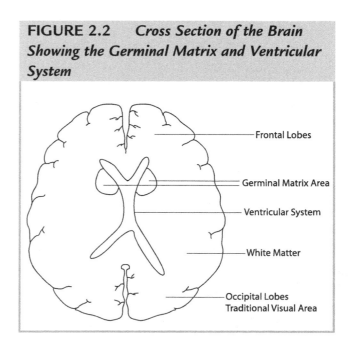

FIGURE 2.2 *Cross Section of the Brain Showing the Germinal Matrix and Ventricular System*

Frontal Lobes

Germinal Matrix Area

Ventricular System

White Matter

Occipital Lobes
Traditional Visual Area

and those weighing less than 1,250 grams are at greatest risk (Shankaran, Bauer & Bain, 1996). The risk of IVH is highest immediately after the infant is born and generally occurs within the initial week of life (Vaucher, 1988).

The severity of IVH is classified by a method described by Papile, Burstein, and Koffler in 1978. The degree of IVH is graded I through IV and is dependent on how widespread the bleeding is, the amount of blood in the ventricular system, and the specific location of the hemorrhage (see Figure 2.3). A Grade I hemorrhage is defined by a small amount of bleeding into the germinal matrix without blood leaking into the ventricles. A Grade II hemorrhage is a larger bleed that may leak into the ventricles but does not fill or expand the ventricle. In a Grade III hemorrhage, blood fills and swells the ventricles. The most damaging hemorrhage is a Grade IV bleed that results in blood spilling out into the surrounding brain tissues. In IVH the blood within the ventricles forms clots and eventually is reabsorbed (Perlman, 2001).

Although seizures, post–hemorrhagic hydrocephalus (excessive accumulation of

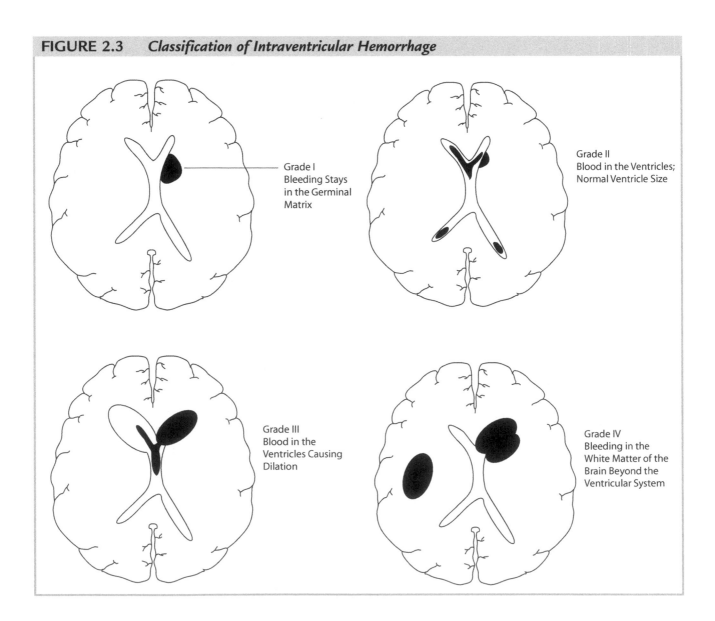

FIGURE 2.3   _Classification of Intraventricular Hemorrhage_

Grade I
Bleeding Stays in the Germinal Matrix

Grade II
Blood in the Ventricles; Normal Ventricle Size

Grade III
Blood in the Ventricles Causing Dilation

Grade IV
Bleeding in the White Matter of the Brain Beyond the Ventricular System

spinal fluid), and developmental delay are negative outcomes associated with Grades III and IV IVH, the most frequently occurring long-term complication is cerebral palsy (Ment, 1985). In infants with Grade III IVH, the incidence of disability is 30 to 40 percent; it is as high as 80 to 100 percent in infants with Grade IV IVH (Volpe, 1987; Vaucher, 1988). CVI has also occasionally been associated with Grade IV bleeds in cases where the blood leaks out of the ventricles into the visual pathways located adjacent to the ventricular area (Lantzy & Roman, 2002–2007).

Post–hemorrhagic hydrocephalus occurs in 40 to 50 percent of infants with Grade III or IV bleeds (Perlman, 2001). It is believed that the normal flow of cerebral spinal fluid in the ventricles is blocked by the presence of a blood clot in the normally free-flowing fluid. The blockage causes spinal fluid to back up into the ventricles, thus increasing the size of the ventricles and creating unusual pressure on other parts of the brain (see Figure 2.4). CVI may also result as a secondary complication of severe post-hemorrhagic hydrocephalus (Huo et al., 1999). In this case, the increased cranial pressure caused by the buildup of fluid surrounding the brain may damage one or more of the visual centers.

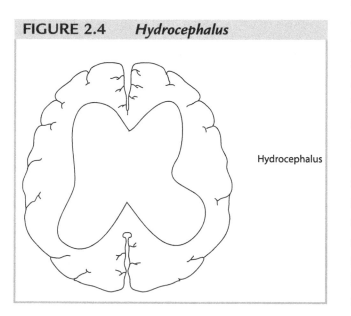

FIGURE 2.4 *Hydrocephalus*

Hydrocephalus

Periventricular Leukomalacia

Matthew was delivered at 32 weeks' gestation as a result of his mother's dangerously high blood pressure. His birth weight was significantly lower than average; otherwise, he was healthy on examination. In Matthew's first week of life, a routine ultrasound was ordered. The ultrasound showed a number of small cystic changes in the white matter of his brain consistent with severe periventricular leukomalacia. Matthew remained in the neonatal intensive care unit an additional four weeks before he was discharged home. Matthew's neonatal follow-up evaluations revealed the presence of spastic quadriplegia, expressive language delays, and CVI.

Periventricular leukomalacia (PVL) is injury to or death of the white matter of the brain. It occurs when low blood flow injures the especially vulnerable cerebral white matter ("leuko" means white) of a premature infant's brain (Volpe, 1997). The areas of the brain associated with PVL consist of a variety of sites, including the most common site, just outside the lateral ventricles where the nerves that control lower extremity function exist (Vaucher, 1988; Brodsky, Fray, & Glasier, 2002). PVL primarily occurs prior to 32 weeks' gestation but also occurs in infants older than 32 weeks' gestation. It is ultimately diagnosed by MRI or neuro-ultrasound (Polin, Yoder, & Burg, 2001). A premature infant is particularly susceptible to PVL because of the immature blood vessel formation, poor control of cerebral blood flow to the brain, and intrinsic vulnerability of the immature brain itself (Volpe, 1997). This is in contrast to the situation in a full-term infant, where the white matter of the brain is much more resistant to hypoxic injury. PVL may coexist with IVH. Clinical conditions associated with PVL may include but are not limited to major systemic low blood pressure caused by difficult resuscitation or serious postnatal illness such as septic shock (the result of severe infection), significant maternal or fetal blood loss, or a collapsed lung (Zupan, Gonzalez, Lacaze-Masmonteil, Boithias, d'Allest, Dehan, & Gabilan, 1996).

According to Brodsky et al. (2002) children with PVL may experience associated developmental and sensory differences, including spastic diplegia, minor neurologic dysfunction and visual differences consistent with CVI. Although difficulties with visual crowding (a phenomenon referred to in this book as *visual complexity*, involving difficulty distinguishing background and foreground visual information) occur most commonly in children with primary visual cortex injury, Brodsky and colleagues indicate that children with PVL may experience this difficulty as well: "Jacobsen et al. have emphasized the difficulties that these children encounter with visual crowding, visuospatial orientation (relating to visual perception of spatial relationships), and interpretation of complex visual patterns such as faces and words" (Brodsky et al., 2002). Jacobsen further describes visual field losses and perceptual difficulties, two additional malfunctions that may also be associated with the unique behavioral and visual difficulties of CVI. Pike, Holmstrom, deVries, Pennock, Drew, Sonksen, & Dubowitz (1994) also report a statistically significant association between PVL and visual behaviors consistent with CVI.

Cerebral Vascular Accident/Cerebral Artery Infarction

Ian was born at 42 weeks' gestation after an uncomplicated labor and delivery. No unusual interventions were required in the delivery room. Within the first 24 hours of life, Ian unexpectedly had seizures and he was transferred to the neonatal intensive care unit. Subsequent testing ruled out meningitis, asphyxia, and metabolic

disorders, but revealed that Ian had suffered a stroke before he was born. After 10 days in the hospital, Ian was discharged with anti-seizure medication and a referral to his local early intervention program. At Ian's first neonatal follow-up appointment he was suspected of having CVI.

More commonly seen in full-term infants, cerebral vascular accident, or "neonatal stroke," is also occasionally seen in premature infants (de Vries, Dubowitz, Dubowitz, & Pennock, 1990). Other than in cases of perinatal asphyxia, the causes of infant stroke are frequently unclear (Rivkin, 1997). Bleeding in the brain from cerebral infarct most frequently occurs in the left hemisphere, subsequently resulting in right hemiplegia, cerebral palsy affecting one side of the body (Rivkin, 1997). Infarct occurs when blood capillaries in the brain are ruptured because of an obstruction, an abnormal increase in blood pressure, or when a small amount of capillary bleeding is not controlled by an intact clotting system (Volpe, 1987). Infant stroke is usually diagnosed by ultrasound after symptoms appear. As with asphyxia and HIE, the extent of long-term damage depends on the severity of the bleeding that has occurred. Infants who have cerebral vascular incidents are likely to have seizures, especially in the first day or two of life (Scher, 2001). The outcomes for children who have these bleeds may include cerebral palsy, developmental delay, and vision differences including CVI (Volpe, 1987).

Infection

Alex was born at 38 weeks' gestation by cesarean section because of decreased fetal heart tones during labor. His birth weight was 6 pounds and he had an unusual rash covering his body. Alex's mother reported feeling healthy throughout her pregnancy. A thorough exam showed that Alex had an enlarged liver and spleen. A brain ultrasound showed calcifications scattered throughout his brain; the lab results confirmed a profile consistent with the diagnosis of congenital cytomegalovirus infection. By age 2, Alex was receiving early intervention services for significant developmental delay, hearing impairment, and CVI.

Infections that place an infant at risk for CVI may be either congenital or acquired after birth. According to Williamson (1992), infections affect at least 40,000 newborns each year. Many of these infections have specific long-term effects on both the ocular and the cortical visual systems.

The TORCH infections (toxoplasmosis, rubella, cytomegalic inclusion disease, and herpes simplex) are a collection of infections that can be passed from mother to fetus in utero and that are known to cause potential damage to the brain, resulting in seizures and permanent brain injury (Scher, 2001). All of these conditions may affect the developing fetus even though the pregnant mother may be asymptomatic. Of the TORCH infections, cytomegalic virus (CMV) may be most closely associated with CVI (Lantzy & Roman, 2002–2007). Children affected by congenital TORCH infections are also commonly at risk for ocular conditions, which may or may not coexist with CVI. The most common ocular conditions associated with TORCH are cataracts and chorioretinitis, an inflammation and scarring of the retina.

Bacterial infections including Group B *streptococcus* and *Escherichia coli* (*E coli*) are known to cause sepsis and meningitis in infants. Group B *streptococcus* is the leading infectious bacterial cause of mortality and morbidity in the newborn period (Farley, Harvey, & Stull 1993). Most infants recover completely from Group B *streptococcus* or *E coli* but some may develop shock and/or meningitis as complications. Shock can result in reduced blood flow

to the brain, potentially causing widespread neuronal damage and potential CVI. Meningitis is an infection that causes inflammation or swelling of the brain and may lead to hearing deficit, cerebral palsy, and CVI (Huo, Burden, Hoyt, & Good, 1999). While mortality has declined over the past four decades, it is estimated that 40 percent or more infants with meningitis exhibit difficulties resulting from brain damage (Heath, Yusoff & Baker, 2003).

Structural Abnormalities

Annie was born at term, but almost immediately physicians suspected that she was at risk. Annie had a weak, high-pitched cry and her facial features looked unusual. Annie's ears were low and her eyes too closely set. Her head circumference measured below the tenth percentile for her age even though her weight and length were within the normal range. Annie was a poor feeder in the neonatal intensive care unit and required a feeding tube to ensure that her nutritional needs were met. Even though she is now receiving specialized instruction in preschool, Annie's head size has never "caught up." She also receives direct services from a teacher of visually impaired students because of her recent diagnosis of CVI.

The development of the human central nervous system is a complex process and has been the subject of numerous in-depth medical reviews (Nickel, 1992). Structures in the brain develop in an orderly sequence beginning at 3 to 4 weeks' gestation and are not completely formed until adulthood (Volpe, 1987). Any alteration in the normal progression of brain development may result in structural abnormalities that have significant developmental and neurological consequences. According to Nickel (1992), "Many of the children in early intervention (E.I.) services have an identifiable disorder of brain development either as an isolated problem or as part of a multiple congenital anomaly syndrome." The most common types of structural brain development disorder include meningomyelocele (spina bifida), Dandy Walker syndrome (a specific type of cyst in the brain), primary microcephaly (small brain), lissencephaly (smooth brain syndrome), schizencephaly (abnormal indentations in the surface of the brain), primary congenital hydrocephalus, polymicrogyria (many abnormally small contours of the surface of the brain), and agenesis of the corpus callosum (lack of connection between the two hemispheres of the brain). Many of these abnormalities are the result of chromosomal disorders; others can result from infections in utero such as CMV or may also occur as an idiopathic, isolated incident.

The developmental outcome of brain structure abnormalities can range from mild impairment to multiple and severe disabilities. Huo et al. (1999) describe CVI in individuals with microcephaly and hydrocephalus. Whiting et al. (1985) also cite structural brain disorders as a potential cause of CVI.

Metabolic Conditions

While medical literature does not commonly describe metabolic disorders as major causes of CVI, it likely that some of the conditions leading to significant neuronal damage and resulting in long-term disability may also be associated with CVI. According to Castano et al. (2000), CVI is usually associated with prenatal infection, hypoxia, trauma, structural defects of the brain, and neurometabolic disease. CVI has been diagnosed in children who have brain damage due to severe hypoglycemia (low blood sugar) and kernicterus (extremely high bilirubin levels) (Lantz & Roman, 2002–2007). According to Volpe (1987), encephalopathy

related to chronically high bilirubin levels results in movement abnormalities, abnormal swallowing and speech, hearing loss, and visual gaze disturbances.

CAUSES OF ACQUIRED CVI

Jack was a typically developing 5-year-old until he was struck by a car. He sustained significant head injury and was hospitalized in intensive care for two months. When he was stable enough to be discharged to a rehabilitation center, Jack's family met with his physicians, who told Jack's parents that in addition to the obvious injuries, Jack also had cortical visual impairment. The doctors were uncertain and not optimistic about the prognosis of Jack's visual recovery.

Janie is an infant who was born full-term with normal weight and length. Six weeks after Janie came home from the hospital, her mother went into Janie's room to check on her during an unusually long nap. Janie's mother panicked when she found her infant daughter limp, bluish, and apparently not breathing. Janie's mother called 911 immediately and although her life was spared from the near-SIDS (sudden infant death syndrome) episode, Janie's brain suffered significant damage due to oxygen deprivation. Janie now has widespread developmental delay, including CVI.

As already indicated, CVI occurs when there is damage to the visual pathways or processing centers of the brain (Good, Jan, Burden, Skoczenski & Candy, 2001). Damage may occur prenatally, perinatally, or anytime throughout life, although CVI is a term most commonly associated with children. Traumatic injury to the brain after the perinatal period can result in CVI and is considered to be an acquired rather than congenital cause of CVI (Huo et al., 1999). The category of trauma includes a broad number of potential causes, including acquired hypoxia (near-drowning, near-SIDS), blows or gunshot wounds to the head, head injury related to auto accidents, shaken baby syndrome, and tumors or optic radiation damage. Childhood infection, encephalitis, or meningitis can also result in short- or long-term CVI. In other words, any serious injury to the brain can potentially threaten the visual processing centers of the brain and, thus, result in CVI.

> Myriad disorders and diseases can destroy neural tissue of the visual system in the retinas, optic nerves, and brain. Mechanical forces, ischemia, anoxia, infection, tumor, degenerative processes, and hemorrhage are among the many prior causes that may lead to photoreceptor or other nerve cell losses anywhere along the visual pathway. In all these situations, the end result is nerve cell death and interruption of the nerve signal transmissions that collectively comprise the visual sense. (Arditi & Zihl, 2000)

CONCLUSION

The body of current medical literature concerning conditions associated with a diagnosis of CVI is most likely incomplete. Medical investigators are just beginning to gather consistent data regarding the causes and conditions associated with CVI. It is important to note that not all researchers agree on the full range of causes, the prognosis or even the proper diagnostic label used to describe vision loss due to brain damage. What is needed is more cooperation and dialogue between members of medical and educational disciplines, and specifically among ophthalmologists, neonatologists, neurologists, and other pediatric specialists, in the hope that timely identification will facilitate appropriate referral to specialists who can undertake early intervention.

3

Visual and Behavioral Characteristics of Children with Cortical Visual Impairment

Given that cortical visual impairment (CVI) is the result of damage to the brain, the nature of the disruption of vision caused by this damage correlates to the location and extent of the damage or injury itself. For this reason, the visual abilities and disabilities of individuals with CVI vary greatly.

Despite this variability, the presence of certain elements or factors will help identify a child with CVI. As explained at the beginning of this book, because CVI is attributable to brain rather than eye dysfunction, children with CVI usually have a normal eye examination with normal pupillary findings (Good, 2004). In addition, because many children have sustained damage or injury to the brain as the result of prematurity or other birth-related conditions, a history of neurological involvement is often present. Finally, children with CVI typically display a number of specific and unique visual behaviors that signal this complex condition. Therefore, when attempting to determine the cause of a child's visual disability, CVI should be considered when the child has:

1. a normal or near normal eye exam that cannot explain the child's impaired vision
2. a history or presence of neurological problems
3. the presence of behavioral responses to visual stimuli that are unique to CVI.

The presence of CVI is indicated when these three criteria are met. In the experience of the Pediatric VIEW Program (Lantzy & Roman, 2002–2007), as well as the ongoing multistate CVI mentor training projects described in "My Introduction to CVI" at the beginning of this book, children's patterns of responses to visual stimuli usually indicate clearly the presence or absence of CVI. Although children may be encountered in various developmental stages and circumstances, and may therefore exhibit variability in their visual behaviors, in general, all ten behavioral characteristics described in this chapter are typically present in children with the most severe forms of CVI. Nevertheless, children with CVI are as different as any other group, and how they manifest the CVI profile is unique to each individual child.

Although the way in which children with CVI respond visually has been the subject of much discussion and the causes behind these responses are subject to much debate (see, for example, Dennison & Lueck, 2006), certain unique visual behaviors that accompany CVI were first identified by Dr. James Jan and his colleagues (Jan, Groenveld, Sykanda, & Hoyt, 1987). These characteristic behaviors are symptoms of visual dysfunction, and they in turn interfere with ongoing visual functioning to varying degrees, depending on the severity of the condition. In order to understand, assess, and provide interventions for children with CVI, it is both helpful and important to become familiar with the following characteristics:

- strong color preference, especially for red or yellow
- need for movement to elicit or sustain visual attention; either the viewer or the object viewed needs to be moving to maximize the viewer's ability to view the object
- visual latency—delayed responses in looking at objects
- visual field preferences—the presence of unusual field locations in addition to loss of visual field
- difficulties with visual complexity—difficulty when an object itself presents a complex display, when an object is viewed within an environment that presents a complex display, or when an object is viewed at the same time that other sensory input is competing for the viewer's attention and ability to manage sensory stimuli
- light-gazing and nonpurposeful gaze
- difficulty with distance viewing
- absent or atypical visual reflexes—the reflex to blink in response to an approaching object is impaired

- difficulty with visual novelty—a preference for viewing familiar objects is shown
- absence of visually guided reach—the ability to look at and touch an object at the same time is not displayed, and these two actions are performed separately. (This characteristic was originally called "atypical patterns of visual-motor behavior" in earlier versions of the author's work and the functional assessment called the CVI Range.)

Overall, children who exhibit any of these characteristics or visual behaviors are usually unable to use their vision consistently in what might be thought of as a "normal" way. That is, they may not look at or pay attention visually to things they might be expected to have an interest in or be able to see. They may fix their attention on something unusual, such as a light or the moving blades of a ceiling fan. Or they may have difficulty perceiving objects under certain environmental conditions, to the extent that observers may conclude that their vision changes from moment to moment. Although medical and educational professionals have observed and studied these characteristics, there is a lack of published data and documented information on the topic.

In general, the greater the severity of CVI, the greater the number of CVI characteristics present. However, these characteristics may change or improve. Some professionals believe that many children with CVI, if not the majority of children, improve, but few develop normal vision, and recovery may take months or years (Good, 2004). In this author's experience, the degree of change experienced by a child without targeted intervention is usually more limited than the improvement generally seen in children who are provided intervention based on a systematic approach relating to the key characteristics of CVI. For this reason, early intervention—the identification of the presence of CVI based on careful assessment, as described in Chapter 5, and planned intervention, as outlined in Chapter 6—can be particularly important to the growth and development of a child. Students who have progressed or have improved their use of functional vision tend to have fewer and milder effects of the unique visual and behavioral traits accompanying CVI, although few progress to the point of having completely typical vision. If these characteristic behaviors diminish, have a reduced effect, or completely disappear, they are said to resolve. As explained in the following chapters, a CVI characteristic is resolved if it no longer interferes with the use of vision and the resolved behavior is similar or identical to typical visual behavior.

By understanding students' visual preferences, aversions, and difficulties, teachers and other professionals can present visual stimuli and environments that are most likely to encourage students to use their vision, and to learn to do so in a sustained way. The following sections describe in more detail the visual behaviors and characteristics typically seen in the presence of CVI.

COLOR PREFERENCE

Individuals with CVI often have a strong attraction to visual targets of a particular color. According to data from the Pediatric VIEW Program of Western Pennsylvania Hospital (Lantzy & Roman, 2002–2007), of 76 children with CVI ages 6 months to 15 years of age, 55 percent were reported to have a preference for red, 34 percent preferred yellow, and 11 percent preferred either green, pink, blue, or no color. Jan et al. (1987) reported attraction to color as a unique characteristic associated with CVI, but it is unclear how or why attraction to a particular color evolves.

According to Norcia, Tyler, and Hamer (1990), a 2-week-old infant can distinguish a red object from a green one, but it remains unclear whether infants actually perceive red better than other bright colors. They discussed the belief that there are numerous factors, including brightness of the object, contrast, and surroundings, that may account for an infant's attraction to a bright target.

Some parents have identified a specific object of their child's favorite color that has been present in a consistent location since the child's infancy, such as a red Elmo doll (based on the red character from the Sesame Street television program) propped in the corner of the child's crib or bed (Roman, 1996). In such cases, it is possible that these children had repeated experiences with the visually simple object and essentially "learned" the color in that way. Whether an individual with CVI demonstrates color preference due to inherent brain functions or because of repeated exposure to an object or objects of a particular color, it is important for professionals working with children with CVI to investigate the question of color preference and, when a preferred color exists, to integrate this color into objects used in daily routines or learning and in leisure. (See color insert, Photo 1.)

Use of the preferred color can serve as a sort of visual "anchor," a way to attract attention toward specific objects or symbols. For example, for the child who prefers red, it will be helpful to use a red spoon, a red toothbrush, a red switch to activate a radio, and a red cup to encourage visual attention to meaningful objects. Favorite color can also be used with a pre-academic student to highlight the salient difference between two similar letters, such as *d* and *b*, as described in the following example.

Nancy, a 6-year-old Chinese student diagnosed with congenital CVI, was unable to recognize black Chinese characters presented on a white background. Although she continued to have difficulty reading the characters used at school, she quickly learned to recognize the same characters written at home by his mother when they were highlighted with red, Nancy's favorite color. Using the symbols outlined in red, Nancy was able to correctly name nearly 100 Chinese word characters.

NEED FOR MOVEMENT

Although in some instances the perception of movement has interfered with the ability of a child with CVI to use his or her vision, the majority of children with CVI have a tendency to be attracted to objects that have properties of movement over those that remain stationary. Many students with CVI can see objects only when they themselves are moving, or when the objects are moving. The rate of movement itself may vary from child to child. It can be said that these children "visually alert" to objects that are in motion—that is, they demonstrate behavior indicating an awareness of the visual stimulus presented. This alerting to motion can take many forms, depending on the child's condition, abilities, and disabilities: the child may smile or become quiet, or have a direct response, such as looking at an object or turning in its direction. For this reason, it is helpful for professionals to be sensitive to any change exhibited by a child.

In general, long before an infant recognizes the details in a children's picture book, he or she will turn and attend to the movement of a mobile suspended over the crib. In early infancy, a baby will watch the *movement* of the objects dangling overhead without any true recognition of what the visual details of the objects themselves are. Movement attracts attention; a person standing on a corner will typically notice a moving car before he or she notices a car that is parked by the curb. The

tendency of many children with CVI to notice movement may be related in some cases to damage to motion centers or other parts of the brain, to their unique visual fields, or to the retention of motion vision in the absence of any other vision that sometimes results from injury to the visual cortex.

For children with CVI, one very important way to begin to activate the visual system is to present objects that have movement properties. Because many children are attracted to movement, educators can make use of this response to help them initiate looking behaviors. Most students with CVI tend to respond more consistently and for longer periods of time to objects that either produce motion or have shiny reflective surfaces that give the illusion of movement. Examples of items with reflective surfaces include single-color Mylar pom-poms, balloons, and papers. Some objects embody a combination of motion and reflection and thus have an extremely strong and invasive effect on the visual system; they are difficult to ignore, and may facilitate a visual response even in children who don't seem to notice other targets. For example, Mylar pinwheels, balloons, and windsocks all have the combined properties of motion and reflection. (See color insert, Photo 2.)

Some students with CVI will increase their ability to function visually by using movement. When objects in the environment are not moving or do not have reflective surfaces, some children will move their head or body in order to provide themselves with visual stimulation. This phenomenon may explain why some children with CVI tend to move randomly through their environment: They move to stimulate themselves or to see better.

Other behaviors that may be related to the need for movement have been reported by parents, including a child's tendency to spend long periods of time gazing out the window of a moving car as objects quickly pass through the visual field and a tendency to spend long periods of time gazing at television. This attention to the television may in turn be related to the movement of colors, objects, or figures across the television screen. Some parents report that their children show particular interest in or attention to television during sporting events. This interest may stem from the display usually presented by most events, consisting of a single-color background with brightly colored figures moving back and forth over a playing field.

Mirrors may be the first objects with reflective surfaces that everyone encounters on a daily basis, but they should be presented to children with CVI with a degree of caution. Although children with CVI may enjoy viewing reflective surfaces, mirrors often present complex visual arrays to the viewer because they reflect back the environment that is opposite to the mirror's surface. Because the human face is a highly complex configuration and many children with CVI have difficulty recognizing faces (Morse, 2006), it is unlikely that most children with CVI will be able to attend to the details of their face reflected in a mirror until much of their CVI has been resolved. It is common, however, for students with CVI to visually attend to the *surface* of a mirror, perhaps in an attempt to engage in light-gazing behaviors rather than in attending to the figures or images present in the mirror's surface.

Similarly, parents and classroom teachers frequently describe students with CVI having a strong attraction to ceiling fans. This attraction may be caused by the continuous movement of a large object that is generally positioned against a single-color background, providing high contrast and little visual complexity.

VISUAL LATENCY

Visual latency refers to delayed response in looking from the time a target is presented to the time the target is visually regarded. An individual exhibiting visual latency has visual responses that are slow and frequently delayed. During the time before a response is exhibited, the student with CVI may act as though no visual target is present. Even if the object is a familiar one, is not visually complex, and is of the child's preferred color, a student may react as though the object is not present at all. If, however, sufficient wait time is permitted, the student may eventually turn in the direction of the target and either localize (turn toward) or fixate (focus) on the object. In general, delayed response is more pronounced in students who have minimal amounts of consistent functional vision and is less pronounced in students whose CVI is more resolved. Visual latency varies from student to student and latency time varies for the individual student as well. For example, visual latency may be more prolonged when a child is tired or overstimulated, or when a child has done little consistent viewing of objects (either in the particular working session or in general) prior to the time a target has been presented. Latency may decrease as a student engages in more purposeful looking, and eventually, latency may become resolved altogether.

Latency may vary with the object, the color of the object, the complexity of the object, or the array—that is, the number of elements involved and the surrounding environment. It is difficult to define the amount of time that should be allotted for waiting for a particular student to visually respond. In general, however, latency is linked to the consistency with which each student uses his or her vision—that is, the frequency and duration of use of vision in functional routines. When working with a student who exhibits visual latency, it is vital that the degree of visual latency be carefully evaluated and that appropriate amounts of time be considered in waiting for the student to respond.

VISUAL FIELD PREFERENCES

According to Jan and Groenveld (1993), visual field preferences are present in almost all students who have CVI. They may ignore information presented in certain areas of their visual field and they may turn their heads to view objects from a particular portion of their field of view. Jan and Groenveld suggest that a child's visual fields be carefully evaluated so that field preferences can be identified and interventions can be planned accordingly. Visual field differences stem from damage affecting the visual pathways and visual processing centers in the brain, and their extent and location are therefore determined by the extent and location of the damage. It is likely that visual field preferences, as with other CVI characteristics exhibited by a child, will change and, in some children, resolve completely.

Many children with CVI may have peripheral field preferences. Peripheral vision regulates seeing in low light, perception of moving targets, and the ability to perceive forms in space. Thus, these individuals tend to orient most consistently to movement and to form rather than detail. Many students tend to show a mixed-field preference (that is, the field preferences are different in each eye), or hemianopsia (lack of vision in half the visual field). In these cases, a student will notice the position of an object using one eye, and then may turn his or her head to use the other eye for examination of the object's details or identity. In students who show a mixed-field preference, a pattern of head turning associated with locating position, and then switching eyes to identify the object, is frequently seen. It is important that professionals working with children identify this pattern, so that the head turning is interpreted correctly, as an intentional attempt on the student's part to use vision, rather than as a random nonvisually associated behavior.

Some professionals find it difficult to imagine that a child has a visual field loss in the presence of a normal eye exam. It is important to remember that all visual functions are primarily regulated in the brain, and it is therefore possible that any of the visual difficulties with which we are familiar in children who have ocular visual impairments may have associated cortical components that are not easily detected through traditional eye examinations.

It is rare that central vision is the preferred visual field in children with CVI. Children who have central field preferences would most likely have little or no difficulty with objects that present visual complexity or with viewing objects at a distance.

DIFFICULTY WITH VISUAL COMPLEXITY

In the context of visual behavior characteristic of children with CVI, visual complexity encompasses three dimensions: complexity of the pattern on the surface of an object; complexity of a visual array—that is, complexity presented by an object within its surrounding environment; and the complexity of the sensory environment. Children with CVI may have difficulty with visual complexity because their visual systems can become overwhelmed by multiple, competing stimuli and they are unable to process what they are seeing.

Complexity of Patterns

Children with CVI in general appear to have the most consistent visual responses to objects with simple patterns or color on their surfaces. Objects with visually simple surfaces, especially those that are of a single color, seem to allow many children to establish and maintain their ability to view them. It is important that the single color of the object presented be matched to the child's identified "favorite" color in cases in which a color preference is known. (See color insert, Photos 1 and 3.)

Complexity of Visual Array

It is also important that the visual array and background be carefully monitored for children with CVI. Even familiar or favorite-color objects presented in a complex array of other objects will not be recognizable by some children with CVI. Jan et al. (1987) referred to this phenomenon as *visual crowding*. For many children with CVI, when an object is placed against a visually complex background, or when objects are placed too close together, no single object can be sorted out from any other. (See color insert, Photo 4.)

The following example may help illustrate the meaning of complexity of visual array. Imagine you are standing in the center field of a large sports stadium during the day. The stands are completely filled. In the huge array of people filling the stands, you are asked to locate your mother. It will be extremely difficult for you—for any individual—to locate one single figure, even a familiar one, within such a complex visual array. For many children with CVI, locating a familiar object when it is placed among an array of three or four other common objects may be as difficult as the task of locating one person in the stands of a sports arena. Now, imagine that your mother is placed in one section of the sports stadium at night and that a spotlight is placed directly on her: You will now be able to locate your mother in this stadium because the complexity of what is viewed has been reduced and the figure of your mother has been highlighted. The intervention for children with CVI in such cases is similar. When an object

to be viewed is placed against a plain background, the child with CVI no longer has to struggle to sort out the object from the background. This simple environmental adaptation can make the difference in whether a child with CVI can visually alert to an object (show through his or her behavior an awareness that something has changed or been introduced into the field of view) and attend to it (turn toward the target or even visually fixate on it).

Another example of the meaning of complexity of array is the children's "hidden picture" puzzle, in which a number of common objects are usually embedded within an illustration. Although these common objects would be quickly recognized if they were presented individually or against simple backgrounds, they appear to be almost lost in the cluttered array of images. Although the viewer's visual acuity has not been altered, nor has the picture been blurred in any way, it requires a good bit of effort to distinguish these common figures and "disembed" them from their background. For many children with CVI, the world may appear as a hidden picture's array, with everyday objects being "hidden" among the colors, patterns, and competing sensory information of the environment. (See color insert, Photo 5.)

Complexity of Sensory Environment

The third dimension involved in visual complexity pertains to competition of additional sensory input. For some children with CVI, the process of visual attention can occur only when there are no distractions from other sensory stimuli. Children who are in the early stages of learning to use their vision may find it very difficult to maintain attention on a target when touch, voice, or even strong olfactory inputs compete for their attention. It is important to assess each student's individual tolerance of additional sensory input and to respect the student's possible need to have other sensory inputs added in a sequential rather than a simultaneous way. Just as many students may be able to see objects only when they are presented to them one at a time, some students may not be able to look at an object and attend to other input or information at the same time. For example, if a student is visually attending to a target, it may be necessary to wait to praise the student verbally for looking until after he or she naturally ends the visual attention to the target. It may also be necessary to withhold praise that includes touching or providing food rewards while the student is actively engaged in looking.

The interventions or approaches for helping children with CVI cope with complexity of the sensory environment are different from the techniques used with students with multiple disabilities. In those cases, a variety of simultaneous sensory inputs are provided to allow for different forms of sensory information that the student may be able to process. Although such techniques may be effective with some student populations, including students with multiple disabilities, children with CVI have unique needs. By providing sequential rather than simultaneous sensory inputs, students with CVI will more likely be able to sustain their visual functioning.

The CVI characteristic of visual complexity is one that requires careful assessment and precise instructional planning. It is the characteristic with the strongest effect and is one of the most prolonged, tending to linger in students even as they approach resolution of their visual difficulties.

LIGHT-GAZING AND NONPURPOSEFUL GAZE

Light-gazing and nonpurposeful gaze are exhibited by many children who have CVI, who spend prolonged periods of time gazing at primary sources of light. The light itself can be either natural light or artificial forms of light; parents report that although their child doesn't appear to fixate on expected targets, he or she may spend long periods of time gazing at light streaming in from a window or at overhead lights. (See color insert, Photo 6.)

Nonpurposeful gaze for a student with CVI refers to the apparent inability to visually attend to any specific target. Other forms of nonpurposeful gaze include apparent visual fixation on a target when, in fact, no target is present. Parents have also reported that it appears as though their child is looking through them or through an object rather than directly at it (Roman, 1996). It may be difficult to discern whether a student is staring at lights as a primary form of visual stimulation or if the student gazes toward light in an attempt to avoid looking at overly visually complex environments. In essence, the light may be a sort of visual "safety zone" in an otherwise visually overwhelming setting. An additional explanation for light-gazing is that some students cannot look and listen simultaneously, and thus will look away from a target toward light or a blank wall when listening to voices, music, or environmental sounds. Students who engage in nonpurposeful gaze or light-gazing behaviors frequently turn their heads away from, rather than toward, an object, figure, or activity, and may appear to be disinterested in the activity when in fact, they may be attempting to process input or information by using some sense other than vision. Light-gazing is a normal behavior in children at birth, and its persistence in many children with CVI signals a delay in their normal visual development.

DIFFICULTY WITH DISTANCE VIEWING

Some students with CVI who have difficulty with distance viewing behave as though they were highly nearsighted. The student may position his or her face within inches of a visual target and have great difficulty recognizing even familiar or large targets when they are presented beyond near space. This characteristic is closely linked to the characteristic of complexity—children who tend to have difficulty with one will have difficulty with the other. (See color insert, Photo 7.) The closer an object is moved toward the face, the more the background is obscured for the viewer. When appropriate objects are presented in environments that are completely free of visual clutter, many students may be able to visually attend to the objects at more typical distances, as described in the following example.

> *Juan had difficulty recognizing any family members when they approached him without speaking. Whether at home, at school, or during an outing, Juan was never quite sure who was present until they spoke to him. During summer vacation, Juan's family spent time at a remote beach with white sand and crystal blue water. While Juan was facing the sand and the sea, he surprised all of his family by being able to point directly at his mother when she was standing approximately 50 feet away. This was quite surprising to family members because Juan's mother did not speak to him, but simply waved to him from a distance. The environmental conditions were perfect for Juan to be able to identify his mother from this distance. Because his mother was positioned on the white sand against a noncomplex blue background, with no intervening visual distractions, Juan had no difficulty identifying the single figure that was his mother.*

As noted, distance viewing and complexity are interrelated characteristics. Juan's inability to notice faces stems from the CVI characteristic of complexity, but his ability to even know whether a person is present is dependent on the number of visual elements between Juan and the target figure. The greater the number of visual details, the greater the difficulty in disembedding the target from the visually complicated background.

ABSENT OR ATYPICAL VISUAL REFLEX RESPONSES

Many students with CVI tend to have atypical responses with regard to two innate reflexes that serve to protect the eyes from potential harm. These are known as the *visual blink reflex* and the *visual threat response*. Both the visual blink and the visual threat responses are examples of innate responses intended to protect the eyes from potential harm.

The first reflex that is atypical in many children is the visual blink. Normally, when a child is touched at the bridge of the nose, he or she blinks simultaneously with the touch. Many students with CVI frequently have either an absent or a delayed blink to an unexpected touch at the bridge of the nose.

The second response that is atypical in some students with CVI is the visual threat response. Typically, when a hand is moved quickly toward the face on midline, children reflexively blink in response to the incoming visual threat. In many students with CVI, the blink to the perceived threat is either absent or occurs with some latency or delay.

DIFFICULTY WITH VISUAL NOVELTY

The human visual system is designed to be alert to targets that are new or unusual or are not automatically perceived as familiar. The more novel the target is, the greater the innate desire experienced by humans to visually investigate (Restak, 2003). According to Thompson, Fagan, and Fulker (1991), infants demonstrate a visual preference for objects that are novel over those that are familiar. These authors' longitudinal studies indicate that novelty preference during the first year of life predicts later IQ and may reflect specific cognitive processes.

The response to novelty begins in infancy and continues throughout adult life. Imagine sitting in a room full of 200 adult learners in a large lecture hall. Most adults view the figures in the room as broad, sweeping "peopleness" rather than seeing 200 individual people; in other words, no single person would tend to emerge as a distinct visual target. Now imagine an Elvis Presley impersonator entering the room, dressed in a spangled white satin costume complete with cape and matching boots. It is likely that everyone in the room will immediately turn to look at this novel, unusual figure.

It should be noted, however, that many children with CVI seem to have an *anti*novelty response. They prefer to visually regard targets that have been viewed over and over and, conversely, to ignore objects or other targets that are new. This behavior may be puzzling to families and professionals, who may at times bombard a child with new stimuli in an attempt to elicit visual attention. Unfortunately, these attempts may result in misperceptions about the child's visual abilities or interest.

Parents are often able to identify a child's "favorite" objects. These familiar or preferred objects often are of the child's favored color, and have features of low visual complexity. For example, the child who may ignore a new multisensory toy may consistently look at a red Elmo doll. It is therefore critical for professionals to understand how to select new objects for the child to view, based on the critical elements of the known objects.

ABSENCE OF VISUALLY GUIDED REACH

Jan and Groenveld (1993) and Dutton (2006), among others, have commented on the tendency of many children with CVI to not look and reach simultaneously. Rather, students with CVI tend to localize or fixate on a target, turn away, and then reach in the direction of the target. This pattern may also be reversed. In such cases, the student will touch an object, and after some moments of touching, turn to visually regard the object that is being touched. Regardless of whether vision or touch leads the sequence of behavior, in many children with CVI, looking and reaching occur as two separate, rather than simultaneous events.

COEXISTING OCULAR CONDITIONS

As professionals work to determine whether the presence of CVI is the cause of a child's visual disability or differences, it is important to note that CVI may coexist with ocular forms of visual impairment. When an eye condition coexists with CVI, it makes it difficult to determine whether a particular behavior is due to the ocular or cortical condition. For example,

- High myopia or hyperopia, optic nerve disorders, cataracts, and in some cases retinitis of prematurity (ROP) may mask the effect of the characteristic of *difficulty with visual complexity.*
- More severe forms of ROP, glaucoma, and retinal disease may mask the effect of the characteristic of *visual field preferences.*
- Low acuity resulting from various disorders may mask the effect of the characteristic of *light-gazing.*

Because the identification of CVI may be missed when other eye conditions are present, a careful assessment is particularly important in this situation. When there is a significant ocular disorder, CVI is frequently not diagnosed because the ocular condition provides a logical explanation for the loss of vision. When CVI is diagnosed, usually the eye condition (or normal eye exam) does not give sufficient evidence or explanation for why the child has so little functional vision. For example, strabismus (eyes not aligned) or Stage I ROP does not result in a child acting "blind." Optic nerve hypoplasia (underdeveloped optic nerve) is also not an adequate reason for profound vision loss. When the child has a history of a brain condition associated with CVI *and* has an ocular issue that generally does not explain the degree of functional vision loss, it may be because the CVI (often undiagnosed) is the actual underlying cause of visual impairment. Coexisting CVI and ocular conditions are discussed further in the section on the CVI Resolution Chart in Chapter 5.

IMPROVEMENT IN CVI

The behavioral characteristics displayed by many children with CVI may resolve over time; that is, they may change or improve to become more typical. In the author's experience, students with CVI who receive systematic intervention with reference to the visual behaviors accompanying CVI show observable and steady progress in the use of their functional vision.

In the author's work with young children with CVI, the visual behaviors associated with the condition tend to become resolved in the following order (Lantzy & Roman, 2002–2007):

- Early resolution: Light-gazing, atypical or absent blink reflex
- Middle resolution: Color preference, visual latency, difficulty with visual novelty, atypical or absent reflex to visual threats, need for movement
- Later resolution: Visual field preferences, absence of visually guided reach, difficulty with visual complexity, difficulty with distance viewing

Before interventions can be tailored to the specific mix of visual behaviors exhibited by an individual student with CVI, it is necessary to do a functional vision assessment with reference to the CVI-related characteristics outlined in this chapter. Assessing the presence and degree of each of these characteristics, as explained in Chapter 5, provides a greater likelihood of appropriate interventions and of improved outcomes as well.

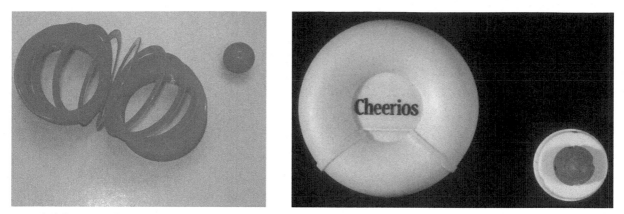

1. Children with CVI typically have strong color preferences and respond best to objects of a single color.

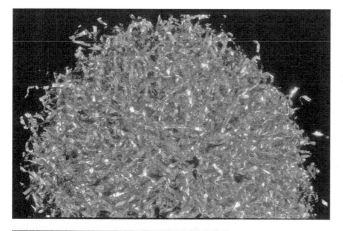

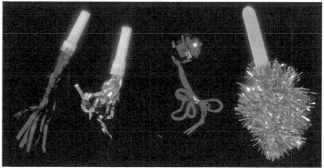

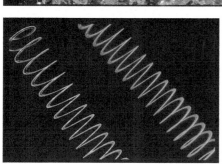

2. Objects such as these that either produce motion or have shiny reflective surfaces, giving the illusion of movement, capture the attention of students with CVI who are attracted to movement.

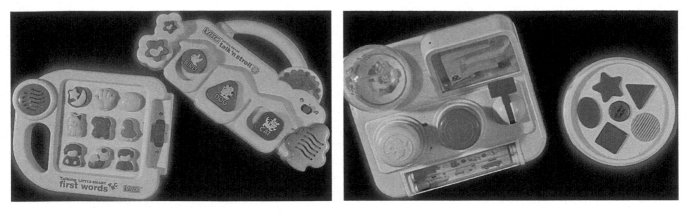

3. Students exhibiting the CVI characteristic of difficulty with visual complexity tend to have trouble perceiving highly patterned, visually complex objects such as these.

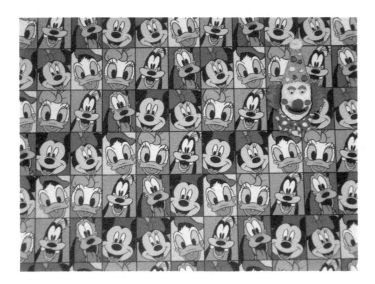

4. Complexity of array is illustrated in this picture, in which a complex object, the clown, becomes lost against the background, which is also visually complex.

5. Many children with CVI may experience the world as a hidden picture (left), in which common objects such as this spoon (right) are hidden among the colors, patterns, and competing sensory information of the environment.

6. Many children with CVI are attracted to light and spend prolonged periods gazing at light sources. For this reason, lightboxes are useful for drawing their attention to objects and images.

7. For a child with CVI, this stop sign may be lost amid the background of a street scene because of the characteristics of difficulty with distance viewing and difficulty with visual complexity. The sign can be seen much more easily in isolation.

8. Activities for students in Phase II CVI are designed to combine vision with touch. This girl is working with her teacher on looking and reaching in an environment of increased visual complexity.

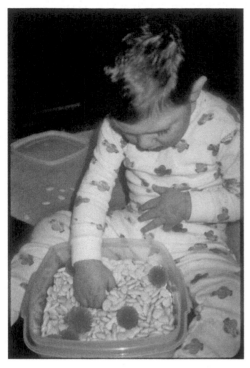

9. In an activity adapted for early Phase II CVI, this boy is able to locate simple red balls in a plain, single-color background of lima beans.

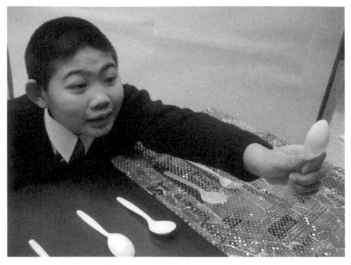

10. In Phase III CVI, this student is able to use visually guided reach to pick up a spoon from a patterned background.

11. Students in early Phase III CVI typically are able to recognize simple images in age-appropriate books.

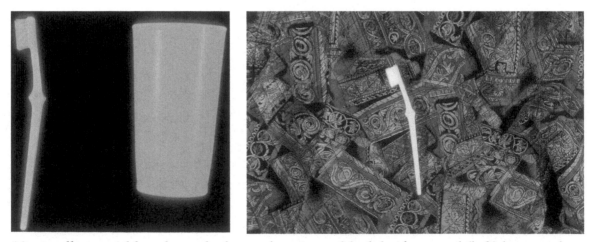

12. A yellow toothbrush can be located against a black background (left) by a student in Phase I CVI. The same student may ignore the toothbrush when it appears against a complex pattern (right).

13. An environmental cue, such as this flag (left), may be seen when it is presented individually, but not in its natural setting of complexity (right).

14. Students in Phase I CVI require environments without visual or auditory distractions. A Level I environmental adaptation, such as isolating the object on a lightbox against a dark background, enables students to focus on the object.

a b

15. Students in Phase II CVI can maintain visual attention in environments with a small degree of visual and auditory competition, such as this Level II environment (a). Only in Phase III CVI can students locate objects in typical or non-adapted settings (b), which are considered Level III environments.

16. Use of objects in the student's preferred color against a plain background promotes visually guided reach in Phase II CVI.

17. In Phase III CVI, this student is able to recognize his face in a mirror, as well as the faces of others.

18. The Mayer-Johnson symbols shown here have been adapted to make them more visually identifiable for some students who have CVI. Mayer-Johnson and other symbol systems are used to facilitate communication or to help students anticipate daily routines.

19. Highlighting salient features in red helps this student learn to recognize a new Chinese character.

20. Practicing sorting skills with these red and blue blocks helps this student learn to differentiate important visual features and understand the concepts of "alike" and "different."

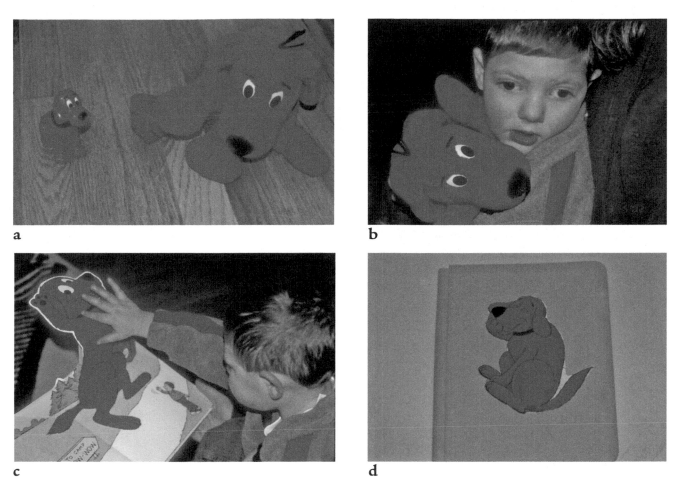

a

b

c

d

21. One strategy for teaching students to recognize salient features uses the children's book character Clifford the Big Red Dog. (a) Start with a stuffed animal or other three-dimensional representation chosen for simplicity. (b) Allow the child to become used to the toy. (c) Introduce the character in a pop-up book, which embodies movement. (d) Isolate the two-dimensional image of the character before finally introducing a two-dimensional image embedded in a more complex picture.

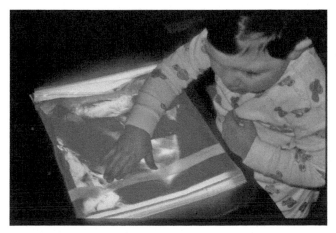

22. Manipulating a bag filled with red gel on a lightbox addresses the CVI characteristics of color preference, need for movement, difficulty with complexity, light-gazing, and difficulty with novelty.

23. Working with translucent color pegs on a lightbox can facilitate the development of visually guided reach, as well as skills in sorting and matching.

a   b   c

24. Students with CVI can learn environmental cues or landmarks first in isolation and then in actual locations with increasing degrees of visual complexity. Features can be presented in a sequence: (a) an isolated image, such as this pole, (b) an image showing more of the background, and (c) in the actual environment.

25. This student with CVI is able to take ski lessons because his ski instructor's orange jacket, in the student's preferred color, serves as a target for the student to follow on the slopes.

CHAPTER

4

The Primacy of Parents

The assessment of children with cortical visual impairment (CVI)—or with any other condition—needs to begin with the child's family. Parents are the true experts when it comes to their children, and the importance of the information they can provide should not be underestimated. Parents and other family members live with their children 24 hours a day, and know how they act and respond under widely varying circumstances. For this reason, any investigation of a child who may have CVI needs to begin at home. Functional vision assessment for CVI is discussed in detail in Chapter 5, but the first step in understanding what may be happening with a child is an interview with the family. Family members will also be involved when the child's behavior is observed and when the child has a direct functional assessment for CVI, so it is important to be aware of their concerns at those times.

Parents' participation in structured intervention, discussed later in Chapter 6, is also a key to success in helping a child learn how to use his or her vision and develop visual skills.

At the same time, the parents of children with CVI need support from professionals that goes beyond educational intervention with their children. Because CVI is not generally well understood, many parents may find that their questions and concerns frequently are not addressed, and that their reports of their experiences with their children are not always believed or taken seriously. They need clear, accurate information; acknowledgment of their child's potential; and help and supportive efforts by advocates who will ensure that children with CVI receive the services that will allow them to develop and improve their visual abilities.

PARENTS AS EXPERTS

Parents are the best reporters about their children. The parents and other family members of children with CVI possess critical information about how their children respond visually and the ways in which the child may display

Assessment of children with CVI needs to begin with the child's family. Parents are the true experts when it comes to their children, and the importance of the information they can provide should not be underestimated.

the specific visual and behavioral characteristics typical of CVI (which are described in Chapter 3). Nevertheless, the following account, provided by a mother of a child diagnosed soon after birth with CVI, may not be an unusual experience for many families.

My 7-year-old daughter, Maria, has severe multiple disabilities, including spastic quadriplegia cerebral palsy and CVI. Maria's disabilities are secondary to birth asphyxia, including HIE [hypoxic-ischemic encephalopathy]. When Maria was discharged from the NICU [neonatal intensive care unit], I distinctly remember nearly all of the hospital staff pretty much looking on us with pity. No one held any expectations for this child I was taking home.

Because of her rough beginning, we were instructed up front that she could experience vision and hearing problems. I think I learned the specific diagnosis of CVI by the time she was 3 months old. What is most troubling is that once we had the diagnosis, we did not receive appropriate instruction or intervention recommendations. Oh, we had "therapy" coming out of our ears—physical therapy, occupational

therapy, speech, vision, water, massage, group vision therapy, special needs playgroup—you name it. If it was recommended for Maria, being good parents doing our good parent job, we said, "Sure, we'll try that." But "therapy," translated into our actual real-life experience, meant take Maria somewhere, have folks do things to her, have her scream the entire time, then scream for the next several hours from the trauma of it all, get ready to do the whole experience again the next day, exist in complete exhaustion, then cry myself to sleep.

Our well-known and well-respected pediatric ophthalmologist would not recommend glasses for Maria because "they would not make a difference." I told my daughter's early intervention team that I thought Maria saw better at night. My observation was pooh-poohed. At another meeting I shared that I thought Maria's eyes worked better when she was in the bathtub. Again my comment was brushed off, and the team responded, "Well, that is not a real-world scenario. Do you want her to spend the rest of her life in a bathtub?" Needless to say, I realized these folks had little use for my opinion.

When Maria was 2 years, 4 months, I stopped all of her so-called therapy. Using parts of what I had learned by previously watching therapists and then modifying what they did, we adopted a highly regimented daily routine, including making modifications to our home environment. We provided low lighting, noise insulation, less clutter, and so on. Within one month, Maria was a totally different child, one who was now playful, cheerful, and pleasant to be around. She was no longer crying 12 of the 24 hours of the day, and, despite having spastic quadriplegia, would let me twist and stretch her into a pretzel shape when the conditions were right.

Maria is now 7½ years old, and knowing that we unknowingly may have missed her greatest window for visual attainment, I feel immensely let down. I wish that at least one person among the very many professionals we dealt with would have known what we should have been doing for Maria, I truly believe that much of the terrible, traumatizing early childhood experience was totally avoidable. No one ever implied to me that there was anything that they or I could do to potentially lessen the severity of Maria's CVI. No one ever suggested to me that CVI and its effects could be diminished and that appropriate intervention was possible. I did know, as a general statement, that some kids with CVI improved, but no one ever suggested that there were strategies for achieving this. And most certainly, no one ever took the general CVI information that we all had access to and applied it to modifying their therapy sessions with my daughter.

—Mother of a child with CVI

This account expresses a frustration that is reported by countless parents in their search for information and assistance from both medical and educational professionals. As eager as parents are to hear answers from experts, it may be more effective for medical and educational professionals to first listen to parents, who are the most reliable observers regarding the effect of CVI on their children. Professionals who work with children who have CVI need to pay careful attention to the experiences and the information supplied by the people who know these children best. And, by listening to and guiding these parents, they will be giving children with CVI the best chance to improve their visual functioning.

THE IMPORTANCE OF INTERVIEWS

Overall, family interviews are an important, if not in some respects the most important, source of assessment information. An interview with family members is the first step in assessing a child for the presence of CVI, and sets the stage for observation and further direct assessment of the child.

Evidence that a parent interview instrument is an effective tool in identifying the unique characteristics of CVI in infants comes from the author's test of a 25-question interview (Roman, 1996). The purpose of the study was to explore whether parent interviews could provide reliable and valid information. Responses to the interview questions were scored as either positive for (or consistent with) a diagnosis of CVI or as negative for CVI. For example, when parents or caregivers were asked, "Do you think your child has a favorite color?" answers such as "red," or "He seems to see yellow best," were scored as positively associated with the presence of the CVI characteristic of color preference. Conversely, answers such as "I never noticed," or, "Yes, he prefers yellow, green, blue, red, and other bright colors," were scored as not associated with the CVI characteristic of color preference. (The original interview questions appear in Sidebar 4.1.)

In the first part of the study, 23 parents were interviewed in their homes. The responses to the interview questions from caregivers of 11 children with a diagnosis of CVI were compared to those from caregivers of 12 children who were diagnosed with an ocular form of visual impairment. When the responses were analyzed, reports from parents or caregivers of infants and children with CVI were very different from the reports of parents or caregivers of children with ocular visual impairments. The results demonstrated that responses of parents or caregivers to a set of interview questions probing for the presence of CVI can reliably differentiate the presence of CVI from the presence of ocular visual impairments. (Test-retest reliability was between 84 percent and 96 percent; the mean percentage of agreement for interscorer reliability was 92 percent.)

SIDEBAR 4.1   *Interview Questions for Parents*

Substitute the child's name for "your child" in the questions.

1. Tell me what you do with a toy to get your child interested in it.
2. When you show your child something, how do you know he or she sees it?
3. Does your child have a favorite side or a favorite head position?
4. Does your child usually find objects by looking or by feeling for them?
5. Do you have concerns about the way your child sees?
6. Where do you usually hold objects for your child to look at?
7. What are your child's favorite things in your house?
8. What, if anything, have doctors told you about your child's eyes?
9. When does your child usually like to look at things?
10. What color are the things your child likes to look at most?
11. What does your child do when he or she is near very shiny or mirrored objects?
12. Describe how your child behaves around lamps or ceiling fans.
13. Are you usually able to identify (be certain of) what your child is looking at?
14. Does your child usually first notice things that move or things that don't move?
15. How does your child position his or her head when you think he or she is looking at something?
16. Do you think your child has a "favorite" color?
17. Does your child seem to notice things more at home or more in new places?
18. Describe how your child positions his or her head when swatting or reaching toward something.
19. How does your child react when you give him or her new things to look at?
20. Do you position your child in a certain way to help him or her see things?
21. Have you ever been concerned about the way your child's eyes move?
22. What does your child do when there are many objects in front of him or her to look at?
23. Tell me about the faces your child prefers to look at.
24. If your child had his or her own object to look at and a new object, which object do you think he or she would prefer?
25. Tell me what your child's favorite objects or toys look like.

In the second part of the study, the interview questions were asked of parents of infants who had experienced neurological insult consistent with the frequent causes of CVI. The oldest child in this part of the study was 6 months old. At the same time that the interview was being conducted with the adult, a functional vision assessment was conducted with the infant in a separate room of the parent's home. The results of both the interview and the functional vision assessment were compared and scored as positive or negative for CVI. The results indicated that parents and caregivers were able to reliably and validly report the typical visual characteristics associated with CVI in their infants, and that the same characteristics reported by parents were also observed in the functional vision assessment. (Agreement between interview scores and behavioral functional vision assessment was significant at the $p = .0001$ level.) In addition, a pattern emerged from the atypical visual responses reported by parents, revealing that what may be considered random visual behaviors by some medical practitioners are, in fact, typical patterns for children with CVI.

The interview questions from this study can be used by teachers of students with visual impairments and other professionals to interview parents as part of their assessment, as discussed in the next chapter. Each open-ended question is presented by the interviewer, and answers provided by the parent or caregiver are assigned a positive score (the response is suggestive of the presence of CVI), or a negative score (the response is not suggestive of CVI). Professionals who conduct the interview may need to take notes, or, with the parent's permission, tape-record the interview in order to carefully score the responses at a later time.

An Answer Guide with samples of responses that would be scored either positive or negative for CVI is provided in the appendix to this chapter. Based on the author's research (Roman, 1996), and on the findings to date from the two multistate CVI training projects discussed in "My Introduction to CVI" at the beginning of this book, this interview protocol tends to reveal either a profile that is very strongly indicative of CVI, with most or all items scored positive for CVI, or the opposite, with very few, if any, items scored positive for CVI. There is no exact number of items that must be marked positive for CVI in order to initiate interventions. The interview is one important indicator that is considered, in conjunction with medical information, direct observation of the child, and information gathered from the functional assessment used in the identification of CVI that is described in Chapter 5.

Because the identification of CVI depends on the recognition of unique characteristics of visual and behavioral activity, a carefully worded interview with a parent or caregiver might be the most appropriate and most easily implemented method of screening for positive indicators of CVI. However, medical experts often favor expensive and less reliable tests or wait months or even years to finally confirm the diagnosis of CVI.

INTERVIEWING FAMILIES

When educators or other professionals attempt to understand what is happening with a child and undertake an assessment of a child who may have CVI, they will usually obtain information from three sources: interviews with family members and others who know the child well, observation of the child, and a direct assessment of the child. As already noted, an interview with the parents often forms the basis for the rest of the assessment. The interview may take place during one or several sessions, and observation of the child may begin at the same time. Whether the professional visits the home or the parent and child come to the assessor's office, there are a number of steps the professional can take to ensure a more successful interview. The following are some suggestions to make the interview go smoothly:

- Come disarmed, with as few professional trappings as possible. Too many forms, folders, or charts may interfere with establishing a rapport with the parents. Inform the parents if you need to take notes.
- Introduce yourself and communicate that you are sincerely interested in the family—by saying, for example, "Thank you for coming. I'm so happy you're here," or "I'm so glad to meet you."
- Begin by making the parent and child comfortable and reassuring them. Make some small talk (practice this, if necessary, beforehand).

- Acknowledge all the family members who are present, and make a special effort to relate to the child who is about to be evaluated.
- Ask if it is all right to have observers, if any are present.
- Try to let the child know that you enjoy his or her company. Touch, talk to, or compliment the child. Parents will appreciate your attention to him or her.

While the assessor is engaged in these preliminaries, he or she can begin to observe the child and note the following:

- Is the child demonstrating visual curiosity?
- Is the child staring at the lights?
- Is the child holding a special object? If so, notice its properties, such as color, complexity of pattern, or movement.
- How is the child positioned?
- Does the child have any medical equipment?
- Is the child alert, fatigued, or anxious?

It is important for the educator or other professional to be aware, as he or she speaks with family members and throughout the session, of how the discussion is affecting the family, and to respond accordingly. As always, when dealing with families of children who have visual impairments, it is important to understand that they will be concerned for their child and may be upset about the prospect of confronting a new diagnosis. Parents of children who may have CVI may have experienced the frustration of having their unique knowledge of their child disregarded and even disparaged (as described in Maria's case study earlier). They may be highly concerned about their child's ability to see, only to have been told, "Her eyes are fine." Thus, it is important to acknowledge the parents' importance as a source of trustworthy information and to be sensitive to their need for information and support. Other suggestions for interacting with parents and family members include the following:

- Be aware of cultural differences. For example, don't place a high value on the development of eye contact in children who are from cultures in which making eye contact is a sign of disrespect.
- Try not to be afraid of the emotional effects of the interview, on either the parents or yourself. It can be helpful for professionals to have a trusted colleague who is willing to listen and share the feelings evoked by families' emotionally charged stories.
- Know when to touch, hug, and make physical contact, and when not to. Let the parents provide the cues or take the lead.
- Give parents credit for the progress their children make—for example, learning to eat with a spoon, taking steps using a walker, or reading his or her name.

When the parents are comfortable, the more formal section of the interview can begin:

- Ask parents why they have come and what are they hoping to gain from this session.
- Allow the family members to tell their story, even if you have already reviewed the medical records.
- Make note of anything you need to add to the child's medical and educational history.
- Don't correct parents' perceptions or terminology unless what is being discussed will result in a critical misunderstanding that may affect the child.

In interviews with parents, as well as with teachers, caregivers, or others who are familiar with the child, the assessor will want to make sure the following information is covered in regard to visual behaviors:

- What is the child's medical background?
- What does the eye care specialist report?
- What are the parents' and teachers' concerns?
- What does the student prefer to look at?
- Does the student have a preferred color?
- When is the student most visually alert?
- Does the student look directly into faces?
- Does the student notice things that move more than things that are stable?
- Does the student seem to "look through" rather than directly at objects?

The interview questions in Sidebar 4.1 cover visual behaviors about which information needs to be gathered.

CONDUCTING ASSESSMENTS

The formal assessment of the child's vision will take place after the initial interview with the family. The same sensitivity and consideration shown to the family during the interview need to be extended to them throughout the assessment. Before beginning the direct assessment and, specifically, a functional vision assessment, in which a variety of objects and visual stimuli are presented to the child, it is important for the professional to let the child and family members know what he or she will be doing and whether he or she will be taking notes. They will also want to know how the findings will be presented: Will comments and explanations be provided as the assessment proceeds, or will findings be summarized when it is completed? It is also important to find out if the child has any medical needs that need to be taken into account during the assessment: For example, is the child prone to seizures, or is any special positioning required? Parents should be asked to tell the assessor if

they notice any signs of stress in their child, such as the child appearing to be tired, hungry, or overstimulated, and they should be encouraged to comfort their child as needed. In addition, parents need to be comfortable with any assessment materials that include food or treats.

Chapter 5 offers suggestions for activities and materials to use in the direct assessment with a child. During this activity, the assessor will want to continue to convey to the child that his or her company is enjoyable and take some time to make small talk, or focus on something the child seems interested in. While working with the child, the professional may also wish to observe the parents' proximity to the child, to see whether they are hovering, far away, or available. The parent's position in relation to the child may be an indication of the parent's comfort with the assessment situation or their confidence in their child's ability to participate or perform the tasks of the evaluation. A parent who is quietly available is one who allows the child to go beyond his or her reach, and who gives the child the opportunity to interact with new people and materials without "rescuing" him or her.

Rapport with family members should be maintained as the formal portion of the assessment ends. The professional will offer any further information, such as how the findings will be reported, and any necessary consent forms will be obtained. The family should be thanked for the opportunity to work with their child. If they have come to a facility, the professional should accompany them to the door in a companionable and reassuring manner when they depart.

SUPPORTING PARENTS

Parents Have a Different View

All parents have hopes and dreams for their children. It is unlikely that any parent anticipates

All parents have hopes and dreams for their children. Parents of children with CVI hope that their child will feel included, have friends, and face some of the same challenges as their nondisabled peers. This boy, who had severe CVI, is now able to go fishing with his dad.

follow some exceptional rules of parenting. But we are all human: It is likely that the parents of children with CVI and other disabilities are more like the parents of children without disabilities than unlike them. They, too, dream about their child going to school on the bus, or learning to ride a bike, or being invited to birthday parties. Parents of children with CVI and other disabilities hope that their child will feel included, have friends, and be allowed to face some of the same challenges as their nondisabled peers. Isn't it also possible that parents wish educational and medical professionals to allow their children to compete, even if that possibly also means failing? The hopes and dreams of parents of children with CVI differ very little from those of all parents, and professionals need to be aware of the similarities.

Parents Need More Than Information

Although on one hand, many parents of children with CVI may experience times when their need for answers is frustrated and confusion abounds, on the other hand, they may become overwhelmed with information related to their child's physical, developmental, and educational status. Descriptions of medical conditions, diagnostic testing, treatments, medications, developmental evaluation, early intervention, and educational programs can include confusing terminology and hundreds of pieces of new information. Furthermore, the information is often given to parents while they are experiencing considerable anxiety. Even when explanations are offered in the clearest possible manner, it should be expected that not all of the information will be understood.

having a child with disabilities. Some parents will recover from the shock of such difficult news more quickly than others, but regardless of the presence of a disability, most families want their child to achieve his or her full potential. However, educators and medical professionals may have very different views about what "full potential" means. The experts may be more likely to see the obstacles facing the child, rather than the possibilities that parents imagine. Professionals may even feel compelled to quash the hopeful statements of parents, believing that it is their duty to prepare parents for the worst. In general, it is appropriate to adopt a sympathetic attitude, encouraging families to maintain expectations for their child, and taking into account a child's abilities as well as his or her disabilities.

Specialists sometimes treat parents of children with disabilities as though they instinctively

The diagnosis of CVI may be especially subject to misinterpretation. Imagine the emotions that some parents may be experiencing when they take their medically complicated child home from the hospital. They are given directions and orders to see a host of medical specialists, interventionists, and educators. It is not difficult to imagine that, after countless appointments filled with disturbing news, they may feel enormous relief when they hear the ophthalmologist say, "Your child's eyes are fine—we just don't know how well he processes what he sees." Even if they are able to hear and process the ophthalmologist's statement, the message they perceive may cause unfounded hope for parents who are eager to hear good news. The misperception of this information may lead some parents to believe that their child's vision is normal and that no further action need be taken.

It is for reasons such as these that it is important for medical and educational professionals to take a leading role in interpreting the information that bombards parents of children with CVI. Professionals need to remember that parents may not understand that the neurological condition that caused their child's cerebral palsy, cognitive delay, or speech and language difficulty may also have caused CVI.

Advocacy and Action

I am the mother of a newly adopted Chinese baby, Rose, whom we received at 8 months of age from Hunan Province. We were told that she was healthy—sitting, crawling, and eating ground-up table foods. But when we arrived in China and received our little bundle of joy, we had immediate concerns. Rose acted more like an infant than an 8-month-old. She could not even hold her head up. We thought that maybe she had spent the 8 months in a crib with no stimulation. My husband and I knew something was very wrong; however, we accepted this child as our baby.

Upon returning home from China, Rose had jerking motions that concerned us. After months of dealing with many doctors, Rose was

diagnosed with double subdural hematomas of the brain. The doctors felt that Rose had suffered this traumatic brain injury while institutionalized. Rose has also been diagnosed with infantile spasms.

My husband and I have been to many doctors, including ophthalmologists, and yet none have ever described Rose as having CVI. Rose's eyes are normal and healthy. The test conducted to check the connection between the optic nerve and the rest of her brain is normal. Rose's eyes look normal, yet there are so many things she cannot do. Based on my own Internet research, I came to the conclusion that Rose's behaviors indicate that she does in fact have CVI, but no doctor would admit that Rose had this condition until she was 13 months old and I insisted that my question about CVI be answered directly. Doctors generally tell us we "just have to wait and see," but I know waiting is not the answer. I realize it is up to us to gain as much information as possible so that I can help my daughter learn to use her vision.

My specific questions are:

1. Who can assess my daughter's vision?
2. How will this assessment be different from the eye exam, which was not useful?
3. Do you know of any organizations that can support our family and help us meet other parents of children with CVI?
4. Who can help our family develop appropriate approaches to improve Rose's vision?

This little girl whom we have been so fortunate to have in our family has endured so much from the time she was born. She is a survivor, and I believe in my heart of hearts that if this little girl could see, she would progress in her developmental skills. It is amazing to see how far she has come since we got her, and I think that if we can get her to use her vision, she will take off with leaps and bounds.

—Parent of a child with CVI

When educators facilitate improvement in children's vision, they are also supporting their participation in their family's life, as well as in school and elsewhere. The children pictured with their families on these pages are some of the same children shown elsewhere in this book facing the challenges of learning to use their vision despite CVI.

Parents of children with the complex condition known as CVI depend on educators to make careful identification, assessment, and intervention of infants, children, and school-age students who have been given eye exams, but with results that do not explain their child's profound vision loss. When educators facilitate improvement in children, they are also facilitating healing in the families, who have watched their children struggle through an obstacle course of medical and developmental challenges. Educators need to maintain a sense of urgency about the needs of individuals with CVI, and to advocate for appropriate intervention in support of the development of visual skills. They can also be advocates for the parents, clearing a path for them through the complex and often confusing world of special education. Educators can ensure that each student receives the appropriate services that can facilitate a student's improvement by "leaps and bounds." Assessment in support of identification and planned intervention, which in turn leads to developmental improvement, is described in the chapter that follows.

The following answer guide provides samples of responses to the Parent Interview questions that would be scored positively or negatively for CVI. However, there is no exact number of items that must be marked positive to suggest that CVI is present; the entire picture, including medical information and information gathered from the functional CVI Range assessment described in the following chapter must be considered.

Substitute the child's name for "your child" in the questions.

Interview Question	Characteristics of CVI or Other Features	Positive for CVI: Sample Responses	Negative for CVI: Sample Responses
1. Tell me what you do with a toy to get your child interested in it.	Movement Visual fields	I move it, or shake it back and forth, or activate it. I present it to my child's right or left side and move it or try to get it to make a motion.	I set it up in the center of where my child is positioned. I put it in his or her hand. I put it in front of him or her. He or she notices the toy and then I bring it to him or her.
2. When you show your child something, how do you know he or she sees it?	Visual attention/ nonpurposeful gaze	I'm not always sure he or she sees what I show to him or her. When I show him or her favorite or familiar objects, he or she stops doing other things. He or she smiles or moves toward the object. I don't think there are many things he or she likes to look at.	He or she likes to see most things as long as I move them close enough. He or she seems to like the same things other babies like. He or she looks right at the toy and gets "excited."
3. Does your child have a favorite side or a favorite head position?	Visual field preference Presence of additional disability	He or she seems to generally keep his or her head positioned to one side. He or she usually notices things when I place the object at the right/left side.	No, he or she uses both/right/left sides. I haven't noticed a favorite side. The physician told me he or she might have trouble seeing at right/left/center.

(continued)

Interview Question	Characteristics of CVI or Other Features	Positive for CVI: Sample Responses	Negative for CVI: Sample Responses
		Yes, I think he or she is going to be right-/ left-handed.	
4. Does your child usually find objects by looking or by feeling for them?	Visually guided reach or visual complexity	He or she usually searches for toys without looking where his or her hand is aiming. If something touches his or her hand, he or she grasps it. He or she seems to look away before moving his or her hand in the direction of the toy.	If the toy is within view, he or she will look and reach for it. No, he or she seems to look and reach/swat/ bat at toys.
5. Do you have concerns about the way your child sees?	Appearance of eyes/ normal eye exam	Yes. The physician told us that his or her eyes are normal, but he or she may not understand what he or she sees. He or she seems to have better and worse times when he or she seems to see. I think he or she will outgrow the problem with his or her eyes.	No, the physician explained that eyeglasses/surgery/ other will help him or her. I was concerned, but I'm not concerned about his or her vision now.
6. Where do you usually hold objects for your child to look at?	Visual field preferences Visual complexity	I usually hold things at right/left/center. He or she seems to pay attention to objects when I hold the toy at right/left/center. I usually hold things close and/or at right/left/center.	I usually hold them up close (or far away) because the physician said he or she has trouble seeing far away (or near). I usually put them where he or she can reach the toys. In the playpen, crib, on the floor, etc.

(continued)

Interview Question	Characteristics of CVI or Other Features	Positive for CVI: Sample Responses	Negative for CVI: Sample Responses
7. What are your child's favorite things in your house?	Light-gazing Nonpurposeful gaze Movement Visual novelty	He or she likes the ceiling fan. He or she looks at overhead lights, lamps, windows. He or she seems to like to watch the television. He or she likes to look at mirrors/shiny, reflective objects.	He or she notices everything around him or her; "never misses a trick." The physician said he or she will notice large or bright things. He or she reacts when someone new comes near.
8. What, if anything, have doctors told you about your child's eyes?	Appearance of eyes/normal eye exam	The physicians told me that his or her eyes are normal, but we can't be sure how well he or she understands what he or she sees. The physicians told me that we will know more about his or her vision as he or she gets older. The physicians say his or her eyes are fine. The physicians say he or she has optic nerve atrophy/hypoplasia/dysplasia.	The physicians say he or she is diagnosed with _____.
9. When does your child usually like to look at things?	Visual novelty Visual array/visual complexity	He or she is most alert when the house is quiet (when other members of the household are at school or work). He or she seems to be more aware at night. He or she likes to look at things after he or she is rested/is fed. He or she likes to look at things when his or her favorite toys are presented.	He or she likes to look at things that are new or he or she is curious about. He or she likes to look at things any time of the day. He or she likes to look at things when the toys are close enough or bright enough (according to the early interventionist or medical suggestion).

(continued)

Interview Question	Characteristics of CVI or Other Features	Positive for CVI: Sample Responses	Negative for CVI: Sample Responses
		He or she likes to look at things in his or her crib (if the same set of toys is generally present in the crib).	
10. What color are the things your child likes to look at most?	Color preference Visual novelty	He or she seems to like things that are yellow/red (or any consistent color). He or she likes black and white objects. He she likes toys that are shiny or mirrored. He or she only likes one or two toys.	I've never noticed that he or she likes a certain color. The physician told me that he or she will see bright colors best.
11. What does your child do when he or she is near very shiny or mirrored objects?	Light-gazing Movement Color preference	He or she turns toward/looks at them. He or she swats at them. He or she smiles, quiets; he or she seems to like shiny things.	The physician told us that he or she might find those toys interesting. They seem to be too bright for him or her. Bright, shiny things seem to bother his or her eyes. He or she likes them about as much as other things.
12. Describe how your child behaves around lamps or ceiling fans.	Light-gazing Nonpurposeful gaze/ visual attention	He or she stares at them, looks at them, notices them often. He or she moves toward them or positions his or her body in the direction of the light. He or she will lie on his or her back and watch the light for long periods of time.	He or she squints or closes his or her eyes. I haven't noticed anything in particular. He or she turns away from the lights. The physician said that he or she might notice lighted things.

(continued)

Interview Question	Characteristics of CVI or Other Features	Positive for CVI: Sample Responses	Negative for CVI: Sample Responses
13. Are you usually able to identify (be certain of) what your child is looking at?	Nonpurposeful gaze/visual attention	I'm not sure what he or she looks at or is interested in. Sometimes it seems like he or she is looking "through" things and not "at" things. I can tell when he or she is looking at things some of the time or when the things are favorite objects. He or she seems to notice things when the house is quiet/when there isn't much activity.	Yes, I am usually able to identify what he or she is looking at. I can identify things if they are close enough to him or her to be able to see the object(s) clearly. He or she seems to be interested in most objects or activities going on around him or her.
14. Does your child usually first notice things that move or things that don't move?	Movement Visual field preferences	He or she likes toys or objects that move/ spin/are activated. He or she seems to notice people/pets as they move around the room. He or she seems to like to watch the action/color/visual array on the television.	I never noticed either way. He or she seems to "lose" where I am in a room unless I stand still. He or she likes his or her stuffed animals that are (in the crib, on the dresser, etc.) The physician told us that he or she sees best using peripheral or movement vision.
15. How does your child position his or her head when you think he or she is looking at something?	Visual field preferences	He or she seems to turn his or her head (slightly) even when the object is straight ahead of him or her. He or she favors his or her right/left side of his or her body.	The physician told us that he/she might see better at his/her right/left/center. No particular position; I just show the toy to him or her as I would with any baby.

Interview Question	Characteristics of CVI or Other Features	Positive for CVI: Sample Responses	Negative for CVI: Sample Responses
		I usually put things at his or her right/left side.	It doesn't seem to matter where I place a toy; he or she notices things he or she is interested in.
16. Do you think your child has a "favorite" color?	Color preference	Yes, yellow/red/blue/other. He or she prefers Big Bird (or any single toy that is primarily *one* color). He or she likes black and white patterned toys.	No, I haven't noticed a favorite color. He or she seems to like toys with lots of colors. The physician told us that he or she might see bright colors best.
17. Does your child seem to notice things more at home or more in new places?	Visual array/visual complexity Nonpurposeful gaze/visual attention	He or she is more alert in the familiar surroundings of home. He or she seems to sleep a lot when we're out in new places. He or she doesn't seem to notice things as much in new places; he or she prefers to be at home. He or she seems bored in new places.	He or she seems more alert in new places. He or she seems to get bored with the things he or she has at home. He or she smiles and seems excited when we're out.
18. Describe how your child positions his or her head when swatting or reaching toward something.	Visual motor Visual field preferences	He or she doesn't usually reach or swat at things. He or she doesn't look in the direction of his or her hand. It seems like he or she looks or swats/reaches but doesn't do them together. He or she turns his or her head when trying to reach for something.	He or she looks at the thing he or she swats/reaches toward. The physician told us that he or she might turn his or her head in order to see or reach for something. He or she positions his or her head in the center of his or her body.

Interview Question	Characteristics of CVI or Other Features	Positive for CVI: Sample Responses	Negative for CVI: Sample Responses
19. How does your child react when you give him or her new things to look at?	Visual complexity/ visual array Visual novelty	He or she doesn't seem to like new things at first. He or she seems to prefer his or her old, favorite toys more than new ones. He or she learns to like them after a while.	He or she loves new toys; he or she gets bored with the old ones quickly. He or she usually likes new toys. He or she smiles and/or gets excited when there are new toys to play with.
20. Do you position your child in a certain way to help him or her see things?	Visual field preferences Visual complexity/ visual array	Usually on the right/ left side. I sometimes position him/her away from things that distract his/her attention. I position him or her close to the things he or she is trying to look at.	No, there isn't a usual or special position. The physician told us that we should move him or her closer to things, or that we should move the things closer to him or her.
21. Have you ever been concerned about the way your child's eyes move?	Normal eye exam/appearance of eyes	No, his or her eyes seem to move together People tell us that his or her eyes are pretty. When he or she was younger, his or her eyes didn't always look straight and seemed to move in an irregular pattern, but he or she has outgrown that.	No, the physician didn't mention that. Yes, the physician said that it's part of his or her eye condition.
22. What does your child do when there are many objects in front of him or her to look at?	Visual complexity/ visual array Visual novelty	He or she usually just plays with the one(s) we place in his or her hand. He or she seems to just look away. He or she can't choose which one to play with.	He or she plays a little bit with each one. He or she picks out his/her favorite one(s) to play with. He or she smiles/ gets excited.

(continued)

Interview Question	Characteristics of CVI or Other Features	Positive for CVI: Sample Responses	Negative for CVI: Sample Responses
		We think he or she likes to play with one or two things at a time. He or she gets fussy when there's a lot going on around him or her.	
23. Tell me about the faces your child prefers to look at.	Visual novelty Visual complexity/ visual array	He or she doesn't usually look at faces. He or she only looks at one or two familiar faces (mom, dad, or siblings). He or she likes his or her own face when I show it to him or her in a mirror.	He or she loves all kinds of faces. He or she enjoys other babies' or children's faces. He or she usually notices voices first because his or her eye condition makes his or her vision less helpful when recognizing people.
24. If your child had his or her own object to look at and a new object, which object do you think he or she would prefer?	Visual novelty Visual complexity/ visual array	I think he or she would prefer his or her own toy. He or she has "strong opinions" about what he or she likes to look at, and he or she likes his or her favorite old toys. We have difficulty finding toys that he or she likes as much at the old ones.	He or she would prefer to look at the new toy. He or she plays with his or her toys for a brief time and then he or she seems to get bored, so we offer him or her something new. I'm not sure. It depends on the toys presented. The physician told us he or she may prefer bright or lighted toys.

(continued)

Interview Question	Characteristics of CVI or Other Features	Positive for CVI: Sample Responses	Negative for CVI: Sample Responses
25. Tell me what your child's favorite objects or toys look like.	Color preference Visual novelty Visual complexity/ visual array Movement	He or she likes objects or toys that produce movement/have a consistent, predominant color. He or she likes objects or toys that are simple in visual array with little pattern change. He or she likes objects or toys that have repetitive black and white patterns. He or she prefers one, two, or three favorite objects or toys with simple color, pattern, or movement features.	He or she likes a variety of objects/toys (with little similarity in features of color or pattern). The physician told us he or she would see lighted/moving/other objects or toys the best. He or she likes anything we give him or her to play with.

‖‖‖‖‖‖‖

5

Functional Vision Assessment: The CVI Range

Although many children with cortical visual impairment (CVI) may appear to those around them to present a constellation of inexplicable or inconsistent visual behaviors, their functional vision can be improved through the use of systematic interventions, tailored specifically for the individual child. In the author's own practice, and in reports from teachers and parents who have used these methods, children have made significant and steady progress in the level of their functional vision after assessment-based intervention begins. And, as discussed in Chapter 1, there is a window of opportunity during infancy when a child's visual system is developing rapidly and is especially receptive to the influence of interventions. During this period, it is possible to influence the development of the visual system of children with CVI by using appropriate stimuli and visual inputs to stimulate the formation and strengthening of synapses—the connections between neurons in the brain—that support the use of vision by increasing neural pathways. This, in turn, helps a child build his or her capacity for vision by mitigating the effects of damage that his or her

visual system may have sustained. Plasticity for vision may extend beyond infancy and, in fact, improvements in visual function may be possible through adolescence or into early adulthood (Dutton, 2006). It is reasonable, therefore, for parents and professionals to have an expectation of improvement in functional vision regardless of the age of the child. Because infancy is the time of greatest receptivity, however, it is still important to assess infants who may be at risk for CVI and to begin appropriate intervention as early as possible.

For these reasons, infants and children who have been found to have some kind of neurological damage also need to have their vision assessed. Children who have atypical visual functioning, yet show no evidence of damage to the eyes, or who exhibit the characteristic behaviors related to CVI, even in the presence of additional ocular damage, need to be evaluated by professionals trained in assessing and working with children who have CVI. Teachers of students with visual impairments and orientation and mobility (O&M) instructors can perform a specialized functional visual assessment that focuses on the visual behaviors and characteristics accompanying CVI, and helps determine whether the child does in fact have the condition, and to what degree he or she is affected by each of the CVI characteristics. The author's approach to this process of functional vision assessment is based on a framework called the CVI Range.

Once an identification of CVI is made, the characteristics the child displays can be mapped on a form known as a CVI Resolution Chart that will help to monitor the child's progress over time. As discussed in Chapter 6, the child's Individualized Family Service Plan (IFSP) or Individualized Education Program (IEP) team can use this information to set goals, and a program of interventions based on the child's individual needs can be mapped out. Once intervention has begun, the child should be reevaluated from two to five times a year.

ASSESSING CHILDREN FOR THE PRESENCE OF CVI

Teachers of students with visual impairments conduct educational and functional vision assessments to determine how an existing or potential visual impairment may affect a student's educational performance. When students have ocular conditions, the question that implicitly drives the evaluation is, "How does damage to or dysfunction of the eye affect the student's ability to perform in school?" To investigate this question, teachers of visually impaired students assess such visual functions as near and distance acuity, visual field, visual motility (the ability to visually follow and track a target), color perception, and contrast sensitivity. Evaluation of these individual components guides the teacher in determining how an eye disorder may interfere with the student's ability to gain access to and benefit from instruction and the educational setting.

When assessing students with CVI, however, the fundamental question to be resolved is, "How does damage to the brain affect vision?" Therefore, the protocol for assessment needs to be driven by something else. The essential focus of assessment shifts to an examination of any visual behaviors that indicate the presence of neurological involvement—that is, to an examination of the unique behavioral characteristics that tend to accompany CVI, as described in Chapter 3. If the key to recognizing CVI is identification of its unique visual and behavioral hallmarks (Jan & Groenveld, 1993), it is critical that teachers of students who are visually impaired integrate these key features into their functional vision assessments. Thus, the protocol for evaluation of students with CVI should include assessment of the following:

- color preference
- need for movement
- visual latency
- visual field preferences
- difficulties with visual complexity
- light-gazing and nonpurposeful gaze
- difficulty with distance viewing
- atypical visual reflexes
- difficulty with visual novelty
- absence of visually guided reach

For students with CVI, this assessment may replace the traditional functional vision assessment, since CVI can mask the symptoms of ocular impairment. This would make it impossible to assess the effects of an eye condition on the student's use of existing vision until most of the effects of CVI were resolved. Nevertheless, children with ocular visual impairments or CVI need to be evaluated by a medical eye care specialist as soon as possible, preferably before undergoing a functional visual assessment. The ophthalmologist or optometrist will be able to examine the health of the eye and determine if there is a refractive error or if there is any eye pathology present that may account for visual dysfunction in the child. In short, when a child sustains neurological damage, the possibility of visual disability and the presence of CVI should be explored. When a child sustains ocular damage or experiences an ocular impairment that does not explain the visual dysfunction displayed, the presence of CVI should be investigated as well.

AN OVERVIEW OF THE CVI RANGE

The assessment instrument that the author has developed over a number of years to determine a student's level of visual functioning and the effect of the various characteristics of CVI on that particular student is known as the CVI Range. The use of the term *range* refers to the use of the assessment to identify students' position on a continuum of visual functioning that they may exhibit, from no functional vision to typical visual functioning. The CVI Range presented in this chapter is the most recently revised version of an evolving protocol. By assessing *both* the presence of the behavioral characteristics associated with CVI *and* the degree of impact that *each* characteristic has on a child, a teacher of students with visual impairments will be able to determine whether the child requires educational vision intervention in his or her living and learning settings and will also obtain a guide to the type of intervention required.

Once the assessment has been completed, utilizing the CVI Range assessment form presented in this chapter, a student's educational team can then prepare a summary of all the information known about his or her visual functioning by using a companion form known as the CVI Resolution Chart, also presented here. This assessment process can, in turn, guide the selection of appropriate interventions to use with the student. Clear and accurate assessment results are crucial to ensuring that interventions are targeted to a student's actual needs. Program planning and intervention are discussed in Chapter 6.

The CVI Range assessment form is structured so that multiple assessments can be collected on a single evaluation form for effective monitoring of a student's progress over time. The protocol is not restricted to students of a particular age; it can be used with infants as well as adults.

This chapter presents the two parts of the CVI Range protocol and gives a detailed explanation of how to determine a student's score on each part. The two sections actually represent two methods of assessing the presence and impact of CVI that, when taken together, present a comprehensive picture of the way in which the student is functioning visually. The summary or overview of a student's characteristics that can be compiled using the CVI Resolution Chart is also explained. A case study is then presented to illustrate the use of the CVI Range and the Resolution Chart.

THE FRAMEWORK FOR ASSESSMENT

Both of the assessment methods used in the CVI Range are completed by gathering information from three sources, as explained in Chapter 4:

1. interviews with parents, caregivers, teachers, paraeducators, or any informant who has in-depth knowledge regarding the child's medical history and day-to-day functioning
2. observation of the child in both living and learning settings
3. direct, face-to-face evaluation

In each instance, and when using each method, the evaluator will be considering the student's visual behavior with regard to each of the CVI behavioral characteristics.

Before assessment is undertaken, the student's medical history should be reviewed to determine whether the student has a neurological diagnosis consistent with CVI, and whether he or she has a normal eye exam or an already identified ocular or visual condition. In addition, the medical and educational histories should be reviewed for evidence of the behavioral indicators of CVI.

Interviews

As noted in Chapter 4, in interviews with parents, teachers, caregivers, or others who are familiar with the child, questions such as the following need to be addressed in regard to visual behaviors:

- What is the child's medical background?
- What does the eye care specialist report?
- What, if anything, does the child prefer to look at?
- What are the concerns of the family and teachers?
- Does the child have a preferred color?
- When is the child most visually alert or interactive?
- Does the child look directly into faces?
- Does the child notice things that move more than things that are stable?
- Does the child seem to "look through" rather than directly at objects?

A detailed interview protocol to use with family members is discussed in Chapter 4.

It should be remembered that parents are important reporters of their children's behaviors and know their children better than anyone else. For this reason, and because children may exhibit behaviors at home or in the presence of their families that any assessment needs to encompass, parents should be regarded as a source of critical information about a child. Attentive and thorough interviews with family members therefore form the cornerstone of careful assessment. As explained in Chapter 4, educators who are interested in determining the presence of the visual characteristics associated with CVI in an individual student can obtain reliable information by asking pivotal questions (Roman, 1996). Properly structured questions can provide information related to color preference, attraction to movement, visual latency, difficulty with distance viewing, and the other possible indications of CVI. In the case of students who are not diagnosed with CVI, but who demonstrate the unique characteristics that accompany it, parents can provide important information to the physician that may help confirm the potential diagnosis of CVI.

Observation

After information has been derived from interviews, students should be observed in both living and learning environments. Observations are gathered throughout the evaluator's time with the child, beginning with the initial contact. Visual behavior needs to be observed in a variety of settings and circumstances, including:

- during quiet and noisy times
- in both near and distance activities
- with familiar and novel objects
- with cluttered and simple backgrounds
- with objects that move and objects that are stationary

Observations should also focus on whether the student demonstrates any of the following behavior:

- interest in objects of a specific color
- light-gazing or nonpurposeful gaze

- attraction to moving or reflective objects
- interest in very few objects or objects that are similar in appearance
- looking away from areas where there is a lot of activity
- looking away while music is playing or when people are talking
- a lack of visual curiosity
- looking at objects or materials at closer than expected distances

Direct Assessment

Direct assessment consists of systematic presentation of visual stimuli that would be expected to evoke behavioral responses typical of CVI, and then noting the student's response. In performing a direct assessment of a student regarding the CVI behavioral characteristics, environments should be selected that will allow the student's best performance in order to determine the student's visual potential. That is, all factors should be eliminated that might interfere with the student's vision, such as complex backgrounds or competing sensory stimuli, as already identified by interview and observation. By providing the most appropriate environmental and material adaptations for a student with CVI, the assessor can discover how well the student can use his or her vision under optimum conditions.

Sidebar 5.1 provides suggestions for use in evaluating each of the visual behaviors typically indicative of CVI. Ideas for a variety of items that might be useful for assessing CVI and that can be put together to form an assessment kit appear in Sidebar 5.2. The case study of Kathy at the end of this chapter provides an example of how one student was evaluated by her teacher of students with visual impairments.

THE CVI RANGE

The CVI Range is an assessment protocol whose structure is based on the visual and behavioral characteristics typically displayed by children with CVI. Chapter 3 detailed these characteristics, which were also listed earlier in this chapter: color preference, need for movement, visual latency, visual field preferences, difficulties with visual complexity, light-gazing and nonpurposeful gaze, difficulty with distance viewing, atypical visual reflexes, difficulty with visual novelty, and absence of visually guided reach. Essentially, the use of the CVI Range involves scoring a child on each of these characteristics in two different ways. The CVI Range uses a 10-point scale of visual functioning. On this scale, 0 represents no functional vision, and 10 represents typical or near-typical visual functioning.

Rating I: Across–CVI Characteristics Assessment Method

In the first section of the CVI Range, the Across–CVI Characteristics method is used (see Figure 5.1). The child is assigned an overall score along a 10-point range after being assessed for each CVI characteristic. The score resulting from this assessment is referred to as Rating I. It provides a "snapshot" or overview of the child's level of functional vision. In this method, five levels of visual functioning are used:

CVI Range 1–2: Student functions with minimal visual response
CVI Range 3–4: Student functions with more consistent visual response
CVI Range 5–6: Student uses vision for functional tasks
CVI Range 7–8: Student demonstrates visual curiosity
CVI Range 9–10: Student spontaneously uses vision for most functional activities

As Figure 5.1 shows, for each of the five levels, the statements specify visual behaviors

The following are suggestions for materials and procedures to use in assessing the influence of each of the visual and behavioral characteristics that typically accompany CVI:

- **Color preference:** Present materials that are made of the student's reported preferred color and then compare the response to behavior when objects of a nonpreferred color are presented.

- **Need for movement:** Present single objects of the preferred color on a stable surface and compare the student's visual response to the response when the same object is moving in space. If the student displays little or no visual attention to the moving object (that is, does not quiet, open his or her eyes, turn in the direction of the target, or make eye-to-object contact), present an object that has shiny or reflective surfaces, such as a Mylar pom-pom or pinwheel.

- **Visual latency:** When presenting both known and novel objects, note the amount of time it takes for the student to notice the presence of the object. Also note when the latency, or slowness to respond, occurs in the session and what conditions or materials are associated with latency.

- **Visual field preferences:** Note preferred visual fields throughout the session. Present a moving object in the right, left, upper, and lower peripheral fields. Note, too, whether the student turns or positions his or her head to align the right or left eye in order to identify or examine the details of the object.

- **Difficulties with visual complexity:** Present objects of a single color (using the student's preferred color when one is reported), then objects that have two colors, and then three colors, and, finally, highly patterned objects.

- **Light-gazing and nonpurposeful gaze:** Position the student near primary sources of natural and artificial light. Compare potential light-gazing behavior under conditions of high illumination with conditions of indirect or subdued lighting. In some cases, students will require low lighting during the assessment to be able to give visual attention.

- **Difficulty with distance viewing:** Place an object that is familiar to the student on a single-color background. If the student can visually locate or fixate on the target, increase the complexity of the background and decrease the size of the target object.

- **Atypical visual reflexes:** Attempt to elicit the visual blink and visual threat reflexes several times in a row—perhaps two or three times—and several times during the assessment session. Be aware of the possibility of habituation; that is, the student's blink responses may lessen if the evaluator repeats the touch or threat too many times in a row.

- **Difficulty with visual novelty:** Present some objects that are familiar and some that are novel. Use visually simple objects for this task.

- **Absence of visually guided reach:** If the student can reach away from his or her body, place a familiar and then a less familiar object on a simple background and observe the type of looking and reaching pattern used by the student. Repeat this activity with the target object presented on a more complex background.

SIDEBAR 5.2   *Suggested Items for an Assessment Kit*

The following are examples of objects that can be gathered into a functional vision evaluation kit to be used in the assessment of children with CVI:

- A favorite toy brought in by the student's parent
- Items in solid colors used in the student's everyday routines, for example, a cup, a spoon, or a toothbrush
- Cereal or other food items, for example, Fruit Loops, red licorice, or banana
- A plastic Slinky in a solid color (a translucent Slinky is a compelling visual object when used with a flashlight or lightbox)
- Black-and-white toys or objects (useful for students who were exposed to black-and-white patterned developmental toys)
- Reflective materials, for example, Mylar balloons, pompoms, or shakers
- Mirrors
- Suspended or moving objects, for example, windsocks or balls on elastic cords
- A pinwheel
- A black, light-absorbing background; black felt or terrycloth work well. (The Invisiboard available from the American Printing House for the Blind [APH; see the Resources section] is useful for this purpose.)
- A small lightbox with clear or translucent colored acrylic objects: for example, translucent pegs or shapes (available from APH) or a colored Slinky
- Sets of red and/or yellow objects, such as blocks, pegs, or crayons, to be sorted into containers of the same color
- Lights with colored caps or filters

relating to the various CVI characteristics. For example, in regard to the characteristic of visual latency, the behavior that would be observed of a student at level 1–2 is "Prolonged periods of latency in visual tasks"; at level 3–4, "Latency slightly decreases after periods of consistent viewing"; at level 5–6, "Latency present only when the student is tired, stressed, or overstimulated"; at level 7–8, "Latency rarely present"; and at level 9–10, "Latency resolved." However, within a given range, some statements may address more than one characteristic, and more than one statement may address a given characteristic. As noted in Chapter 3, the behaviors characteristic of CVI tend to resolve in a particular order, so that the characteristics reflected in the statements for each CVI range

vary somewhat at the different levels. The evaluator scores each statement, starting from the beginning of the assessment instrument, until he or she reaches a point where the statements no longer apply to the student (see the following section on scoring).

In the lower number ranges, the statements describe behavioral responses indicating that the CVI characteristic in question has an intense effect on the student's visual functioning. As the numbers increase through the levels, the behaviors described in the statements indicate that the CVI characteristic is having a less intense effect as the characteristics resolve—that is, as the students' behaviors and visual skills change or improve. As the student's visual functioning approaches 10 on the scale,

THE CVI RANGE

Student/child's name:_____ Age:_____

Evaluator(s):_____ Evaluation Date: _____

This assessment protocol is intended for multiple evaluations over a period of time. Suggested scoring (no less than three times per school year):

a. Initial assessment (red)
b. Second assessment (blue)
c. Third assessment (green)
Further assessments will require a new form.

Totals:	Evaluation #1 (red)	Evaluation #2 (blue)	Evaluation #3 (green)
1. Range for Rating I			
2. Total for Rating II			
3. Combine both ratings to get overall CVI Range			

```
      0    1    2    3    4    5    6    7    8    9    10
```

No functional
vision

Typical or
near-typical
visual functioning

The CVI Range: Across–CVI Characteristics Assessment Method

Rating I
Rate the following statements as related to the student/child's visual behaviors by marking the appropriate column to indicate the methods used to support the scores:

O = information obtained through observation of the child/student
I = information obtained through interview regarding the child/student
D = information obtained through direct contact with the child/student

In the remaining columns, indicate the assessed degree of the CVI characteristic:

- **R**   The statement represents a resolved visual behavior
- +   Describes current functioning of student/child
- +/–   Partially describes student/child
- –   Does not apply to student/child

(continued)

CVI Range 1–2: Student functions with minimal visual response

O	I	D	R	+	+/–	–	
							May localize, but no appropriate fixations on objects or faces
							Consistently attentive to lights or perhaps ceiling fans
							Prolonged periods of latency in visual tasks
							Responds only in strictly controlled environments
							Objects viewed are a single color
							Objects viewed have movement and/or shiny or reflective properties
							Visually attends in near space only
							No blink in response to touch or visual threat
							No regard of the human face

CVI Range 3–4: Student functions with more consistent visual response

O	I	D	R	+	+/–	–	
							Visually fixates when the environment is controlled
							Less attracted to lights; can be redirected
							Latency slightly decreases after periods of consistent viewing
							May look at novel objects if they share characteristics of familiar objects
							Blinks in response to touch and/or visual threat, but the responses may be latent and/or inconsistent
							Has a "favorite" color
							Shows strong visual field preferences
							May notice moving objects at 2 to 3 feet
							Look and touch completed as separate events

(continued)

CVI Range 5–6: Student uses vision for functional tasks

O	I	D	R	+	+/–	–	
							Objects viewed may have two to three colors
							Light is no longer a distractor
							Latency present only when the student is tired, stressed, or overstimulated
							Movement continues to be an important factor for visual attention
							Student tolerates low levels of background noise
							Blink response to touch is consistently present
							Blink response to visual threat is intermittently present
							Visual attention now extends beyond near space, up to 4 to 6 feet
							May regard familiar faces when voice does not compete

CVI Range 7–8: Student demonstrates visual curiosity

O	I	D	R	+	+/–	–	
							Selection of toys or objects is less restricted; requires one to two sessions of "warm up"
							Competing auditory stimuli tolerated during periods of viewing; the student may now maintain visual attention on objects that produce music
							Blink response to visual threat consistently present
							Latency rarely present
							Visual attention extends to 10 feet with targets that produce movement
							Movement not required for attention at near distance
							Smiles at/regards familiar and new faces
							May enjoy regarding self in mirror
							Most high-contrast colors and/or familiar patterns regarded
							Simple books, picture cards, or symbols regarded

(continued)

FIGURE 5.1   *CVI Range: Cover Sheet and Across–CVI Characteristics Assessment Method (Rating I) Form (continued)*

CVI Range 9–10: Student spontaneously uses vision for most functional activities

O	I	D	R	+	+/–	–	
							Selection of toys or objects not restricted
							Only the most complex environments affect visual response
							Latency resolved
							No color or pattern preferences
							Visual attention extends beyond 20 feet
							Views books or other two-dimensional materials, simple images
							Uses vision to imitate actions
							Demonstrates memory of visual events
							Displays typical visual-social responses
							Visual fields unrestricted
							Look and reach completed as a single action
							Attends to two-dimensional images against complex backgrounds

his or her overall visual functioning improves, and the effects of the characteristics of CVI interfere less with his or her use of vision.

Scoring

The Across-CVI Characteristics Assessment Method, Rating I, is scored using a series of symbols: R (resolved), + (plus), +/– (plus/minus), and – (minus). For each statement, the evaluator assigns the symbol that most accurately indicates the student's relationship to the visual functioning described in that statement:

- A score of **+** is assigned if the statement accurately describes the current functioning of the student. In other words, if the statement describes a behavior that is

actually occurring in the present time, a score of + is assigned.

- A score of +/– is assigned if the statement partially describes a behavior demonstrated by the student. It may also be assigned if the behavior occurs occasionally, but is neither strongly present nor strongly absent.

- A score of – is given if the statement does not currently apply to the student. In other words, if the statement represents a level of functioning not yet obtained by the student, a score of minus is assigned.

- Finally, the first column of the assessment form is for a score of R, which is assigned if the statement represents a behavior that was previously present but is now resolved for the student—that is, if the behavior has improved and no longer interferes with visual functioning. The score of R is different from the score of – in that, although an R rating also applies to behavior that is not present at the current time, the R describes behavior that the student no longer demonstrates because the student's visual functioning is more advanced than that described in the statement.

It is important, too, that evaluators indicate the method used to assign a score to a student to provide documentation of how the score was determined, whether it be through interview, observation, or direct assessment. This information is also useful when different methods of assessment provide conflicting reports about the presence of a characteristic. For this reason, the CVI Range rating form provides columns that indicate which methods were used to obtain the score of R, +, +/–, or – (see Figure 5.1). An X should be placed in the appropriate columns to designate whether the score was obtained through observation of the child or student (*O*), interview with parents, caregivers, or school personnel (*I*), or direct face-to-face assessment techniques (*D*) or some combination of the three. In the initial assessment, scores of R would be assigned based on interviews, since the resolved behaviors would not have been observed by the assessor.

The CVI Range Scoring Guide (see Appendix 5A at the end of this chapter) is used during assessment to help assign scores to a student. To assist evaluators, the guide provides examples of visual behaviors that would correspond to each possible score of R, +, +/–, or –. The chart also indicates which CVI characteristics are encompassed by each of the statements.

An additional component—that of phases of visual functioning—completes the scoring protocol. The Scoring Guide is organized by phases of CVI. A phase is a period in the resolution of

CVI that broadly indicates the level or severity of the CVI characteristics experienced by a student. The three phases each correspond to specific score ranges on the CVI Range. The phases and their themes are as follows:

Phase I (Ranges 0–3): Building visual behavior
Phase II (Ranges 4–7): Integrating vision with function
Phase III (Ranges 8–10): Resolution of remaining CVI characteristics

These phases form the conceptual framework and, in a sense, the backdrop, for the broad themes of the intervention that needs to be used to help students develop their visual skills. They are used for program planning and intervention and are noted in the CVI Resolution chart. Phases are discussed in more detail in Chapter 6.

Establishing a Range of Functioning

An evaluator can establish a sense of a child's range of visual functioning by examining the pattern of the scores assigned to the child's visual behaviors. The individual statements that describe visual behaviors are matched to the child's visual responses and scored until a "ceiling effect" has been reached. A ceiling effect occurs when the pluses that indicate the student's current level of functioning end, and a cluster of minuses occur for four or more consecutive items. The minuses indicate that the student has not yet reached the level of functioning described in that range. The student's score on this section of the assessment is determined by the number of the CVI Range in which the last plus (+) item occurs prior to the shift to scores of plus/minus (+/–) and minus (–). Since each group of statements is identified by a range of two scores, the lower number of the range is assigned if the plus statements end in the middle of the cluster; the higher number is used if the plus-scored statements are marked to the end of the cluster.

For example, in the CVI Range completed for Kathy later in this chapter, the ceiling is reached at level 6 (see Figure 5.2). In the 5–6 range, Kathy has six items marked with a + and three items marked +/–. In range 7–8, Kathy's first statement is marked +, followed by four statements marked –. The remainder of the items in the 7–8 cluster are marked either +/– or –. Thus, the level at which the last plus item occurred prior to the shift to plus/minus or minus items is the end of the 5–6 Range; therefore, the ceiling for Rating I, the Across–CVI Characteristics Assessment Method, for Kathy is 6. The single item marked plus in the 7–8 range is not sufficient to edge Kathy's overall score above 6.

Evaluators need to use clinical judgment and their knowledge of students in determining when the ceiling effect has been reached; it is common for occasional outlier ratings (unusual observations that don't fit the pattern of the rest of the data) of pluses, plus/minuses, or R's to exist past the point where the ceiling effect occurs. For example, a Phase I or II student may have an intact ability to look directly into faces or may never have demonstrated a preferred color. Evaluators should score items in accordance with the behaviors the student demonstrates, even if they seem somehow out of context in the overall level of the student's functional vision. Given that CVI is caused by injury to the visual processing and visual pathways of the brain, and given the wide variability or degree of injury to the brain, it is not unexpected that some students will manifest outlier or unexpected behaviors. Ultimately, these outliers will not affect the overall score.

This method of interpretation is not intended to determine a precise score; rather, it is more useful in identifying the general range of functioning for a student. It is also important to remember that a student's level of visual functioning may be between two ranges

rather than within one number range. For example, a student's score using the Across-CVI Characteristics Assessment Method may be determined to be 2–3. Again, evaluators should use their judgment and consider the assessment to be a tool to help guide educational practices. Once the score from the Across-CVI Characteristics Assessment Method is determined, it is recorded in the space labeled "Range for Rating I" on the CVI Range cover sheet shown in Figure 5.1.

Rating II: Within–CVI Characteristics Assessment Method

In the Across-CVI Characteristics Assessment Method just described, a student's level of visual functioning is assigned an overall score based on a consideration of each of the CVI visual characteristics. This score provides an overview or composite perspective of the overall extent to which the impact of CVI is interfering with the student's use of vision. Once this score is obtained, an additional assessment is undertaken to examine the *specific degree* to which each individual CVI characteristic is affecting the child. This assessment is the Within-CVI Characteristics Assessment Method, and is completed by using a different but complementary scoring system, shown in Figure 5.3. The score resulting from this assessment is referred to as Rating II. By completing both methods of assessment, educators can obtain a comprehensive and helpful description of a child's current visual functioning that will provide a foundation for planning educational interventions.

In the Within-CVI Characteristics Assessment Method, the evaluator assesses the degree to which each of the ten behavioral characteristics of CVI is interfering with a student's functional vision—that is, the level of each CVI characteristic is determined. For each of the CVI characteristics, a numerical value from 0 to 1 is assigned that corresponds to the level of

FIGURE 5.2   The Ceiling Effect: Kathy's CVI Range

CVI Range 5–6: Student uses vision for functional tasks

O	I	D	R	+	+/–	–	
X		X			+/–		Objects viewed may have two to three colors
X	X	X		+			Light is no longer a distractor
	X	X		+			Latency present only when the student is tired, stressed, or overstimulated
		X		+			Movement continues to be an important factor for visual attention
X		X		+			Student tolerates low levels of background noise
		X			+/–		Blink response to touch is consistently present
		X		+			Blink response to visual threat is intermittently present
X	X	X		+			Visual attention now extends beyond near space, up to 4 to 6 feet
X		X			+/–		May regard familiar faces when voice does not compete

CVI Range 7–8: Student demonstrates visual curiosity

O	I	D	R	+	+/–	–	
X		X		+			Selection of toys or objects is less restricted; requires one to two sessions of "warm up"
X	X	X				–	Competing auditory stimuli tolerated during periods of viewing; the student may now maintain visual attention on objects that produce music
		X				–	Blink response to visual threat consistently present
	X	X				–	Latency rarely present
X	X	X				–	Visual attention extends to 10 feet with targets that produce movement
X		X			+/–		Movement not required for attention at near distance
X	X	X			+/–		Smiles at/regards familiar and new faces
X	X	X				–	May enjoy regarding self in mirror
X		X				–	Most high-contrast colors and/or familiar patterns regarded
	X	X				–	Simple books, picture cards, or symbols regarded

The CVI Range: Within–CVI Characteristics Assessment Method

Rating II

Determine the level of CVI present or resolved in the 10 categories below and add to obtain total score. Rate the following CVI categories as related to the student/child's visual behaviors by circling the appropriate number (the CVI Resolution Chart may be useful as a scoring guide):

    0   Not resolved; usually or always a factor affecting visual functioning
  .25   Resolving
   .5   Resolving; sometimes a factor affecting visual functioning
  .75   Resolving
    1   Resolved; not a factor affecting visual functioning

		Not Resolved		Resolving		Resolved
1.	Color preference	0	.25	.5	.75	1
	Comments:					
2.	Need for movement	0	.25	.5	.75	1
	Comments:					
3.	Visual latency	0	.25	.5	.75	1
	Comments:					
4.	Visual field preferences	0	.25	.5	.75	1
	Comments:					
5.	Difficulties with visual complexity	0	.25	.5	.75	1
	Comments:					
6.	Light-gazing and nonpurposeful gaze	0	.25	.5	.75	1
	Comments:					
7.	Difficulty with distance viewing	0	.25	.5	.75	1
	Comments:					
8.	Atypical visual reflexes	0	.25	.5	.75	1
	Comments:					
9.	Difficulty with visual novelty	0	.25	.5	.75	1
	Comments:					
10.	Absence of visually guided reach	0	.25	.5	.75	1
	Comments:					

functioning observed, based on a continuum from full effect of the characteristic to either no effect, or resolution of, the characteristic. (See Figure 5.3)

Scoring

Scoring for the Within-CVI Characteristics Assessment Method is as follows:

   0 Not resolved, usually or always a factor affecting visual functioning

.25 Resolving

 .5 Resolving, sometimes a factor affecting visual functioning

.75 Resolving

   1 Resolved, not a factor affecting visual functioning

Thus, a score of 0 is assigned if a characteristic is not at all resolved and is always or usually a factor affecting visual functioning. A score of 1 is assigned if the characteristic no longer interferes with the student's visual functioning; it therefore signifies a resolved characteristic. If a score of 1 is assigned, no specially designed instruction is required to address the characteristic.

For example, if Maria originally looked only at objects that were red (scored as 0), but now will look at simple objects of any single color, then in Maria's case, the CVI characteristic of color preference may be considered to have been resolved. Even though other CVI visual behaviors and characteristics may not yet have become resolved, if Maria is able to visually attend equally well to simple objects of any color, that characteristic is scored as a 1.

Scoring values between 0 and 1 represent degrees of resolution. Determining how much a characteristic is interfering with a student's vision, and thus whether it is resolved to a .25, .5, or .75 degree, requires careful assessment. In order to gather the best assessment data, it is vital that the evaluator observe the student in a number of different settings and at different time. Information obtained from interviews of individuals who are well acquainted with the student is invaluable in this process. Guidelines for scoring the Within-CVI Characteristics Method are provided later in this chapter, when the CVI Resolution Chart is described. An example of scoring for the CVI characteristic of color preference is the following:

Score = 0	Score = .25	Score = .5	Score = .75	Score = 1
Objects viewed are generally a single consistent color	Student has a "favorite" color	Objects viewed may have two to three colors	More colors and familiar patterns are regarded	Student has no color or pattern preferences

Once each characteristic has been evaluated, and a number value has been assigned for each, all the number values are added and a total score is given. The range of possible scores, therefore, is 0 to 10. The total score on the Within-CVI Characteristics method is then recorded on the CVI Range cover sheet shown in Figure 5.1.

THE COMBINED CVI RANGE SCORE

The two scores obtained from using the Across- and Within-CVI Characteristics Methods are next combined, as shown on the CVI Range cover sheet. In doing so, the evaluator determines an overall score range that represents the effect of CVI for the individual student. Although the scores derived from the two assessment methods will tend to be similar, they generally are not identical. The lower score and the higher score comprise the CVI Range for a student, and this set of numbers is recorded on the 0–10 number scale on the cover sheet, which indicates where on the continuum of visual functioning the student falls (see Figure 5.1). This range can be indicated by marking the two end points representing the student's lowest and highest scores and drawing a line or a bracket between them. Each score should be clearly dated. If evaluators choose to, multiple assessments can be marked on a single assessment form, so that cumulative changes over several assessments can be recorded together. Marking the scores for the different assessments in different colors, as indicated in the key on the CVI cover sheet where the scores are recorded, makes them easy to differentiate. In this way, the number line can reveal the student's progress over time. Evaluators who wish to check that their assessment of a child is complete can use the CVI Range Assessment Review, shown in Figure 5.4.

Overall, the CVI Range assessment protocol described in this chapter incorporates two methods of looking at a child's visual behaviors that, when used together, determine the presence or absence of the individual characteristics associated with CVI, as well as the overall degree or level to which each characteristic is affecting the student's ability to use functional vision. The result of the assessment allows a professional to determine a child's level of functional vision or overall degree of CVI.

THE CVI RANGE PHASE III EXTENSION

Many educators working with children with CVI find that when their students' CVI behavioral characteristics begin to be resolved and they reach Phase III in their level of visual functioning, the educators need to consider more specific detail in their assessments in order to plan interventions. While not a mandatory part of the CVI Range assessment protocol, the Phase III Extension Chart in Figure 5.5 offers an option for professionals who wish to gather more information about a student. It can be used as a guide to obtain more detailed data when a student scores 7–10 on the CVI Range.

Although all improvements in visual ability support literacy, particularly literacy pertaining to accessing print materials, as students with CVI progress into Phase III, their ability to discern, focus on, and discriminate between letters and shapes improves. They begin to have the skills to use symbols and words and to learn from imitation. In other words, they are now in a preliteracy or early literacy and pre-reading phase of their growth and development. The use of the Phase III Extension is a way for educators to gather information to help there students make the transition into early reading or literacy tasks. The format of the Phase III Extension and the methods used to gather information (interviews, observations, and direct assessment) are similar to those of the Across-CVI Characteristics Assessment Method, Rating I. However, no separate score is derived from the extension; rather, it is used to provide a more detailed summary of the student's visual behavior and ability to recognize the salient or distinguishing features of objects in Phase III, when the effects of CVI may be subtler, to help the teacher plan practical interventions.

The CVI visual characteristics considered in the extension are difficulties with visual complexity, difficulty with distance viewing, visual field preferences, and absence of visually guided reach. The other CVI characteristics are generally resolved by Phase III. The Phase III Extension focuses on the integration of vision with higher-level visual, cognitive, O&M, and social tasks.

FIGURE 5.4 *CVI Range Assessment Review*

CVI RANGE ASSESSMENT REVIEW

This worksheet can be used as a quick review for evaluators who wish to double-check the completeness of the CVI Range.

Interview and Observation Check-Off

The following chart can be used to check off whether the presence of a medical cause for CVI has been determined as well as whether all the information has been obtained from the interview and observation portions of the assessment. (Not all characteristics are represented, only those determined by interview or observation.) For the CVI behavioral characteristics, the chart can be used as follows:

Yes: information from interview and observation suggests the possibility of the presence of this characteristic

No: information from interview and observation does not suggest the presence of this characteristic

Pending: information from interview and observation is incomplete

Recheck: information gathered from interview and observation is conflicting, more information needed

	Yes	No	Pending	Recheck
Medical cause				
Interview and observation				
Color preference				
Need for movement				
Visual latency				
Visual field preferences				
Difficulties with visual complexity				
Light-gazing and nonpurposeful gaze				
Difficulty with distance				
Atypical visual reflexes				
Difficulty with visual novelty				
Absence of visually guided reach				

Direct Assessment Guide

The following Direct Assessment guideline questions can be reviewed by the evaluator as a quick self-check of key information that must be gathered prior to the completion of the CVI Range. These questions represent behaviors frequently demonstrated by students in Phases I to III. Answers to the guiding questions may also provide useful information for report preparation.

(continued)

FIGURE 5.4 *CVI Range Assessment Review (continued)*

Phase I: Building Visual Behavior

Did I check . . . ?

- Are viewed objects primarily one color?
- Are the objects similar to one another in degree of complexity?
- Is the child/student able to look toward parent or my face?
- Can the child/student simultaneously look and process other sensory information?
- Is a black or nonpatterned background required?
- Is there persistent latency?
- Is movement or shiny or reflective material required?
- Is light a significant motivator, and is it also interfering with visual attention?
- Do materials always have to be presented within 18 inches?

Phase II: Integrating Vision with Function

Did I check . . . ?

- Is the preferred color still important?
- Can the student look at two- or three-color items?
- Is movement or shiny or reflective material less critical?
- Is latency decreasing?
- Is light-gazing decreasing or resolved?
- Is look and reach occasionally completed as a single action?
- Is the child/student able to look toward or into faces?
- Is the child/student able to look while voices or music occur?
- Is the child/student able to locate an object in the presence of several additional objects?
- Does the child/student have a repertoire of objects that resemble one another?
- Does distance viewing now extend as far as 10 feet?

Phase III: Resolution of CVI Characteristics

Did I check . . . ?

- Can objects be presented against increasingly complex backgrounds?
- Are novel objects preferred over familiar objects?
- Is light-gazing almost never or never present?
- Is visually guided reach seen more frequently, or is it related to motor rather than visual issues?
- Can the child/student now use vision even in the presence of voices or music?
- Do highly complex environments (such as malls, assemblies, or parties) continue to affect visual performance?
- Is distance viewing now extended up to or beyond 20 feet?
- Are simple two-dimensional images discriminated, recognized, or identified?
- Are small objects placed on patterned backgrounds located?
- Are small, single-color images found in two-dimensional backgrounds?
- Is the child/student able to locate salient features in two-dimensional materials or in the environment?
- Is the child/student able to differentiate faces?

FIGURE 5.5   *CVI Range: Phase III Extension*

CVI RANGE: PHASE III EXTENSION CHART

Approaching Literacy

This chart can be used as a guide to obtain more detailed information when a student scores 7–10 on the CVI Range, a phase in which he or she may be developing the visual skills for literacy activities. The CVI characteristics considered in this extension are difficulties with visual complexity, visual field preferences, difficulty with distance viewing, and absence of visually guided reach. No separate score is derived from the Extension; it is used to help organize appropriate interventions. This extension may not be appropriate for Phase III students who have both CVI and co-existing ocular visual impairment.

Recognition of Salient Features with Increasing Levels of Complexity at Near							
O	*I*	*D*	R	+	+/–	–	Statement
							Visually discriminates between same and different objects ("Show me one like . . . ")
							Visually recognizes same and different objects ("Show me the _____"). Recognition can be based on object name, color name, or shape
							Visually identifies object, color, or shape in three dimensions ("What is this?")
							Visually discriminates between same and different symbols in two dimensions, such as photographs
							Visually recognizes symbols in two dimensions, such as photographs
							Visually identifies symbols of two dimensions, such as photographs
							Visually discriminates "same" three-dimensional object (1 inch or smaller) from a field of 10 or fewer objects
							Visually discriminates "same" three-dimensional object (1 inch or smaller) from a field of 11 or more objects
							Visually recognizes a named object (1 inch or smaller) from a field of 10 or fewer objects
							Visually recognizes a named object (1 inch or smaller) from a field of 11 or more objects
							Visually identifies objects (1 inch or smaller) from a field of 10 or fewer objects

(continued)

FIGURE 5.5   *CVI Range: Phase III Extension (continued)*

							Visually identifies objects (1 inch or smaller) from a field of 11 or more objects
							Visually discriminates "same" two-dimensional picture or symbol from a field of 10 or fewer images
							Visually recognizes a named two-dimensional picture or symbol from a field of 11 or more images
							Visually identifies pictures or symbols from a field of 10 or fewer images
							Visually identifies pictures or symbols from a field of 11 or more images
							Visually discriminates hidden or embedded pictures or symbols when provided an identical prompt
							Visually recognizes hidden or embedded pictures or symbols when provided a verbal prompt ("Find the ____")
							Visually identifies hidden or embedded pictures or symbols without visual or verbal prompt ("Can you find the hidden pictures/symbols?")
							Visually discriminates, recognizes, and identifies faces in three dimensions
							Visually discriminates, recognizes, and identifies two-dimensional images of faces
							Visually discriminates, recognizes, and identifies their name, sight words, or communication symbols
							Visually recognizes, identifies, and functionally uses words or symbols presented in a group of two to five symbols
							Visually recognizes, identifies, and functionally uses words or symbols presented in a phrase or group of six or more symbols

Recognition of Salient Features with Increasing Levels of Complexity at a Distance (O&M)

							Visually recognizes or identifies three-dimensional landmarks in familiar indoor settings at distances up to 20 feet
							Visually recognizes or identifies three-dimensional landmarks in familiar indoor settings at distances beyond 20 feet

(continued)

FIGURE 5.5   *CVI Range: Phase III Extension (continued)*

								Visually recognizes or identifies two-dimensional signs, symbols, or pictures in familiar indoor settings at distances up to 20 feet
								Visually recognizes or identifies two-dimensional signs, symbols, or pictures in familiar indoor settings at distances beyond 20 feet
								Visually recognizes or identifies three-dimensional landmarks in familiar outdoor settings at distances up to 20 feet
								Visually recognizes or identifies three-dimensional landmarks in familiar outdoor settings beyond 20 feet
								Visually recognizes or identifies three-dimensional landmarks in unfamiliar indoor settings up to 20 feet
								Visually recognizes or identifies three-dimensional landmarks in unfamiliar indoor settings beyond 20 feet
								Visually recognizes or identifies three-dimensional landmarks in unfamiliar indoor settings beyond 20 feet with low levels of sensory complexity
								Visually recognizes or identifies three-dimensional landmarks in unfamiliar indoor settings beyond 20 feet with high levels of sensory complexity
								Visually recognizes or identifies three-dimensional landmarks in outdoor settings beyond 20 feet with low levels of sensory complexity
								Visually recognizes or identifies three-dimensional landmarks in outdoor settings beyond 20 feet with high levels of sensory complexity
								Visually locates three-dimensional moving or reflective objects presented in upper, lower, right, and left peripheral visual fields
								Visually locates three-dimensional stable objects presented in upper, lower, right, and left peripheral visual fields
								Visually locates two-dimensional moving or reflective materials presented in upper, lower, right, and left peripheral visual fields
								Visually locates two-dimensional stable materials presented in upper, lower, right, or left peripheral visual fields

(continued)

FIGURE 5.5   *CVI Range: Phase III Extension (continued)*

						Moves through familiar indoor or outdoor settings without unintended contact with walls, doorways, or objects on the floor
						Moves through unfamiliar indoor or outdoor settings without unintended contact with walls, doorways, or objects on the floor
						If appropriate, ascends and descends stairways safely and without assistance
Visually Guided Reach with Increasing Levels of Complexity						
						Visually guided reach occurs when a 1-inch target is presented on a visually noncomplex background
						Visually guided reach occurs when a 1-inch target is presented on a moderately patterned or cluttered background
						Visually guided reach occurs when a 1-inch target is presented on a nonadapted, highly patterned, or cluttered background

However, the use of the Extension may not be appropriate for Phase III students who have both CVI and ocular visual impairments.

ENVIRONMENTAL CONSIDERATIONS

When assessing students for the presence of CVI, it is extremely important to take into account the influence of the environment on their visual functioning. There is a common, and perhaps inaccurate, belief that students with CVI have vision that varies from minute to minute, hour to hour, and day to day. However, it is essential to consider the factors that create such apparent variability in a child's vision.

In general, in cases in which a student's visual abilities seem highly variable, it is likely that the student's ability to utilize his or her vision may be greatly dependent on the influences of the environment. It is not uncommon for parents to report that their children seem more visually alert at night (Roman, 1996). The alertness that parents observe in their children at night may be associated with lower levels of environmental stimulation that occur during the routines of the evening or late at night, versus those that occur during the daylight hours. Students who have difficulty with visual complexity and who are not able to easily sort out the complex patterns presented by an object, the array in which the object exists, or the sensory environment, may tend to be faced with great challenges in navigating their learning environments. The need to attend to competing stimuli may overwhelm or greatly fatigue a student. Thus, it is important to consider when assessing a student's behavior whether it is the student who has changed or, more likely, the environment that has changed in some critical way, as in the following case study.

> *Jeremy is a 12-year-old student who has CVI. His classroom teacher feels that Jeremy uses his vision so irregularly that it is difficult to know when to expect him to use it at all. His teacher noted that Jeremy was able to locate his yellow toothbrush when it was presented on a black towel in the bathroom but moments later, when he was asked to reach for the toothbrush, he acted as though it had disappeared. The question to be considered was whether Jeremy's vision had changed, or whether something in the environment had changed. Interestingly, when Jeremy reached for the toothbrush on the black background he was able to do so because of the appropriate adaptation—the use of the black towel—that reduced visual complexity for him. Moments later, when the teacher held the yellow toothbrush up and asked Jeremy to reach, she was holding the yellow toothbrush against her paisley shirt. By doing so, she had changed the degree of visual complexity that Jeremy had to deal with, and Jeremy's inability to locate the toothbrush now was more likely due to the change in his near environment than to a change in his vision.*

In general, the more affected by CVI a student is, the greater the need for environmental adaptations. For example, students in Phase I are unable to use vision consistently unless they are positioned away from all visual and auditory distractions. Conversely, students who are in Phase III are able to use vision in many functional tasks, with only occasional need for reduction of the visual or auditory information in the classroom or home setting. Consider a student who acts as though she is visually inattentive during class. She may turn her face away from an activity or engage in nonpurposeful gaze. It is difficult to know whether the student is unwilling or unable to attend to the classroom activity unless careful analysis of the student's ability to handle the complexity of the setting has been considered.

The degree to which the environment must be controlled or adapted for students with CVI to be able to function visually is represented by a conceptual framework involving of three levels of environmental considerations. The need for Level I environmental adaptations is associated with Phase I CVI; students in this phase require complete reduction of visual, auditory, and tactile inputs while attempting to look at a single, selected target. Level II environmental considerations are associated with Phase II CVI. In this phase, the student is able to use vision to look at from two to four targets when visual, auditory, and tactile inputs are reduced, but not eliminated. Finally, Level III environmental considerations, associated with Phase III CVI, refer to an environment in which very few if any adaptations are necessary while the student is engaged in visual activities. These environmental levels are incorporated into the CVI Resolution Chart discussed in the following section. Methods of implementing environmental adaptations in educational programs or functional routines are discussed in Chapter 6.

THE CVI RESOLUTION CHART

The CVI Resolution Chart is a table that summarizes all information for a child regarding CVI phases, CVI number ranges, CVI characteristics, and CVI environmental considerations in a single document (see Figure 5.6). There are more items on the CVI Resolution Chart than in the CVI Range; it is not intended to be a copy of the assessment. This chart is intended to be used over time as a reference in writing Individualized Education Programs (IEPs) or Individualized Family Service Plans (IFSPs) and in planning specific instructional activities. It is used as a working and planning chart following the administration of the CVI Range assessment protocol. For each visual or behavioral characteristic typically associated with CVI, a summary statement is provided to describe the visual behavior of a student in each of the ranges for that characteristic. For example, the first row of boxes in the Resolution Chart contains descriptions of how a student reacts to color if he or she is in Range 1–2, Range 3–4, Range 5–6, Range 7–8, or Range 9–10.

Drawing an X through a box indicates that a student has either resolved the behavior or that the behavior no longer interferes with visual functioning. Highlighting the outline of the box indicates current functioning. Thus, once the Resolution Chart is marked to show the behaviors of an individual student, it is possible to see at a glance where the student falls on the CVI Range for each characteristic. The Resolution Chart can be posted in the classroom and used to guide program planning on a day-to-day basis. As indicated earlier, the CVI Range scoring sheets and the CVI Resolution Chart are similar but not identical; because the Resolution Chart is used to guide and monitor improvement, there are more items on the Resolution Chart than on the CVI Range assessment forms.

The Resolution Chart is marked using the following guidelines. Some boxes contain more than one statement describing visual behavior. In such cases, individual statements or the entire box can be marked accordingly.

1. *Draw an X through boxes that represent resolved visual behaviors or visual behaviors that no longer interfere with visual functioning.* An X indicates that the statement may have once been true of the student and that the student now functions at a higher level than the statement indicates. For example, if an X is marked in the first item for the characteristic of difficulty with distance viewing at the Range 1–2 level, "Visually attends in near space only," it

indicates that the student is now consistently able to attend to visual targets at distances beyond 18 inches from the student's face.

2. *Use highlighter to outline boxes describing current visual functioning.* Highlighting or outlining a box indicates that the statement describes a visual or behavioral trait that is consistently true of the student at this time. For example, if the box for the characteristic of color preference at the Range 5–6 level is highlighted, it indicates that the student continues to have a favorite color whose appearance is associated with increased visual attention, but is also able to demonstrate visual attention to objects that have a color similar to the favorite color or can visually attend to objects that have the favorite color plus one or two additional color.

3. *Draw an O in boxes describing visual skills that may never resolve because of co-existing ocular conditions.* The designation of O in a box is used when a student has both CVI and any form of ocular visual impairment. This indicator provides a way to specify visual behaviors that could be the result of either the cortical or the ocular visual impairment. The confounding effect of ocular visual impairment may make it impossible to know whether an atypical visual behavior is due to CVI or the student's eye condition. If the student's initial assessment is marked with highlighted O and X boxes, it is not easy to determine the differential effects of ocular visual impairment versus CVI. However, if the same student is reassessed after a period of intervention and now has boxes that are marked with X well into Phase III, except for the boxes originally marked O, it is likely that the CVI has essentially resolved and that the visual difficulty that remains can be explained by the ocular condition. At this point, the intervention approach should focus on methods and materials used with students with ocular visual impairments, rather than CVI.

FIGURE 5.6 CVI Resolution Chart

CVI RESOLUTION CHART

Use the following chart to help develop areas of needs for development of IEP goals and objectives.

CVI Characteristics	**Phase I:** Building Visual Behavior Level I Environmental Considerations		**Phase II:** Integrating Vision with Function Level II Environmental Considerations		**Phase III:** Resolution of CVI Characteristics Level III Environmental Considerations	
	Range 1–2 (0)	Range 3–4 (.25)	Range 5–6 (.50)	Range 7–8 (.75)	Range 9–10 (1)	
Color preference	Objects viewed are generally a single color	Has "favorite" color	Objects may have two to three favored colors	More colors, familiar patterns regarded	No color or pattern preferences	
Need for movement	Objects viewed generally have movement or reflective properties	More consistent localization, brief fixations on movement and reflective materials	Movement continues to be an important factor to initiate visual attention	Movement not required for attention at near	Typical responses to moving targets	
Visual latency	Prolonged periods of visual latency	Latency slightly decreases after periods of consistent viewing	Latency present only when student is tired, stressed, or overstimulated	Latency rarely present	Latency resolved	
Visual field preferences	Distinct field dependency	Shows visual field preferences	Field preferences decreasing with familiar inputs	May alternate use of right and left fields	Visual fields unrestricted	
Difficulties with visual complexity	Responds only in strictly controlled environments Generally no regard of the human face	Visually fixates when environment is controlled	Student tolerates low levels of familiar background noise Regards familiar faces when voice does not compete	Competing auditory stimuli tolerated during periods of viewing; student may now maintain visual attention on musical toys	Only the most complex visual environments affect visual response Views books or other two-dimensional materials	

(continued)

FIGURE 5.6 *CVI Resolution Chart (continued)*

CVI Characteristics	Phase I: Building Visual Behavior — Level I Environmental Considerations		Phase II: Integrating Vision with Function — Level II Environmental Considerations		Phase III: Resolution of CVI Characteristics — Level III Environmental Considerations	
	Range 1–2 (0)	Range 3–4 (.25)	Range 5–6 (.50)	Range 7–8 (.75)	Range 9–10 (1)	
				Views simple books or symbols	Typical visual/social responses	
				Smiles at/regards familiar and new faces		
Light-gazing and nonpurposeful gaze	May localize briefly, but no prolonged fixations on objects or faces. Overly attentive to lights or perhaps ceiling fans	Less attracted to lights; can be redirected to other targets	Light is no longer a distractor			
Difficulty with distance viewing	Visually attends in near space only	Occasional visual attention to familiar, moving, or large targets at 2 to 3 feet	Visual attention extends beyond near space, up to 4 to 6 feet	Visual attention extends to 10 feet with targets that produce movement	Visual attention extends beyond 20 feet. Demonstrates memory of visual events	
Atypical visual reflexes	No blink in response to touch and/or visual threat	Blinks in response to touch, but response may be latent	Blink response to touch consistently present. Visual threat response intermittently present	Visual threat response consistently present (both reflexes near 90 percent resolved)	Visual reflexes always present; resolved	

	Only favorite or known objects elicit visual attention	May tolerate novel objects if the novel objects share characteristics of familiar objects	Use of "known" objects to initiate looking sequence	Selection of objects less restricted, one to two sessions of "warm up" time required	Selection of objects not restricted
Difficulty with visual novelty					
Absence of visually guided reach	Look and touch occur as separate functions Look and touch occur with large and/or moving objects	Look and touch occur with smaller objects that are familiar, lighted, or reflective Look and touch are still separate	Visually guided reach used with familiar objects or "favorite" color	Look and touch occur in rapid sequence, but not always together	Look and touch occur together consistently

Key:

- Draw an X through boxes that represent resolved visual behaviors
- Use highlighter to outline boxes describing current visual functioning
- Draw an O in boxes describing visual skills that may never resolve because of coexisting ocular conditions

For example, if it is known that a student has optic nerve atrophy, it will be difficult to determine whether the student's inability to look directly into a face is because of the ocular condition or CVI. Therefore, an O should be marked over the statement "regards familiar face when voice does not compete" for the characteristic of visual complexity at the 5–6 Range level. Another example might involve a child who has retinopathy of prematurity (ROP). This individual has experienced damage to the retina that may result in retinal detachment. If both ROP and CVI are present, many of the statements about visual fields will be confounded by the inability to know whether the visual field preferences displayed by the student is due to the ocular or the cortical involvement. Such statements will be marked with an O.

For a student who scores 7–8 on the Within–CVI Characteristics Assessment Method, Rating II of the CVI Range assessment, the CVI Resolution Chart would be marked as shown in Figure 5.7. Another example, shown in Figure 5.8, is marked for a student with CVI and cataracts who scored 3 on the Within–CVI Characteristics Assessment Method, Rating II, of the CVI Range.

A discussion of how to use the CVI Resolution Chart in program planning and intervention appears in Chapter 6. In the following section, the example of Kathy illustrates the use of the CVI Range and the CVI Resolution Chart to assess the visual functioning of a child who has been diagnosed with CVI. This example demonstrates the procedures used in evaluating a student and completing these instruments.

APPLYING THE CVI RANGE: KATHY

Kathy is a 6-year-old girl who has a history of congenital hydrocephalus. She was diagnosed with CVI when she was 2 years of age. Kathy received early intervention services as an infant and then special education services in a preschool for students with disabilities. She has received vision-related support from a teacher of visually impaired students and an O&M specialist since she was 3. Her initial score on the CVI Range was 2–3. Kathy has continued to improve her functional vision; her most recent CVI Range score was 5–6. Kathy's most recent completed CVI Range appears in Figure 5.9. The narrative report written regarding Kathy's latest CVI Range assessment appears in Appendix 5B at the end of this chapter. The report is organized according to the CVI characteristics. Present findings and educational recommendations are provided characteristic by characteristic.

The following procedures describe the methodology used by Kathy's teacher of students who are visually impaired to obtain this score. It includes statements representing information gathered by observation or interview, along with the teacher's interpretation of the information regarding possible changes in CVI status, and procedures that she planned to follow up on through direct assessment. The teacher considered all of the information obtained in the final scoring of the CVI Range.

Interview or Observation Information

Kathy's parents were contacted to get an update of Kathy's most recent medical and ophthalmologic information. Kathy's status has remained stable, seizures are generally under control and no new medicines have been prescribed. Kathy's eye specialist continues to report that Kathy's eye exam is normal, although her right eye does occasionally turn inward when she is especially fatigued. The ophthalmologist is not recommending treatment at this time.

FIGURE 5.7 *Example of CVI Resolution Chart for a Student Who Scored 7–8 on the CVI Range*

CVI RESOLUTION CHART

Use the following chart to help develop areas of needs for development of IEP goals and objectives.

CVI Characteristics	Phase I: Building Visual Behavior — Level I Environmental Considerations		Phase II: Integrating Vision with Function — Level II Environmental Considerations		Phase III: Resolution of CVI Characteristics — Level III Environmental Considerations	
	Range 1-2 (0)	Range 3-4 (.25)	Range 5-6 (.50)	Range 7-8 (.75)	Range 9-10 (1)
Color preference	Objects viewed are generally a single color	Has "favorite" color	Objects may have two to three favored colors	More colors, familiar patterns regarded	No color or pattern preferences
Need for movement	Objects viewed generally have movement or reflective properties	More consistent localization, brief fixations on movement and reflective materials	Movement continues to be an important factor to initiate visual attention	Movement not required for attention at near	Typical responses to moving targets
Visual latency	Prolonged periods of visual latency	Latency slightly decreases after periods of consistent viewing	Latency present only when student is tired, stressed, or overstimulated	Latency rarely present	Latency resolved
Visual field preferences	Distinct field dependency	Shows visual field preferences	Field preferences decreasing with familiar inputs	May alternate use of right and left fields	Visual fields unrestricted
Difficulties with visual complexity	Responds only in strictly controlled environments / Generally no regard of the human face	Visually fixates when environment is controlled	Student tolerates low levels of familiar background noise / Regards familiar faces when voice does not compete	Competing auditory stimuli tolerated during periods of viewing; student may now maintain visual attention on musical toys	Only the most complex visual environments affect visual response / Views books or other two-dimensional materials

(continued)

CVI Characteristics	Phase I: Building Visual Behavior Level I Environmental Considerations		Phase II: Integrating Vision with Function Level II Environmental Considerations		Phase III: Resolution of CVI Characteristics Level III Environmental Considerations
	Range 1–2 (0)	Range 3–4 (.25)	Range 5–6 (.50)	Range 7–8 (.75)	Range 9–10 (1)
				Views simple books or symbols Smiles at/regards familiar and new faces	Typical visual/social responses
Light-gazing and nonpurposeful gaze	May localize briefly, but no prolonged fixations on objects of faces. Overly attentive to lights or perhaps ceiling fans	Less attracted to lights; can be redirected to other targets	Light is no longer a distractor		
Difficulty with distance viewing	Visually attends in near space only	Occasional visual attention to familiar, moving, or large targets at 2 to 3 feet	Visual attention extends beyond near space, up to 4 to 6 feet	Visual attention extends to 10 feet with targets that produce movement	Visual attention extends beyond 20 feet Demonstrates memory of visual events
Atypical visual reflexes	No blink in response to touch and/or visual threat	Blinks in response to touch, but response may be latent	Blink response to touch consistently present Visual threat response intermittently present	Visual threat response consistently present (both reflexes near 90 percent resolved)	Visual reflexes always present; resolved

	Difficulty with visual novelty	Absence of visually guided reach
	Only favorite or known objects elicit visual attention	Look and touch occur as separate functions Look and touch occur with large and/or moving objects
	May tolerate novel objects if the novel objects share characteristics of familiar objects	Look and touch occur with smaller objects that are familiar, lighted, or reflective Look and touch are still separate
	Use of "known" objects to initiate looking sequence	Visually guided reach used with familiar objects or "favorite" color
	Selection of objects less restricted, one to two sessions of "warm up" time required	Look and touch occur in rapid sequence, but not always together
	Selection of objects not restricted	Look and touch occur together consistently

Key:

- Draw an X through boxes that represent resolved visual behaviors
- Use highlighter to outline boxes describing current visual functioning
- Draw an O in boxes describing visual skills that may never resolve because of coexisting ocular conditions

FIGURE 5.8 Example of CVI Resolution Chart for a Student with CVI and Cataracts Who Scored 3 on Rating II of the CVI Range

CVI RESOLUTION CHART

Use the following chart to help develop areas of needs for development of IEP goals and objectives.

CVI Characteristics	Phase I: Building Visual Behavior Level I Environmental Considerations		Phase II: Integrating Vision with Function Level II Environmental Considerations		Phase III: Resolution of CVI Characteristics Level III Environmental Considerations	
	Range 1–2 (0)	Range 3–4 (.25)	Range 5–6 (.50)	Range 7–8 (.75)	Range 9–10 (1)	
Color preference	Objects viewed are generally a single color	Has "favorite" color	Objects may have two to three favored colors	More colors, familiar patterns regarded	No color or pattern preferences	
Need for movement	Objects viewed generally have movement or reflective properties	More consistent localization, brief fixations on movement and reflective materials	Movement continues to be an important factor to initiate visual attention	Movement not required for attention at near	Typical responses to moving targets	
Visual latency	Prolonged periods of visual latency	Latency slightly decreases after periods of consistent viewing	Latency present only when student is tired, stressed, or overstimulated	Latency rarely present	Latency resolved	
Visual field preferences	Distinct field dependency	Shows visual field preferences	Field preferences decreasing with familiar inputs	May alternate use of right and left fields	Visual fields unrestricted	
Difficulties with visual complexity	Responds only in strictly controlled environments Generally no regard of the human face	Visually fixates when environment is controlled	Student tolerates low levels of familiar background noise Regards familiar faces when voice does not compete	Competing auditory stimuli tolerated during periods of viewing; student may now maintain visual attention on musical toys	Only the most complex visual environments affect visual response Views books or other two-dimensional materials	

					Typical visual/social responses
Light-gazing and nonpurposeful gaze	May localize briefly, but no prolonged fixations on objects or faces. Overly attentive to lights or perhaps ceiling fans	Less attracted to lights; can be redirected to other targets	Light is no longer a distractor		
Difficulty with distance viewing	Visually attends in near space only	Occasional visual attention to familiar, moving, or large targets at 2 to 3 feet	Visual attention extends beyond near space, up to 4 to 6 feet	Visual attention extends to 10 feet with targets that produce movement	Visual attention extends beyond 20 feet; Demonstrates memory of visual events
Atypical visual reflexes	No blink in response to touch and/or visual threat	Blinks in response to touch, but response may be latent	Blink response to touch consistently present; Visual threat response intermittently present	Visual threat response consistently present (both reflexes near 90 percent resolved)	Visual reflexes always present; resolved
Typical visual/social responses				Views simple books or symbols; Smiles at/regards familiar and new faces	

CVI Characteristics	Phase I: Building Visual Behavior / Level I Environmental Considerations	Phase II: Integrating Vision with Function / Level II Environmental Considerations		Phase III: Resolution of CVI Characteristics / Level III Environmental Considerations	
	Range 1–2 (0)	Range 3–4 (.25)	Range 5–6 (.50)	Range 7–8 (.75)	Range 9–10 (1)
Difficulty with visual novelty	Only favorite or known objects elicit visual attention	May tolerate novel objects if the novel objects share characteristics of familiar objects	Use of "known" objects to initiate looking sequence	Selection of objects less restricted, one to two sessions of "warm up" time required	Selection of objects not restricted
Absence of visually guided reach	Look and touch occur as separate functions Look and touch occur with large and/or moving objects	Look and touch occur with smaller objects that are familiar, lighted, or reflective Look and touch are still separate	Visually guided reach used with familiar objects or "favorite" color	Look and touch occur in rapid sequence, but not always together	Look and touch occur together consistently

Key:

- Draw an X through boxes that represent resolved visual behaviors
- Use highlighter to outline boxes describing current visual functioning
- Draw an O in boxes describing visual skills that may never resolve because of coexisting ocular conditions

FIGURE 5.9   *Kathy's CVI Range Form*

THE CVI RANGE

Student/child's name: _Kathy Wong_ _____ Age: ___ _6 years_ _____
Evaluator(s): ___ _Ann Dimitri_ _____ Evaluation Date: ___ _12/12/07_ _____

This assessment protocol is intended for multiple evaluations over a period of time. Suggested scoring (no less than three times per school year):

 a. Initial assessment (red)
 b. Second assessment (blue)
 c. Third assessment (green)
 Further assessments will require a new form.

Totals:	Evaluation #1 (red)	Evaluation #2 (blue)	Evaluation #3 (green)
1. Range for Rating I	5+		
2. Total for Rating II	6		
3. Combine both ratings to get overall CVI Range	5-6		

		10/18/04			12/12/07					
0	1	2 ⟷ 3	4	5 ⟷ 6	7	8	9	10		

No functional
vision

Typical or
near-typical
visual functioning

The CVI Range: Across–CVI Characteristics Assessment Method

Rating I
Rate the following statements as related to the student/child's visual behaviors by marking the appropriate column to indicate the methods used to support the scores:

 O = information obtained through observation of the child/student
 I = information obtained through interview regarding the child/student
 D = information obtained through direct contact with the child/student

In the remaining columns, indicate the assessed degree of the CVI characteristic:

 • **R**   The statement represents a resolved visual behavior
 • +   Describes current functioning of student/child
 • –   Does not apply to student/child
 • +/–   Partially describes student/child

FIGURE 5.9 *Kathy's CVI Range Form (continued)*

CVI Range 1–2: Student functions with minimal visual response

O	I	D	R	+	+/-	–	
X		X	R				May localize, but no appropriate fixations on objects or faces
X	X	X	R				Consistently attentive to lights or perhaps ceiling fans
		X	R				Prolonged periods of latency in visual tasks
X		X	R				Responds only in strictly controlled environments
	X	X	R				Objects viewed are a single color
X	X			+			Objects viewed have movement and/or shiny or reflective properties
X		X	R				Visually attends in near space only
		X	R				No blink in response to touch or visual threat
	X	X	R				No regard of the human face

CVI Range 3–4: Student functions with more consistent visual response

O	I	D	R	+	+/-	–	
X		X		+			Visually fixates when the environment is controlled
X	X	X	R				Less attracted to lights; can be redirected
X		X	R				Latency slightly decreases after periods of consistent viewing
X	X	X	R				May look at novel objects if they share characteristics of familiar objects
		X			+/-		Blinks in response to touch and/or visual threat, but the responses may be latent and/or inconsistent
X	X	X		+			Has a "favorite" color
	X	X		+			Shows strong visual field preferences
X	X	X	R				May notice moving objects at 2 to 3 feet
X		X		+			Look and touch completed as separate events

(continued)

FIGURE 5.9 *Kathy's CVI Range Form (continued)*

CVI Range 5–6: Student uses vision for functional tasks

O	I	D	R	+	+/–	–	
X		X			+/–		Objects viewed may have two to three colors
X	X	X		+			Light is no longer a distractor
	X	X		+			Latency present only when the student is tired, stressed, or overstimulated
		X		+			Movement continues to be an important factor for visual attention
X		X		+			Student tolerates low levels of background noise
		X			+/–		Blink response to touch is consistently present
		X		+			Blink response to visual threat is intermittently present
X	X	X		+			Visual attention now extends beyond near space, up to 4 to 6 feet
X		X			+/–		May regard familiar faces when voice does not compete

CVI Range 7–8: Student demonstrates visual curiosity

O	I	D	R	+	+/–	–	
X		X		+			Selection of toys or objects is less restricted; requires one to two sessions of "warm up"
X	X	X				–	Competing auditory stimuli tolerated during periods of viewing; the student may now maintain visual attention on objects that produce music
		X				–	Blink response to visual threat consistently present
	X	X				–	Latency rarely present
X	X	X				–	Visual attention extends to 10 feet with targets that produce movement
X		X			+/–		Movement not required for attention at near distance
X	X	X			+/–		Smiles at/regards familiar and new faces
X	X	X				–	May enjoy regarding self in mirror
X		X				–	Most high-contrast colors and/or familiar patterns regarded
	X	X				–	Simple books, picture cards, or symbols regarded

(continued)

FIGURE 5.9 *Kathy's CVI Range Form (continued)*

CVI Range 9–10: Student spontaneously uses vision for most functional activities

O	I	D	R	+	+/–	–	
X	X	X				–	Selection of toys or objects not restricted
X		X				–	Only the most complex environments affect visual response
		X				–	Latency resolved
X	X	X				–	No color or pattern preferences
X	X	X				–	Visual attention extends beyond 20 feet
X		X				–	Views books or other two-dimensional materials, simple images
X		X				–	Uses vision to imitate actions
X	X					–	Demonstrates memory of visual events
X	X	X				–	Displays typical visual-social responses
X		X				–	Visual fields unrestricted
X	X					–	Look and reach completed as a single action
X	X	X				–	Attends to two-dimensional images against complex backgrounds

The CVI Range: Within–CVI Characteristics Assessment Method

Rating II

Determine the level of CVI present or resolved in the 10 categories below and add to obtain total score. Rate the following CVI categories as related to the student/child's visual behaviors by circling the appropriate number (the CVI Resolution Chart may be useful as a scoring guide):

    0 Not resolved; usually or always a factor affecting visual functioning

  .25 Resolving

   .5 Resolving; sometimes a factor affecting visual functioning

  .75 Resolving

    1 Resolved; not a factor affecting visual functioning

		Not Resolved	Resolving			Resolved
1.	**Color preference**	0	.25	.5	<u>.75</u>	1

Comments: *Color highlighting of new materials*

		Not Resolved	Resolving			Resolved
2.	**Need for movement**	0	.25	<u>.5</u>	.75	1

Comments: *Kathy moves her body or head to create movement if the target does not have movement*

(continued)

FIGURE 5.9   *Kathy's CVI Range Form (continued)*

	Not Resolved		Resolving		Resolved
3. **Visual latency**	0	.25	<u>.5</u>	.75	1
Comments:					
4. **Visual field preferences**	0	.25	.5	.75	1
Comments: *Kathy turns her head to the right to locate targets*					
5. **Difficulties with visual complexity**	0	.25	<u>.5</u>	.75	1
Comments: *1-2 colors, present on plain background, low levels of voice tolerated during viewing*					
6. **Light-gazing and nonpurposeful gaze**	0	.25	.5	<u>.75</u>	1
Comments: *Seat Kathy with her back to the windows*					
7. **Difficulty with distance viewing**	0	.25	.5	<u>.75</u>	1
Comments:					
8. **Atypical visual reflexes**	0	.25	.5	<u>.75</u>	1
Comments:					
9. **Difficulty with visual novelty**	0	.25	<u>.5</u>	.75	1
Comments: *Select red and or yellow objects that have movement or reflective surfaces—no "noisy" objects*					
10. **Absence of visually guided reach**	0	.25	<u>.5</u>	.75	1
Comments:					

Implications or Conclusions

■ *Kathy's medical history continues to support a diagnosis of CVI.*

Interview or Observation Information

Kathy's parents and classroom teacher report that Kathy continues to prefer yellow objects over objects of all other colors. However, the teacher of visually impaired students has noticed Kathy glancing at several red objects and the red shirt her classroom aide sometimes wears. Kathy's mother also reports that her daughter has several new, favorite toys that are primarily bright red.

Implications or Conclusions

■ *Information from observation and report support possible improvement in the CVI characteristics of color preference and difficulty with visual novelty.*

■ *The teacher of visually impaired students will directly assess Kathy by presenting both familiar and novel objects that are yellow and/or red.*

Interview or Observation Information

Kathy's classroom aide, O&M specialist, and occupational therapist report that Kathy continues to be highly distracted by the movement of people and materials in the classroom. Her aide reports that on warm days, if the fan is on, Kathy seems to be overly attentive to the movement of student art projects suspended from the room's lights. Her O&M specialist continues to mark environmental landmarks with gold reflective paper to help Kathy more accurately identify and travel to indoor destinations.

Implications or Conclusions

■ *Kathy continues to be highly affected by movement. Movement can help Kathy direct her visual attention to salient targets, and it can also act as an unintentional interference or distraction.*

■ *The teacher of visually impaired students will present Kathy with yellow or red materials that are stable and that move in order to determine the effect of movement. She will also assess the need to position Kathy in the classroom in an area that has less movement of people and materials.*

Interview or Observation Information

Kathy's classroom teacher reports that Kathy seems a "little slow to notice things" right after lunch and sometimes before dismissal time.

Implications or Conclusions

■ *Kathy may be experiencing fatigue and visual latency after the noisy, non–visually friendly period in the school cafeteria.*

■ *The teacher of visually impaired students will plan to observe Kathy at these times of the day and will directly assess her to determine if visual latency occurs with familiar and novel materials.*

Interview or Observation Information

The occupational therapist, physical therapist, and O&M specialist all report that Kathy seems to be much slower to respond to activities or materials when they are at her left side. The physical education teacher states that he feels Kathy notices moving balls much more quickly when they are rolled at her right side.

Implications or Conclusions

■ *Kathy may have a dominant peripheral visual field on her right side even though she does eventually look at targets approaching from her left side.*

■ *The teacher of visually impaired students will conduct a modified confrontation field test using moving yellow and red filtered lights or objects.*

Interview or Observation Information

Kathy's father reports that Kathy can feed herself using her fingers when the two of them have a meal together, but she seems less able to find her food on her plate when sharing a meal with her parents and three sisters. Kathy's mother says that Kathy's favorite things continue to be her yellow rubber ducky, yellow tambourine, and yellow and red ball. She has started playing with other simple yellow or red things, but many of those objects are not typical playthings. For example, Kathy likes to remove the red coat hangers from the closet and move them back and forth in front of her face. Kathy's teacher has noticed that recently Kathy has shown interest in a *Sesame Street* book that has a pop-up picture of the red character Elmo.

Implications or Conclusions

- *Kathy continues to have difficulty looking at objects when there is too much sensory competition going on and she needs to process information to other sensory systems. Because of the effect of the complex sensory environment, Kathy may have trouble looking at her food on the plate when there is a significant amount of conversation at mealtimes.*
- *Kathy continues to have a small set of preferred objects that are primarily of a single color, yellow or red, because of the CVI characteristic of difficulty with visually novel items, as well as color preference and degree of complexity.*
- *Kathy uses movement to begin or sustain visual attention or looking behavior.*
- *Kathy is beginning to look at two-dimensional materials, although her preferred image is Elmo, a character that is a single red color, and that pops up in a book, creating movement.*
- *The teacher of visually impaired students will directly assess how well Kathy can look at familiar or novel materials when there is competition to other sensory systems. She will also evaluate Kathy's response to the variable of complexity of array by placing single-color objects against backgrounds that increase in complexity. Kathy will be presented with materials that are familiar but have some internal details. For example, the teacher will show Kathy several different Elmo pictures to see if she will look at or identify Elmo when the image has slightly more or different details.*

Interview or Observation Information

The O&M specialist states that Kathy can move her wheelchair from her classroom to the music room, but cannot reverse the route. On the return route, Kathy is facing a large, wall-sized window, which seems to capture her full attention. Kathy's mother also reports that Kathy will occasionally stare at ceiling lights.

Implications or Conclusions

- *Kathy continues to have some degree of light-gazing behavior. The teacher of visually impaired students will observe Kathy in her school and at home to determine the degree of her light-gazing behavior and make recommendations regarding how to position Kathy in the classroom. The teacher and the O&M specialist will evaluate together the need for adaptations, assistance, or route changes.*

Interview or Observation Information

The O&M specialist and the physical therapist have reported that Kathy seems able to visually locate and move her wheelchair toward gold reflective targets placed on environmental landmarks at distances up to 6 to 8 feet away. Kathy's parents report they believe Kathy notices them when they enter a room from at least 6 feet away.

Implications or Conclusions

- *Kathy's distance vision is improving, especially in low-complexity settings. The teacher of visually impaired students will use familiar moving and nonmoving targets to determine how far away Kathy can visually locate and/or move to them. She will also provide suggestions to the classroom staff regarding the most appropriate distances for instruction that occurs at near and beyond arm's reach.*

Interview or Observation Information

The teacher of visually impaired students observed Kathy in physical education class and outdoors on the playground. In games involving balloons or sponge balls that moved quickly, Kathy occasionally blinked in anticipation of the objects moving quickly toward her face, and always blinked when they actually touched her face.

Implications or Conclusions

- *The teacher of visually impaired students will reassess Kathy's blink-to-touch and visual threat reflexes.*

Interview or Observation Information

Kathy's mother described a set of objects that Kathy seems to prefer over all other objects. Her dad reports that at Kathy's last birthday party, Kathy was more excited by the lit birthday candles than any of her new gifts. Kathy's classroom teacher says that sometimes in morning circle activities, they often start out by showing Kathy one of her favorite things to help her "start looking."

Implications or Conclusions

- *Kathy's ability to visually recognize or to look at objects or other visual targets may be affected by the CVI characteristic of difficulty with visual novelty.*
- *The teacher of visually impaired students will assess how well Kathy can look at objects that share traits with her familiar favorite objects. The teacher will systematically present a range of objects that have greater degrees of novelty—objects that differ from ones already known to Kathy.*

Interview or Observation Information

The teacher of visually impaired students and the occupational therapist both observe how Kathy frequently looks toward an object, looks away, and then reaches for the object without looking. However, Kathy's mother and her classroom aide report that Kathy uses a visually guided reach when reaching for her favorite yellow Gummy Bear candies when they are presented one at a time on her plain black placemat.

Implications or Conclusions

- *Kathy demonstrates the CVI characteristic of absence of visually guided reach in a number of circumstances. Kathy is able to use a visually guided reach when highly familiar, motivating objects are placed against a background of low complexity.*
- *The teacher of visually impaired students will assess the CVI characteristic of absence of visually guided reach by presenting both familiar and less familiar items on some backgrounds that are simple and some that increase in complexity to determine conditions that can be duplicated to facilitate more eye-hand coordination.*

After Kathy's teacher scored CVI Range, Ratings I and II, on the basis of her observations, interviews, and assessments, she reviewed her rating sheets to determine Kathy's overall score. In looking at Kathy's ratings on the Across-CVI Characteristics portion of the CVI Range (see Figure 5.9), she concluded that Kathy had reached a ceiling effect with a string of minus ratings in Range 7-8. Therefore, Kathy's score is 5-6. Her score on the Within-CVI portion is 6. Therefore, Kathy's overall score for the CVI Range is 5-6. This overall score places Kathy in Phase II CVI, in which the overall goal is to integrate vision with function. (See Chapter 6 for more on phases and program planning.)

The next step is to score Kathy's CVI Resolution Chart (see Figure 5.10). As noted earlier, this chart is used as a classroom guide and can be posted as a reminder of Kathy's

FIGURE 5.10   Kathy's CVI Resolution Chart

Date ____ 12/12/07 ____   Student's Name ____ Kathy Wong ____   Evaluator ____ Ann Dimitri ____

CVI RESOLUTION CHART

Use the following chart to help develop areas of needs for development of IEP goals and objectives.

	Phase I: Building Visual Behavior Level I Environmental Considerations		**Phase II:** Integrating Vision with Function Level II Environmental Considerations		**Phase III:** Resolution of CVI Characteristics Level III Environmental Considerations
CVI Characteristics	**Range 1–2 (0)**	**Range 3–4 (.25)**	**Range 5–6 (.50)**	**Range 7–8 (.75)**	**Range 9–10 (1)**
Color preference	Objects viewed are generally a single color	Has "favorite" color	Objects may have two to three favored colors	More colors, familiar patterns regarded	No color or pattern preferences
Need for movement	Objects viewed generally have movement or reflective properties	More consistent localization, brief fixations on movement and reflective materials	Movement continues to be an important factor to initiate visual attention	Movement not required for attention at near	Typical responses to moving targets
Visual latency	Prolonged periods of visual latency	Latency slightly decreases after periods of consistent viewing	Latency present only when student is tired, stressed, or overstimulated	Latency rarely present	Latency resolved
Visual field preferences	Distinct field dependency	Shows visual field preferences	Field preferences decreasing with familiar inputs	May alternate use of right and left fields	Visual fields unrestricted

(continued)

FIGURE 5.10   Kathy's CVI Resolution Chart (continued)

CVI Characteristics	Phase I: Building Visual Behavior / Level I Environmental Considerations		Phase II: Integrating Vision with Function / Level II Environmental Considerations		Phase III: Resolution of CVI Characteristics / Level III Environmental Considerations
	Range 1–2 (0)	Range 3–4 (.25)	Range 5–6 (.50)	Range 7–8 (.75)	Range 9–10 (1)
Difficulties with visual complexity	Responds only in strictly controlled environments; Generally no regard of the human face	Visually fixates when environment is controlled	Student tolerates low levels of familiar background noise; Regards familiar faces when voice does not compete	Competing auditory stimuli tolerated during periods of viewing; student may now maintain visual attention on musical toys; Views simple books or symbols; Smiles at/regards familiar and new faces	Only the most complex visual environments affect visual response; Views books or other two-dimensional materials; Typical visual/social responses
Light-gazing and nonpurposeful gaze	May localize briefly, but no prolonged fixations on objects or faces. Overly attentive to lights or perhaps ceiling fans	Less attracted to lights; can be redirected to other targets	Light is no longer a distractor		
Difficulty with distance viewing	Visually attends in near space only	Occasional visual attention to familiar, moving, or large targets at 2 to 3 feet	Visual attention extends beyond near space, up to 4 to 6 feet	Visual attention extends to 10 feet with targets that produce movement	Visual attention extends beyond 20 feet; Demonstrates memory of visual events

Atypical visual reflexes	No blink in response to touch and/or visual threat	Blinks in response to touch, but response may be latent	Blink response to touch consistently present Visual threat response intermittently present	Visual threat response consistently present (both reflexes near 90 percent resolved)	Visual reflexes always present; resolved
Difficulty with visual novelty	Only favorite or known objects elicit visual attention	May tolerate novel objects if the novel objects share characteristics of familiar objects	Use of "known" objects to initiate looking sequence	Selection of objects less restricted, one to two sessions of "warm up" time required	Selection of objects not restricted
Absence of visually guided reach	Look and touch occur as separate functions Look and touch occur with large and/or moving objects	Look and touch occur with smaller objects that are familiar, lighted, or reflective Look and touch are still separate	Visually guided reach used with familiar objects or "favorite" color	Look and touch occur in rapid sequence, but not always together	Look and touch occur together consistently

Key:

- Draw an X through boxes that represent resolved visual behaviors
- Use highlighter to outline boxes describing current visual functioning
- Draw an O in boxes describing visual skills that may never resolve because of coexisting ocular conditions

current CVI functioning status. Kathy's CVI Resolution Chart includes highlighted behaviors representing current levels of visual functioning, resolved behaviors that are crossed off, and unmarked behaviors that may represent future visual functioning. If Kathy had a coexisting ocular condition affecting her functional vision, certain items would be marked with an O to identify visual behaviors that may not be resolved because of the coexisting ocular condition.

Kathy may need to be reassessed two or more times within the school year, depending on observations and interactions that indicate that Kathy's functional vision is improving. For example, if Kathy's mother reports that her daughter recently started looking at her cup when it was moved from the table to the kitchen counter 15 feet away, it is important that Kathy's educational team perform a new assessment to find out if Kathy's visual behavior has improved with regard to distance and her overall level of CVI.

Once the CVI Range, the CVI Resolution Chart, and the narrative report are completed, the educational team will use them to plan educational interventions to address Kathy's visual functioning in each area of CVI, and to integrate them into her daily routines. This aspect of Kathy's story is continued in Chapter 6.

The CVI Range and CVI Resolution Chart can play a central role in working with students who have CVI. The CVI Range provides a framework for understanding seemingly random behaviors so that they can be seen as what in all likelihood are behaviors associated with the unique visual and behavioral characteristics of children with CVI. Only by using an assessment methodology that is specific to CVI, and that identifies the extent to which CVI is affecting a student, can appropriate interventions be designed to mitigate the effects of this condition, as is described in the next chapter.

This Scoring Guide is used to help assign scores to a student during assessment. For each statement in the CVI Range assessment form, it indicates which CVI characteristics the statement encompasses and provides examples of visual behaviors that correspond to each possible score of R, +, +/-, or −.

Phase	Range	Statement	CVI Characteristic	R	+	+/-	−
I	1–2	**May localize, but no appropriate fixations on objects or faces**	Color, movement latency, visual fields, complexity, novelty	Fixates on objects or faces	May occasionally glance in the direction of an object or face, but attention is intermittent and eye-to-object attention occurs rarely	Gives brief, inconsistent attention toward an object or face (may be determined by report only, not observation)	No attention in the direction of any object or face, either by report or observation
I	1–2	**Consistently attentive to lights or perhaps ceiling fans**	Movement, complexity, light-gazing	Able to look at targets in the presence of primary sources of light	Stares into sources of indoor or outdoor light and is unable to attend to other targets unless the lights are turned off or the student is positioned away from the light	Occasionally able to attend to nonlighted targets, even in the presence of primary sources of light	No attention to light or any other target
I	1–2	**Prolonged periods of latency in visual tasks**	Latency	Little or no delay in directing vision to a target	Demonstrates a delay in directing vision to a target every time or nearly every time a new object is presented or a new activity begins	Delay in directing vision to a target occurs only when tired, stressed, ill, hungry, or overstimulated	Profound delay in directing vision to a target; only rarely seems to view a target
I	1–2	**Responds only in strictly controlled environments**	Complexity	Attends to visual targets in the presence of more than one visual target, sound, or touch	Attends to visual targets only when there are no visual, auditory, or tactile distractions	Occasional attention to visual targets in the presence of certain or familiar visual, auditory, or tactile distractions	No consistent visual attention to any visual targets

(continued)

*An asterisk after a statement in column 3 indicates that the CVI characteristic associated with the statement may not resolve if the student has a co-existing ocular visual impairment.

APPENDIX 5.A   *CVI Range Scoring Guide (continued)*

Phase	Range	Statement	CVI Characteristic	R	+	R	+/-	–
I	1–2	**Objects viewed are a single color**	Color, complexity, novelty	Looks at objects that are any color and/or more than a single color	Glances at or briefly fixates on single-color objects; may be reported to be a favorite color		Glances at or briefly fixates on objects of favorite color, and occasionally on objects of other colors. May also glance at or briefly fixate on objects that have more than a single color	No consistent visual attention to visual targets of any particular color
I	1–2	**Objects viewed have movement and/or shiny or reflective properties**	Movement	Looks at objects that are neither moving nor shiny or reflective	Only looks at objects that move, have moving parts, or are made of shiny or reflective materials		May need movment and/or shiny or reflective objects to initiate visual attention. Occasionally attends to objects without movement properties	No consistent visual attention to moving or nonmoving targets
I	1–2	**Visually attends in near space only***	Complexity, distance viewing	Looks at objects that are beyond 18 inches away	Glances at or briefly fixates on objects only when they are presented within 18 inches		Occasional glances at or fixates on objects beyond 18 inches	No consistent visual attention to objects at any distance
I	1–2	**No blink in response to touch or visual threat'**	Visual reflexes	Blinks when touched at bridge of the nose or in response to a target moving on midline toward the face	Fails to blink		Occasionally blinks in response to touch or threat	Eyes not open

I	1–2	**No regard of the human face***	Complexity, novelty	Looks directly into faces, even if briefly or inconsistently	No attention to human faces, may seem to "look through" people	Occasionally glances into faces, even if without eye-to-eye contact	No consistent attention to targets of any kind
I–II	3–4	**Visually fixates when the environment is controlled**	Complexity	Establishes eye-to-object contact with familiar or novel objects or human faces, even in the presence of visual or other sensory stimuli	Intermittent eye-to-object contact, but only when visual, auditory, and tactile distractors are reduced or eliminated. A small degree of additional sensory input may be tolerated while viewing	Occasional eye-to-object contact, but conditions for fixations may vary	May turn in the direction of a target, but no eye-to-object contact
I–II	3–4	**Less attracted to lights; can be redirected**	Light-gazing	Does not stare at primary sources of light	May stare at lights, but is able to shift attention from lights when appropriate visual targets are presented in controlled environments	Primary sources of light must be eliminated only on rare occasions for visual attention to a target to occur	All primary sources of light must be eliminated for visual attention to a target to occur
I–II	3–4	**Latency slightly decreases after periods of consistent viewing**	Latency	A delay in directing vision toward a familiar object is rarely, if ever, present	Demonstrates a delay in directing vision to a target some of the time or for shorter durations of time. Latency may fade as vision is used more consistently	Delay in directing vision toward a target occurs frequently, but not every time a familiar target is presented	Delay in directing vision toward a target is always present

(continued)

Phase	Range	Statement	CVI Characteristic	R	+	+/-	−
I–II	3–4	**May look at novel objects if they share characteristics of familiar objects**	Novelty	Is able to glance toward or have eye-to-object contact with objects never previously seen that may or may not resemble "favorite" objects	Is able to glance toward or have eye-to-object contact with new objects if they have matching features of color, movement, or low complexity	Is able to glance toward or have eye-to-object contact with objects that have few similar traits, but may share at least one matching element of color, movement, or complexity	Is able to glance toward or have eye-to-object contact only with a small set of highly familiar objects
I–II	3–4	**Blinks in response to touch and/or visual threat, but responses may be latent and/or inconsistent**	Visual reflexes	Blinks immediately when touched at the bridge of the nose and/or when a target moves quickly toward face	Blinks to touch at bridge of the nose and possibly to the quick movement of a target toward the face, but responses may be delayed or slightly inconsistent	Blinks to touch, but not to a target moving quickly toward the face	Does not blink consistently to either touch at the bridge of the nose or to a target moving quickly toward the face
I–II	3–4	**Has a "favorite" color**	Color	Visual attention to objects is not dependent on a particular color	Continues to most consistently glance toward or have eye-to-object contact with targets made of a single, preferred color, over objects of all other colors	Favorite color may be necessary to initiate looking. Some part of the target may be made of the "favorite" or preferred color for visual attention to occur	No consistent attention to objects

I–II	3–4	**Shows strong visual field preferences***	Visual field preferences	Visual attention occurs equally in all fields	Glances toward or has eye-to-object contact when presented in specific positions of peripheral and/or central viewing fields / Preferences not as rigid as in Range 1–2	Glances toward or has eye-to-object contact with targets in most viewing positions, with a slight preference for the original preferred position	Glances toward or has eye-to-object contact in one viewing field only
I–II	3–4	**May notice movement objects at 2 to 3 feet**	Movement, complexity	Pays visual attention to objects that do not move or have reflective properties at distances up to 3 feet or beyond	Glances toward or has eye-to-object contact with objects that move in space or are made of shiny or reflective materials and are at distances up to 3 feet	Movement or reflective properties are required to initiate visual attention / One element of the object may be moving, shiny, or reflective for visual attention to occur	Movement or reflective materials are necessary for visual attention, and viewing distance is within 18 inches of face
I–II	3–4	**Look and touch completed as separate events**	Visually guided reach	Reach and touch occur simultaneously, even if used inconsistently	Attempts to reach or swat at a target, but does not use a visually guided reach / Look, look away, then reach pattern is used	Occasionally uses visually guided reach	Makes no attempts to reach or swat at targets
II	5–6	**Objects viewed may have two to three colors**	Color, complexity	Pays visual attention to multicolor or multipattern objects, with or without preferred color	Looks directly at targets that have a pattern of 2 two to three colors / Preferred color is at least one element of the pattern	Looks directly at targets that have two and occasionally three colors / Preferred color is always one of the colors	Pays visual attention only to objects of a single preferred color

(continued)

CVI

Phase	Range	Statement	Characteristic	R	+	+/-	-
II	5–6	**Light is no longer a distractor***	Light-gazing	Normal responses to high and low levels of light	No light-gazing behavior	Occasional gazing at primary sources of light	Light-gazing occurs consistently
II	5–6	**Latency present only when the student is tired, stressed, or overstimulated**	Latency, complexity	No delay in directing visual attention to a familiar or noncomplex target	Delay in directing visual attention toward a target only when experiencing fatigue or inappropriate levels of multisensory input	Occasional delay in directing visual attention to a target	Consistent delay in directing visual attention to a target
II	5–6	**Movement continues to be an important factor for visual attention**	Movement	Moving, shiny, or reflective materials are not required for visual attention at near or up to 6 feet away	Visual attention most consistent with materials that move or are shiny or reflective. Some element of movement is necessary; entire target does not have to be moving, shiny, or reflective for visual attention to occur	A small element of movement may help establish or maintain visual attention	Only materials with elements of movement establish or maintain visual attention
II	5–6	**Student tolerates low levels of background noise**	Complexity	Visual attention established and maintained in typical multisensory environments	Visual attention is maintained even in the presence of low-volume sound, familiar voices, or familiar environmental sounds	Occasionally is able to maintain visual attention in the presence of sound. One or two particular sounds are tolerated during viewing; many are not tolerated	No or little visual attention in the presence of other sensory inputs

	Age	Skill	Category				
II	5–6	**Blink response to touch is consistently present**	Visual reflexes	Blink-to-touch response present; blink-to-visual-threat response (when target moves quickly toward face) inconsistently present	Blinks simultaneous to touch at bridge of nose consistently	Emerging pattern of blink-to-touch response present	Occasional or absent blink-to-touch response
II	5–6	**Blink response to visual threat is intermittently present**	Visual reflexes	Blink-to-visual-threat response consistently present	Blink-to-visual-threat response present in 50 percent of attempts	Blink-to-threat response occurs, but in fewer than 50 percent of attempts	No blink-to visual-threat response present
II	5–6	**Visual attention now extends beyond near space, up to 4 to 6 feet***	Complexity, distance viewing	Visual attention or eye-to-object contact with targets beyond a distance of 6 feet	Can visually locate or fixate on certain targets at distances as far as 6 feet away / Ability to detect objects or movement at 4 to 6 feet may depend on the degree of environmental complexity	Occasional ability to locate or fixate on targets as far as 6 feet away, even when the background is visually noncomplex	Visual attention or eye-to-object contact within 3 feet
II	5–6	**May regard familiar faces when voices do not compete**	Complexity, novelty	Makes eye-to-face contact, even if inconsistent, and maybe simultaneously with speech	Glances at or looks directly into faces of familiar people, but only when the familiar person is not speaking	Glances at or looks directly into faces, but responses are inconsistent or fleeting	No regard of the human face

(continued)

APPENDIX 5.A   CVI Range Scoring Guide (continued)

CVI

Phase	Range	Statement	Characteristic	R	+	+/-	-
III	7–8	**Selection of toys or objects is less restricted; requires one to two sessions of "warm up"**	Complexity, novelty	Novel objects that match complexity requirements are visually regarded	Looks at new objects that have attributes of familiar objects Recognizes new object immediately after one to two presentations	Look at new objects that have attributes of familiar ones, but requires more than two presentations before object is recognized immediately	Looks at familiar objects; novel objects must closely resemble familiar ones
III	7–8	**Competing auditory stimuli tolerated during periods of viewing; may now maintain visual attention on objects that produce music**	Complexity	No amount of sensory information interferes with visual attention	Is able to look at objects that simultaneously produce music or other sounds	Occasionally is able to maintain visual attention while other sensory input competes Particular types of sensory inputs may continue to interfere with visual attention	Visual attention depends on low or no additional sensory input
III	7–8	**Blink response to visual threat consistently present**	Visual reflexes	Blinks to approach of unexpected inputs within a complex environment	Blinks simultaneous to the approach of an object or open hand moving quickly on midline toward the face	Occasionally blinks to the approach of an object or hand moving quickly on midline toward the face	No blink-to-threat response
III	7–8	**Latency rarely present**	Latency	Delayed response to visual input never occurs	Seldom demonstrates a delay in detecting a target after it is presented	Novel objects, complex environments, or fatigue may increase degree of delayed response	Delayed response to new and familiar targets continues to exist

III	7–8	**Visual attention extends to 10 feet with targets that produce movement***	Movement, complexity, distance viewing	Visual attention even beyond 10 feet and/or visual attention up to 10 feet with targets that are stable	Is able to visually locate and/or fixate on certain targets at distances as far as 10 feet away, especially with targets that produce movement Attention at this distance may depend on the degree of complexity of the environment	Occasionally gives visual attention to targets at 10 feet, generally when the environment is controlled for other sensory inputs	No visual attention to any targets at distances as far as 10 feet
III	7–8	**Movement not required for attention at near**	Movement, complexity	Is able to detect targets that do not have moving, shiny, or reflective properties beyond near distance	Is able to visually detect and attend to objects or visual targets that do not move or are not made of shiny or reflective materials within 18 to 24 inches	Occasionally is able to detect and attend to visual targets beyond 2 feet	Is not able to detect or attend to nonmoving targets beyond 2 feet
III	7–8	**Smiles at/regards familiar and new faces***	Complexity, novelty	Has eye-to-eye contact with most faces; discriminates new from known people	Glances at and/or has eye-to-eye contact with familiar and new faces	Occasionally glances toward and/or makes eye contact with familiar faces	Gives no attention to faces
III	7–8	**May enjoy regarding self in mirror***	Complexity, novelty	Maintains consistent eye-to-eye contact with self in mirror	Consistently glances and/or looks directly at mirror image even though eye-to-eye contact may not occur	Inconsistently glances at own image in mirror	Mirror primarily serves as a light-gazing device

(continued)

APPENDIX 5.A   CVI Range Scoring Guide (continued)

CVI

Phase	Range	Statement	Characteristic	R	+	+/-	–
III	7–8	**Most high-contrast colors and/or familiar patterns regarded**	Color, complexity, novelty	Is able to visually attend to materials that have more than two to three colors that may not include the preferred color	Is able to visually attend to objects of any bright color or objects that have simple, multicolor patterns	Is able to visually attend to some simple patterns, especially familiar ones or those that are highlighted with the preferred color	Preferred color continues to be necessary as an element of an object
III	7–8	**Simple books, picture cards, or symbols regarded***	Complexity, novelty	Is able to visually identify elements of age-appropriate books or other two-dimensional materials	Visually attends to two-dimensional materials that have little complexity and that include one- to two-color images	Visually attends to a small set of two-dimensional materials; is not able to generalize the images to new contexts. May use lightbox and lightbox pictures to facilitate attention to two-dimensional details	Is visually inattentive to two-dimensional materials
III	9–10	**Selection of objects not restricted**	Complexity, novelty	Demonstrates visual curiosity and seeks out novel objects or materials	Is able to visually examine and/or interact with objects of any color and of any surface pattern, even if they are novel	Recognizes and/or attends to visually novel objects with a single previous experience	Visually attends to objects that share elements of familiar objects

Level	Score	Item	Category				
III	9–10	**Only the most complex environments affect visual response**	Complexity, novelty	Demonstrates visual curiosity in complex environments, identifies or attends to novel elements within 20 feet	Demonstrates visual curiosity in familiar and novel environments, except those with an extreme degree of visual and other sensory complexity	Demonstrates visual curiosity in familiar environments that have low degrees of sensory complexity	Does not demonstrate visual curiosity
III	9–10	**Latency resolved**	Latency	Directs vision to indicate wants or needs	Demonstrates no delay in visually detecting a target after it is presented	Rarely demonstrates a delayed visual response to a target	Demonstrates a delayed visual response to targets when tired or overstimulated
III	9–10	**No color or pattern preferences**	Color	Demonstrates typical abilities to attend to colors or patterns,	Color highlighting or pattern adjustment or highlighting is not required for visual attention	Some novel patterns or symbols require color highlighting for visual attention	Color highlighting of salient features or details is required for visual attention
III	9–10	**Visual attention extends beyond 20 feet***	Distance viewing	Is able to visually locate and/or fixate on targets at distances commensurate with peers	Is able to visually locate and/or fixate on targets at distances up to and possibly beyond 20 feet away	Is able to visually locate and/or fixate on targets that produce movement or are shiny or reflective at distances of 20 feet away Is able to visually locate and/or fixate on targets without movement 10 to 19 feet away; complexity of environment will continue to affect distance	Is able to visually locate and/or fixate on targets up to 10 feet away

(continued)

APPENDIX 5.A CVI Range Scoring Guide (continued)

CVI

Phase	Range	Statement	Characteristic	R	+	+/-	–
III	9–10	**Views books or other two-dimensional materials, simple images**	Complexity	Identifies salient features of two-dimensional materials with no adjustment or adaptation	Detects or identifies pictures or symbols in books with simple configurations	Detects or identifies familiar elements in familiar two-dimensional, simple materials	Is visually inattentive to two-dimensional materials
III	9–10	**Uses vision to imitate actions***	Complexity	Repeats actions in response to an indirect, incidental model	Repeats actions in response to a direct model	Repeats actions in response to a visual and physical prompt model	Does not imitate visual actions
III	9–10	**Demonstrates memory of visual events***	Complexity, distance viewing	Anticipates an action or event based on environmental visual cues	Demonstrates recognition of a person, place, or event that has occurred in the past	Demonstrates recognition of a person, place, or event that occurs in a rote routine	Demonstrates no recognition of actions or events that occur as a rote routine
III	9–10	**Displays typical visual-social responses***	Complexity	Initiates social contact or demonstrates withdrawal from unfamiliar individuals	Demonstrates appropriate affective social responses to input from facial expressions or gestures of adults or peers	Demonstrates appropriate affective social responses with familiar people	Demonstrates no reliable affective or social responses to peers or adults
III	9–10	**Visual fields unrestricted***	Visual fields	Has full use of both central and peripheral visual fields	Has full functional use of peripheral visual fields; some central visual difficulties related to complexity	Demonstrates greater reliance on peripheral fields; may continue to use near viewing for two-dimensional materials	Demonstrates visual field preferences

III	9–10	**Look and reach completed as a single action**	Visually guided reach	Consistently uses visually guided reach, regardless of the size of target or complexity of background	Uses visually guided reach, but may be affected by size of target or complexity of background	Uses visually guided reach only when the background complexity is reduced	Rarely uses visually guided reach
III	9–10	**Attends to two-dimensional images against complex backgrounds***	Complexity	Is able to identify salient features and additional details in unadapted, two-dimensional materials with backgrounds of high visual complexity	Is able to identify salient features and additional details in age-appropriate two-dimensional materials with minor or no adaptations	Is able to identify salient features in adapted two-dimensional materials with backgrounds of low complexity	Is not able to identify salient features in two-dimensional materials

PEDIATRIC PROGRAM VISIT

Student Name: <u>Kathy Wong</u>   **Student Age:** <u>6</u>

Parent/Guardian Name: <u>Cam Wong</u>

Address: <u>566 Middleton Road, Woburn, KS 12345</u>   **Telephone:** <u>(222) 456-7890</u>

Assessor: <u>Ann Dimitri</u>   **Date:** <u>December 12, 2007</u>

<u>Teacher of Students with Visual Impairments</u>

Kathy was seen at the Pediatric Program on December 12, 2005. At today's evaluation, Kathy was 6 years of age. She came to this evaluation with her parents. The primary goal of this session was to determine functional vision abilities and to identify potential characteristics of CVI that may be interfering with Kathy's visual performance.

Kathy's medical history is complex and consistent with the neurological disorders often associated with CVI. Kathy has a normal eye exam; she does not wear corrective lenses. Kathy receives educational services from her school district. These services include special instruction in a life skills classroom, as well as physical therapy, occupational therapy, and consultation from a teacher of students with visual impairments.

The evaluation was conducted over a $2\frac{1}{2}$-hour time period. In my initial observation, I watched Kathy playing with objects that were primarily yellow or red in color. Her play schemes included shaking, banging, and producing movement-type actions with the objects. Kathy frequently checked in with her parents by looking at, speaking with, or walking over to them, and responded to all of their verbal requests with accuracy. Kathy appeared relaxed throughout our session and she did not have difficulty making transitions from activity to activity.

During this evaluation, Kathy demonstrated all of the visual behaviors and characteristics typically associated with CVI. The remainder of this report will be organized according to these characteristics.

Color preference: Like most children who have CVI, Kathy seems to respond more quickly to objects of a particular color. In Kathy's case, the preferred color is yellow. Although her responses to the objects that are yellow occur more quickly and spontaneously, this characteristic has begun to resolve. Kathy's visual responses to red objects are almost as quick as to yellow, but she tends to ignore objects of almost all other colors. Yellow or red highlighting of objects, symbols, or environmental features may facilitate increased looking behaviors.

Need for movement: Many children with CVI respond best visually to targets that move in space or that have reflective surfaces. Reflective or shiny materials are likely to be interpreted in the brain as "super-charged movement" and thus elicit and sustain greater visual attention. In our session today, Kathy repeatedly oriented to objects that had properties of movement. For example, I observed that Kathy ignored even familiar objects until the objects were moved back and forth in Kathy's peripheral visual fields.

Visual latency: The characteristic of visual latency is one in which there is a delayed response between the time a target is presented and the time the individual first notices it. Kathy demonstrated latency only occasionally in our session today. Her parents report that she shows greater

(continued)

latency when she is especially tired or stressed, or after a seizure. She also has increased latency if the environment is very noisy or visually cluttered. This delayed response is an important factor that must be considered in instruction and in Kathy's daily life. Kathy should be afforded greater waiting time under conditions that cause latency to increase, such as when she is presented with novel targets or when she is fatigued or overstimulated.

Visual field preferences: Many children with CVI have strong visual field preferences. These field differences typically are not due to damage to the retina or other structures of the eye; they are caused by damage to the visual pathways in the brain. Kathy shows a significant delay when targets are presented in her left peripheral field, but finds them within normal limits when presented at the right. She also has difficulty locating targets in her lower visual fields, even when the targets are yellow, reflective, and moving. This finding has implications for O&M instruction and safety issues, because Kathy may not be able to detect objects or drop offs in her lower visual field or at her left side. It also suggests that she should be positioned in the classroom so that her dominant lateral field is closest to classroom instruction. It is also suggested that Kathy have near-vision activities positioned within 18 inches and off midline, slightly to her right or left.

Difficulties with visual complexity: Difficulties with visual complexity can mean difficulty with complexity of the surface of an object, of the viewing array, or of the sensory environment. Kathy has difficulty with all three components. First, when objects are highly patterned, Kathy tends to avoid them or act inattentive. She is able to participate in activities when materials have no more than two or perhaps three colors. Second, Kathy has significant difficulties disembedding targets presented on patterned backgrounds. For example, when a yellow Gummy Bear was presented on a four-color background, Kathy attempted to pick up the cloth and move it in front of her face. However, when the same object was placed on a black cloth, Kathy visually located and retrieved the object without hesitation. It is suggested that Kathy have a clutter-free work surface and that when necessary, a 12-inch trifold board be placed between Kathy and the source of visual clutter to reduce complexity of array. Third, Kathy's ability to use her vision appears to be highly dependent upon the degree of visual and auditory distraction in her workspace. When music was playing or conversations took place, Kathy tended to move away from the activity and toward the auditory or visual distraction. It is therefore recommended that all sources of sensory competition be monitored in the classroom, and that Kathy not be required to engage in visually based tasks during times of a high degree of visual or auditory activity.

Light-gazing and nonpurposeful gaze: Some children with CVI spend prolonged periods of time gazing at primary sources of light. In our session today, Kathy was not observed engaging in light-gazing behavior at any time. However, according to Kathy's parents and based on school reports, Kathy does occasionally stare at overhead lights. Again, this behavior may occur or increase if Kathy is overstimulated or if she is fatigued or not feeling well. Light-gazing behavior should signal to classroom personnel that Kathy either needs a break from activity or that the classroom activity is not conducive to sustaining her visual attention.

Difficulty with distance viewing: Kathy was able to locate objects presented against relatively simple backgrounds at distances as great as 6 feet away. The assessment environment was visually simple; therefore, it cannot be assumed that she can perform tasks in which she locates objects in nonadapted environments. In more cluttered settings, Kathy was unable to locate her favorite 3-inch high yellow Big Bird toy. Her ability to use distance vision is highly dependent upon the complexity of the setting, as well as familiarity with and color of the target. In general, Kathy is most able to locate objects from distances within 4 feet.

Atypical visual reflexes: There are two responses whose lack is often associated with CVI. The blink reflex is one in which the individual blinks simultaneously to a touch at the bridge of the nose. The second reflex occurs when an individual blinks as a target (usually an open hand) moves quickly toward the face at midline. Kathy blinked occasionally to both of these stimuli, but never consistently. There is no direct instruction that occurs to address these reflexes; they are monitored over time and usually resolve at the student's other visual behaviors improve.

Difficulty with visual novelty: Many children with CVI tend to visually attend to objects or targets seen previously, but may ignore visually novel or new things. Kathy only examined objects that were highly familiar to her or those that were very similar in color, simplicity, and movement traits to familiar objects. Items selected for school activities should also meet these important criteria or be adapted with yellow, red, or shiny materials.

Absence of visually guided reach: Kathy typically looks toward a target, glances away, and then reaches for the object without looking at it. Her ability to use a visually guided reach increased when simple, colored materials were presented individually on a black background.

Based on the CVI Range assessment of 12/12/05, Kathy scored at 5–6 out of a possible 10 (10 represents typical or near-typical visual functioning, with little or no effect of CVI). Kathy requires specially designed instruction and adaptations to address the presence of CVI and to help her develop visual skills, and these adaptations should ideally be integrated throughout her daily routines.

Thank you for providing me with the opportunity to meet and evaluate Kathy and to spend time with her parents. If I can be of any further assistance, please do not hesitate to contact me.

Ann Dimitri, 12/12/07

CHAPTER 6

Program Planning and Intervention

While knowledge of cortical visual impairment (CVI) continues to evolve, professionals who are working with students with CVI are often challenged to come up with different, innovative, and effective approaches. For educational professionals conducting assessments and planning intervention, certain traditional frameworks and assumptions need to be complemented by an awareness of the complex nature of CVI. Typically, children and adults with ocular visual impairments are helped to make optimal use of their functional vision and to learn alternative and adaptive techniques for performing life's activities. However, another rehabilitative dimension needs to be brought into play while working with students with CVI, as will be discussed in this chapter.

Unlike the majority of ocular disorders, CVI is a condition in which improvement in vision is not only possible, but is likely. Educators therefore have the opportunity to plan interventions that will bring about lasting improvement in a student's functional vision, as opposed to facilitating the maximum use of existing functional vision. This opportunity requires bringing to bear an awareness of the remarkable plasticity of the brain, and the significance of neuronal growth, and specialization.

As discussed in Chapter 1, when damage interferes with the brain's ability to process visual information through the centers and pathways normally dedicated to this activity, the brain is capable of developing new and additional synapses (connections between neurons) to sustain visual functions (Schwartz & Begley, 2002). If increased synapses create increased vision, how can the formation of new synapses be stimulated? Their development is spurred by the activity of looking itself. For this reason, the first aims in interventions with children with CVI need to be to facilitate a child's ability to look and to motivate the child to use his or her vision. Through a child's repeated experiences in looking, and by encouraging and supporting the child to use vision to the greatest degree possible, new synapses are formed and visual functioning is strengthened. Presented with objects that they can look at throughout the day, and with methods of using their vision that are integrated into their daily lives, the children's own brains can be engaged to improve their visual power.

RATIONALE BEHIND THE CVI RANGE

Work with children with CVI is in many ways no different from work with children with other conditions. That is, careful assessment needs to take place, and interventions need to be planned with a critical awareness of the needs assessed. For children with CVI, it is important to determine where they are on the continuum of possible impact of CVI, to identify in this way what they are able to look at or are interested in looking at, and to give them as many opportunities to look as possible, by integrating motivating activities and materials into their daily lives. The goal is to facilitate looking.

The CVI Range and CVI Resolution Chart provide supporting structures for this kind of rehabilitative work with a child. The essential approach is to determine where a child may be in terms of the impact of CVI on his or her visual behavior, and then to chart movement and progress in reference to the visual behaviors that typically accompany CVI and interfere with a child's ability to function visually. As indicated in Chapter 5, there are three phases of visual functioning in the progression of CVI that form the conceptual backdrop against which interventions can be planned. In Phase I, which focuses on building visual behavior, all intervention activities are designed to help the student who uses vision infrequently to become more consistent in looking at a small repertoire of specific objects. In Phase II, the goal is integrating vision with function. The student now has enough consistent looking behaviors that all activities can integrate vision with activation or manipulation of some object. The student is no longer passively looking, but is now actively

eliciting a response from a target. For example, the student who once only looked at a red Mylar pompom now touches a red Mylar-covered switch that turns on a radio. Even if a student does not have the ability to reach away from his or her body, making choices using visual regard is a form of integrating vision with function. Finally, the goal in Phase III is the resolution of the remaining CVI characteristics. This is the refinement phase in which fine-tuning of the characteristic visual behaviors takes place. The student now functions visually and might not be readily recognized by casual observers as someone with CVI. The overall goal of intervention is to help a child move through these phases.

Once a student has been assessed, and the CVI Range and CVI Resolution Chart have been completed, the student's educational team can begin to use those documents as the basis of planning for the student's educational program in the form of the goals of an Individualized Family Service Plan (IFSP) or Individualized Education Program (IEP). These goals then need to be translated into specific interventions, tailored to the student's needs. Because the CVI Range and CVI Resolution Chart indicate how much the student is affected by each of the CVI behavioral characteristics, the teacher can plan interventions at the appropriate levels indicated. The flowchart presented in Figure 6.1 provides an overview of the entire process, from efforts to identify whether a child has CVI to program planning and intervention and continued assessment.

Overall, when dealing with children with CVI, it is important to remember that it is not merely exposure to visual stimuli that matters, it is the *type* of visual input (Hubel & Wiesel, 1970). In addition, most children with CVI may not be able to benefit from typical unadapted environments; they may require specialized and controlled sensory inputs in order to visually attend.

FIGURE 6.1 *CVI: From Identification to Intervention*

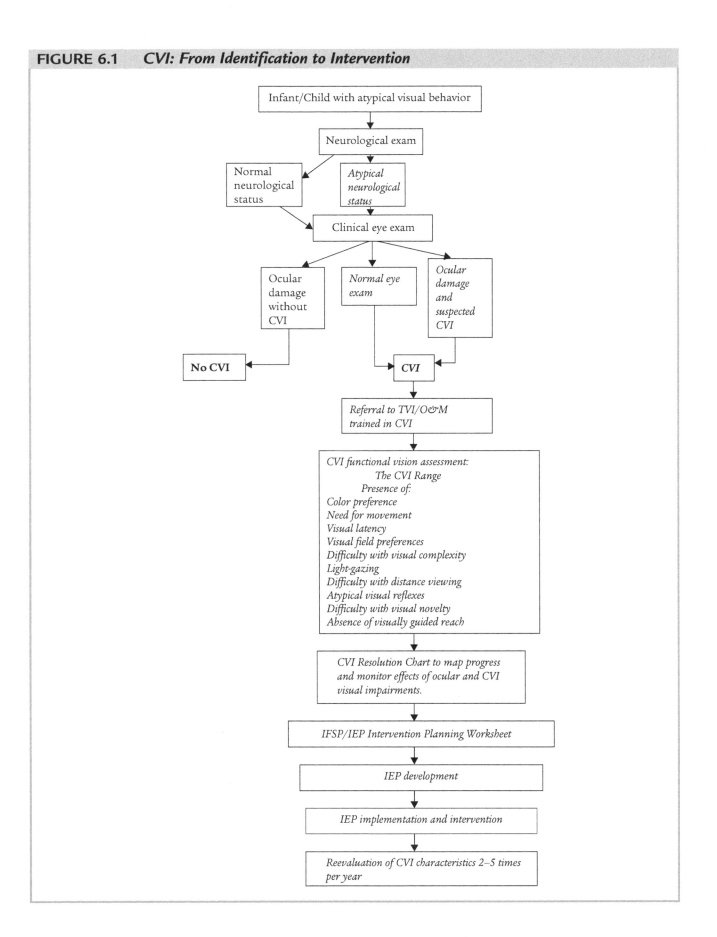

Although the visual behaviors of most children with CVI may sometimes be similar to those of children with ocular visual conditions, the source of the behavior is different, and therefore the interventions need to be different as well. For example, although both a student with CVI and a student with an ocular disorder may benefit from the use of a lightbox, the reasons are very different, as may be the outcomes. The child with an eye disorder may need the lightbox for the provision of increased contrast, and is likely to need this degree of contrast for the foreseeable future. The student with CVI may need a lightbox only if the student demonstrates light-gazing behavior, and then the lightbox serves as a motivator for attention. In addition, this behavior is expected to be resolved over time, so the lightbox is, in effect, a temporary intervention tool. Although the behavior—interest in light—is a shared characteristic, the diagnoses and rationales are different.

This chapter will explain how to use the information in the CVI Range and the CVI Resolution Chart, as well as the data summarized on these forms from observations and interviews, to set goals and objectives for a student's educational program (the IFSP or IEP), as well as how to translate that information into specific, targeted interventions.

DESIGNING INTERVENTIONS: THE CVI RESOLUTION CHART

In using results from the CVI Range to design interventions for students with CVI, it is important to consider all CVI characteristics (except atypical visual reflexes) that are scored lower than 1 in Part II of the assessment, the Within-CVI Characteristics method. The score for atypical visual reflexes is not considered because automatic responses are not directly influenced by instruction. Based on the experience at the Pediatric VIEW program at Western Pennsylvania Hospital (Lantzy & Roman, 2002–2007), it can be concluded that the two reflexes of blinking in response to touch and blinking to visual threat improve as the overall level of CVI improves. Thus, it is not effective, or appropriate, for educators to attempt to "teach" a student to alter the visual blink or the visual threat reflexes.

The example in Figure 6.2 shows the areas scored lower than 1 on Part II of the CVI Range by a student named Jasmine. Jasmine had a total score of 4 on Part II of the Range, and has only one characteristic, that of light-gazing, scored at the 1 level. Therefore, her IFSP or IEP should include goals that relate to color preference, need for movement, visual latency, visual field preferences, difficulties with visual complexity, difficulty with distance viewing, difficulty with visual novelty, and absence of visually guided reach, based on both the scores and the comments on Part II of the CVI Range.

At this point, after the assessment and scoring of both parts of the CVI Range, the evaluator may find it helpful to plot the student's CVI scores on the CVI Resolution Chart, introduced in Chapter 5, in preparation for developing the IFSP or IEP. Jasmine's CVI Resolution Chart, shown in Figure 6.3, shows at a glance that Jasmine is emerging from Phase I into Phase II. Most of her scores are on the border, with some still in Phase I and some distinctly in Phase II. Thus, although some of her activities may continue to be designed to build visual behavior, many will also be planned to meet the goal of integrating vision with function; for example: "During mealtime routines, Jasmine will look and reach toward her single-color orange spoon placed against a black placemat or table cover."

FIGURE 6.2 *Jasmine's Scores on Part II of the CVI Range*

The CVI Range: Within—CVI Characteristics Assessment Method

Rating II

Determine the level of CVI present or resolved in the 10 categories below and add total score.
Compare to the Overall CVI Range obtained in Part I.

Rate the following CVI categories as related to the student/child's visual behaviors by circling the appropriate number:

0	Not Resolved; usually or always a factor affecting visual functioning
.25	Resolving
.5	Resolving; sometimes a factor affecting visual functioning
.75	Resolving
1	Resolved; not a factor affecting visual functioning

	Not Resolved		Resolving		Resolved
1. Color preference	0	<u>.25</u>	.5	.75	1

Comments: Her preferred color is fluorescent orange

	Not Resolved		Resolving		Resolved
2. Need for movement	0	<u>.25</u>	.5	.75	1

Comments: Attracted to bright orange Slinky and orange Mylar.

	Not Resolved		Resolving		Resolved
3. Visual latency	0	.25	<u>.5</u>	.75	1

Comments: Increased latency at beginning of school day, after lunch, and after physical therapy session.

	Not Resolved		Resolving		Resolved
4. Visual field preferences	0	<u>.25</u>	.5	.75	1

Comments: Increased attention in right peripheral and left central visual fields.

	Not Resolved		Resolving		Resolved
5. Difficulties with visual complexity	0	<u>.25</u>	.5	.75	1

Comments: Single-color objects, black background, no auditory or touch distractors while looking.

	Not Resolved		Resolving		Resolved
6. Light-gazing and nonpurposeful gaze	0	.25	.5	.75	<u>1</u>

Comments: Resolved

	Not Resolved		Resolving		Resolved
7. Difficulty with distance viewing	0	<u>.25</u>	.5	.75	1

Comments: Best distance = 12 to 18 inches

	Not Resolved		Resolving		Resolved
8. Atypical visual reflexes	0	.25	<u>.5</u>	.75	1

Comments: Blink to touch and threat reflexes present some of the time.

(continued)

FIGURE 6.2   *Jasmine's Scores on Part II of the CVI Range (continued)*

	Not Resolved		Resolving		Resolved
9. Difficulty with visual novelty	0	.25	<u>.5</u>	.75	1

Comments: Select orange, moving or shiny, single-color objects.

10. Absence of visually guided reach	0	<u>.25</u>	.5	.75	1

Comments: Occasional visually directed reach toward orange moving objects only when placed against a black background

SETTING GOALS: IFSP/IEP DEVELOPMENT

After information from the CVI Range is gathered and plotted on the CVI Resolution Chart, the educational team will be ready to develop the child's IFSP or IEP. The information obtained from the CVI Range and the CVI Resolution Chart can be directly applied to the development of goals. Teachers will also want to check their observational and other data to determine the best way of proceeding to work with a child.

If the student demonstrates characteristics related to CVI and the IFSP/IEP team agrees that intervention should begin, as already indicated, long-range goals are written for all behavioral characteristics that have received a score lower than 1 on Part II of the CVI Range assessment—that is, for any behavioral characteristic that remains unresolved. The themes of Phases I–III, which broadly indicate the level of CVI experienced by the student (and are listed at the head of the CVI Resolution Chart), guide the development of the student's long-range goals, as explained in the sections that follow.

Phase I (Range 0 to about 3)

In Phase I, the goal is building consistent visual behavior for children who barely use their vision

at all, except in the most controlled situations. Most students in Phase I appear to have a dominant color preference, show greatest interest in objects with strong movement properties, seem to ignore objects with either highly patterned surfaces or presented against patterned backgrounds, require significant wait-time even when familiar objects are presented, and have certain objects they recognize before all others, especially before new or novel objects.

- In this phase, all activities should be designed to increase visual attention and to build stable and sustained looking, even if the selection of viewable targets is narrow. For example, a student may look at a yellow pompom, a yellow Slinky, and a yellow lighted ball, but ignore all other objects presented. Typically, the student begins with brief localizations (turning in the direction of the object), with only occasional eye-to-object contact or direct fixation on any object.
- In Phase I, most students require significant control of sensory input in the environment in order to use vision.

Phase II (Range 3 + to about 7)

The goal in Phase II is integrating vision with function. Students in Phase II tend to demonstrate more consistent eye-to-object contact

FIGURE 6.3 Jasmine's CVI Resolution Chart

Date ___ 6/7/07 ___ Name: ___ Jasmine Douglas ___ Evaluator ___ C. Roman ___

CVI RESOLUTION CHART

Use the following chart to help develop areas of needs for development of IEP goals and objectives.

	Phase I: Building Visual Behavior Level I Environmental Considerations		Phase II: Integrating Vision with Function Level II Environmental Considerations	Phase III: Resolution of CVI Characteristics Level III Environmental Considerations	
CVI Characteristics	**Range 1–2 (0)**	**Range 3–4 (.25)**	**Range 5–6 (.50)**	**Range 7–8 (.75)**	**Range 9–10 (1)**
Color preference	Objects viewed are generally a single color	Has "favorite" color	Objects may have two to three favored colors	More colors, familiar patterns regarded	No color or pattern preferences
Need for movement	Objects viewed generally have movement or reflective properties	More consistent localization, brief fixations on movement and reflective materials	Movement continues to be an important factor to initiate visual attention	Movement not required for attention at near	Typical responses to moving targets
Visual latency	Prolonged periods of visual latency	Latency slightly decreases after periods of consistent viewing	Latency present only when student is tired, stressed, or overstimulated	Latency rarely present	Latency resolved
Visual field preferences	Distinct field dependency	Shows visual field preferences	Field preferences decreasing with familiar inputs	May alternate use of right and left fields	Visual fields unrestricted

(continued)

FIGURE 6.3 *Jasmine's CVI Resolution Chart (continued)*

	Phase I: Building Visual Behavior Level I Environmental Considerations		Phase II: Integrating Vision with Function Level II Environmental Considerations		Phase III: Resolution of CVI Characteristics Level III Environmental Considerations
CVI Characteristics	Range 1–2 (0)	Range 3–4 (.25)	Range 5–6 (.50)	Range 7–8 (.75)	Range 9–10 (1)
Difficulties with visual complexity	Responds only in strictly controlled environments ~~Generally no regard of the human face~~	Visually fixates when environment is controlled	Student tolerates low levels of familiar background noise. Regards familiar faces when voice does not compete	Competing auditory stimuli tolerated during periods of viewing; student may now maintain visual attention on musical toys. Views simple books or symbols. Smiles at/regards familiar and new faces	Only the most complex visual environments affect visual response. Views books or other two-dimensional materials. Typical visual/social responses
Light-gazing and nonpurposeful gaze	May localize briefly, but no prolonged fixations on objects or faces. ~~Overly attentive to lights or perhaps ceiling fans~~	~~Less attracted to lights; can be redirected to other targets~~	~~Light is no longer a distractor~~		

Difficulty with distance viewing	Visually attends in near space only	Occasional visual attention to familiar, moving, or large targets at 2 to 3 feet	Visual attention extends beyond near space, up to 4 to 6 feet	Visual attention extends to 10 feet with targets that produce movement	Visual attention extends beyond 20 feet Demonstrates memory of visual events
Atypical visual reflexes	No blink in response to touch and/or visual threat	Blinks in response to touch, but response may be latent	Blink response to touch consistently present Visual threat response intermittently present	Visual threat response consistently present (both reflexes near 90 percent resolved)	Visual reflexes always present; resolved
Difficulty with visual novelty	Only favorite or known objects elicit visual attention	May tolerate novel objects if the novel objects share characteristics of familiar objects	Use of "known" objects to initiate looking sequence	Selection of objects less restricted, one to two sessions of "warm up" time required	Selection of objects not restricted
Absence of visually guided reach	Look and touch occur as separate functions Look and touch occur with large and/or moving objects	Look and touch on smaller objects that are familiar, lighted, or reflective Look and touch are still separate	Visually guided reach used with familiar objects or "favorite" color	Look and touch occur in rapid sequence, but not always together	Look and touch occur together consistently

Key:

- Draw an X through boxes that represent resolved visual behaviors
- Use highlighter to outline boxes describing current visual functioning
- Draw an O in boxes describing visual skills that may never resolve because of co-existing ocular conditions

with objects of their favorite color and begin to look at objects with one to two additional colors and simple patterns.

- In this phase, all activities should be designed to encourage the student to use vision to make something happen. The student should be presented with objects that will not respond in the intended way unless the student acts on them. Pressing a lever in order to activate a fan or a vibrating toy are examples of vision plus function. (See color insert, Photo 8.)
- Activities should now be designed to combine vision with touch, swat, reach, grasp, or even eye-gaze in order to accomplish a task. (See color insert, Photo 9.) The tasks can pertain to choice making, self-help routines, fine-motor development, cognitive tasks, or self-amusement. A student reaching for a comb wrapped in Mylar of the preferred color and placed on a black washcloth is an example of integrating vision with function in a self-help routine.
- Students in Phase II typically improve in their ability to maintain visual contact with people and objects even while there are low levels of familiar background sounds present or they are using the sense of touch while looking.

Phase III (Range 7+ to 10)

The goal in Phase III is to facilitate the resolution of the CVI characteristics that remain active and that affect the student. Students in Phase III tend to have difficulties with complexity in two-dimensional materials, with visual complexity and distance viewing in unfamiliar indoor and outdoor areas, with specific areas of visual fields (most commonly lower fields [Dutton, 2006]), and with visually guided reach when the object is very small or placed against a patterned or complex background. (See color insert, Photo 10.)

- In Phase III, background details in two-dimensional materials (images, photographs, print, and symbols) should be added in discrete amounts until the student is able to find salient features or details in unadapted or traditional presentations. For example, the Phase III student may initially be able to locate an image of a boat when it is presented by itself on a black background. The professional should introduce additional details and observe if the student can find the boat against backgrounds of increasing complexity: against waves; against waves and clouds in the sky; against waves and clouds with a person added in the boat; against waves and clouds with a person in the boat and a fish added in the water; and so on. (See color insert, Photo 11.)
- The same fundamental issue of complexity must also be addressed as it relates to the environment. The student should be able to demonstrate that he or she can locate the salient feature in an unfamiliar indoor or outdoor environment. For example, the Phase III student who is able to visually locate a stop sign will learn to recognize the stop sign when it occurs in a natural setting with additional details. The complexity of the setting is gradually increased in a procedure similar to that for learning to recognize salient features in two-dimensional materials.
- Students in Phase III may have difficulty noticing descending steps, drop-offs at curbs, or surface changes. These students require O&M evaluation and frequently direct services from an O&M professional. (See the section on O&M later in this chapter.)

Using the CVI Resolution Chart, long-range goals can be planned, based on consideration of a student's CVI behavioral characteristics and their corresponding scores, as well as any comments noted in the second part of the CVI Range—Rating II, Within–CVI Characteristics—and using the data gathered in the assessment interviews and observations to fill in the details of the student's specific preferences and tendencies. Each characteristic that currently affects the visual functioning of the student should be considered in IFSP or IEP development. The following are examples of goals written for different characteristics for three different students in each of the three phases.

Phase I Example: Juan

Juan scored 3 on the CVI Range, placing him in Phase I. His goals should therefore emphasize building consistent visual behavior. Two of Juan's CVI behavioral characteristics are color preference (score of .25) and need for movement (Score of 0). The IEP team set Juan's long-range goal as follows:

Juan will increase his use of vision in functional academics, self-help, and leisure routines.

The team also specified the following activities and interim objectives for Juan that matched his CVI behavioral characteristics:

- For the characteristic of color preferences: *Juan will visually attend to fine-motor activities that involve the use of single-color, red materials.* Examples might include opening a door whose handle is adapted with red material; activating a red switch; and locating, reaching for, and grasping a red toothbrush, cup, and spoon.
- For the characteristic of need for movement: *Juan will visually attend to leisure activities that involve movement or*

movement-like properties and/or red reflective surface. For example, Juan will activate a red switch to turn on a radio or pull a yellow lever to obtain water from a cooler.

Phase II Example: Jennifer

Jennifer has scored 6 on the CVI Range, putting her in Phase II. Her goals and activities should therefore emphasize integrating vision with function. Two of Jennifer's CVI visual characteristics include difficulty with visual complexity (score of .5) and visual field preferences (score of .75). The IFSP team set the following for her long-range goal:

Jennifer will integrate vision with gross and fine-motor movements.

The team also chose the following activities and objectives for Jennifer:

- For difficulties with visual complexity: *Jennifer will look at and reach for a single-color object (such as a cup) presented in an array of no more than three objects (for example, a cup, napkin, and spoon) that are placed on a high-contrast, light-absorbing background (such as a black fabric placemat), with increasing independence, and decreasing prompt.*
- For visual field preferences: *Jennifer will look at and reach in her left lower visual field to activate switches (in her preferred color) and to obtain objects (such as a comb) for fine-motor or self-help routines.*

Phase III Example: Ruby

Ruby scored 9 on the CVI Range, indicating she is close to the resolution of CVI visual behaviors. Her scores on the Within–CVI Characteristics portion of the CVI Range included a score of .75 in difficulty with distance vision and a score of .75 in absence of visually guided reach. The IEP team assigned her the following long-range goal:

Ruby will refine visual skills in near and distance activities.

The activities chosen to help Ruby reach her goals were as follows:

- For the characteristic of difficulty with distance vision: *Ruby will visually locate and identify functional indoor landmarks (such as an exit sign) at distances up to 20 feet and will travel with decreasing amounts of assistance to the landmark destinations.*
- For the characteristic of absence of visually guided reach: *Ruby will coordinate movements of looking and reaching by maintaining visual attention while reaching for targets that decrease in size or that are presented in backgrounds of increasing complexity, for example, reaching while looking for a Cheerio presented on a three-color placemat.*

Some educators may find it useful to list the CVI-specific adaptations in the section of the IFSP or IEP used for specially designed instruction (SDI), which is used to list modifications and adaptations. The modifications listed in the SDI section of the IEP are considered accommodations that must be in place in order for the learner to be able to access the educational program. Examples of SDIs for Phase I, II, or III students are the following:

Phase I SDIs

- select objects that are the same shade of yellow as the student's "favorite" object, Big Bird
- suspend or move objects and present them in the student's right peripheral field
- provide up to 60 seconds wait time to allow for latency in visual response
- select objects that do not have sound components

Phase II SDIs

- select objects that are highlighted with yellow
- move objects slightly in the right or left peripheral visual field
- provide 15–30 seconds wait time to provide for latency in visual response
- select objects that have low-volume sound components

Phase III SDIs

- use bright colors to outline or highlight two-dimensional symbols
- present materials in all visual fields except lower field
- provide wait time to provide for visual latency after seizure activity

PROGRAM DESIGN AND INTERVENTION

As explained earlier, the purpose of the interventions designed for students with CVI is to encourage them to use their vision as much as possible. Only by looking will these students actually learn to look. Through use of vision, increased synapses are developed in the visual areas of the brain. Increased firing of the neurons across the synapses increases visual capacity. Therefore, students are given visual targets that will stimulate them to look. The CVI Range and CVI Resolution Chart are used to determine the extent of each characteristic's influence on the student and then to intervene at the appropriate levels indicated. Essentially, students must be given something to look at that they are *able* to look at. If a child's highest level of visual functioning is to regard the color red, then the plan for intervention will be to provide red objects within his or her daily activities.

Interventions should be designed to meet, but not to exceed, the assessed level of function. That is, educators must follow the lead of the student; activities must "meet" the student where he or she happens to be. For example, if a student demonstrates increased visual attention to objects that are red, but disregards objects of other colors, it is critical to select red objects when planning interventions, rather than attempt to "train" the student to attend to other colors. After a period of using his or her vision to look at the red objects, the student may suddenly be observed looking at an object that is red and yellow. This is a sign that the student may benefit from reevaluation to see if he or she has progressed to a new level of the CVI Range, requiring new interventions. At that point, an educator would usually do a complete reassessment, because improvements in vision tend to occur in clusters. It is important to remember that the student's own behavior will provide cues regarding changes in how to approach the CVI characteristics.

Some professionals may find this concept of intervention difficult to adjust to, because they are accustomed to challenging their students to go beyond their current abilities. But in the author's experience, the mechanism for learning to use vision in most students with CVI is different than it is for other kinds of learning. If the visual targets provided are items that a child avoids looking at, he or she will not be practicing using vision. A systematic approach based on assessed levels of CVI characteristics will be more likely to facilitate improved visual outcomes in the student.

Improvement in CVI can be facilitated through this approach, although there is no certainty regarding an individual's potential "recovery." Interventions will vary depending on the individual student's CVI-related characteristics and CVI phase, as well as his or her age and level of developmental, pre-academic, or academic functioning; however, all CVI program planning should adhere to the guiding principles described later in this chapter.

It is also crucial to realize that intervention for students with CVI as explained in this book is an *approach,* not a therapy. The strategies used for improving vision should be integrated into daily, functional activities of learning, self-help, leisure activities, and so forth. Isolated, meaningless activities, such as asking a student to gaze into a flashlight, do not easily translate into meaningful function. Conversely, if a student visually attends to a red Mylar balloon, red Mylar can be used in routine activities by wrapping it around a toothbrush, tying it on a drinking cup, and using it to highlight symbols on a communication board, therefore providing numerous meaningful opportunities for the student to display visual attention—to look—throughout the day. Rather than being stand-alone activities in themselves, interventions for CVI provide adaptations—an overlay that may determine *how* already occurring activities or routines take place. For example, an activity may be reaching for a spoon. The CVI intervention doesn't change this activity. However, by wrapping the spoon in blue Mylar, the CVI intervention changes how it takes place, to give the student visual access to the activity. Note, too, that CVI characteristics rarely occur in isolation from one another, and, therefore, adaptations or interventions frequently address more than one characteristic, as the examples throughout this chapter illustrate. For example, selecting a single-color, yellow, non-noise-making, shiny object to use with a student addresses the characteristics of color preference, difficulty with complexity of the surface pattern of the object and with complexity of the sensory environment, and need for movement, all at the same time.

It is also important to note that, despite the common impression to the contrary, students with CVI do not have visual function that constantly varies. As explained in Chapter 5, subtle but important changes in the environment are as likely to be responsible for a student's changing visual attention or behavior as are changes within the child. For example, when a yellow toothbrush is presented against a black washcloth, the student may look at and reach toward the toothbrush. However, if the same toothbrush is offered to the student by an adult, and the adult happens to be wearing a patterned shirt, the student may ignore the toothbrush. (See color insert, Photo 12.) The guiding question should be "What changed in the environment?" rather than "What changed in the child?"

GUIDING PRINCIPLES

Program planning and intervention with children with CVI need to follow a number of guiding principles in order to be successful. These principles include:

- precision
- intentionality
- reciprocity
- expectation of change
- attention to the total environment

Precision

First, it is critical that educators consider precision. One of the main purposes of the CVI Range assessment protocol is to determine the degree to which CVI is affecting the student in order to design a program for intervention that matches the student's level of visual functioning. As in many areas of educational intervention, a random approach in intervention for CVI is unlikely to be effective. A student who scores 1–3 on the CVI Range will typically not benefit from an intervention that includes the use of mirrors or two-dimensional materials. Merely presenting an activity on a lightbox or asking a student to look at a Mylar pompon are not appropriate CVI-related interventions.

Without reference to assessment results, it is likely that interventions will not be appropriate and will not address the actual needs of the student.

Intentionality

The second guiding principle is intentionality. Teachers who work with students with CVI need to be highly intentional and specific about why and how interventions are selected. Random teaching will not be effective. It is important to know where the student currently functions and where you expect the student to function next. Imagine a couple driving through a foreign country without a map or the ability to speak the language. One member of the couple seems to think they have lost their way and asks, "Are we lost?" and the other cheerfully responds, "Yes, we're lost, but we're making good time." So, too, an educator who works diligently to provide activities and collect data without knowing at what phase the student is functioning or what activities or adaptations should come next is "lost," but working steadily to "make good time."

Reciprocity

The third guiding principle is reciprocity. Reciprocity is the process of sharing and considering another's point of view. Educators who work with students with CVI need to be sensitive to the students' cues. For example, if a student with CVI seems generally able to move her wheelchair into the classroom, but occasionally appears unable to perform the same task without becoming disoriented, it is important for the instructor to try to analyze the environment from the student's perspective for potential changes in degree of complexity, new sources of movement, or novel features. Suppose that, to celebrate Valentine's

Day, the teacher has taped red and pink Valentine hearts on the classroom doorway. Although the students without CVI may be delighted with the decorations, the student with CVI may now be unable to recognize and move through the classroom door. The increased complexity, color, and movement result in a new and very different appearance of the doorway, and therefore the student becomes disoriented. Did the student change or did the environment change? In this and similar examples, as noted earlier, inattentive behavior may not be a signal that the student's visual behavior *changes* from hour to hour or day to day; rather, it may be a sign that the activity or the environment is not visually accessible. It requires reciprocity, or sensitivity to the student's perspective, to enable an educator to determine what has actually changed.

Expectation of Change

Change is the fourth guiding principle. The expectations for students with CVI are improvement in visual functions. In many cases, teachers of students with visual impairments traditionally have thought of ocular vision differences as static conditions, or, in some cases, as conditions that worsen over time. CVI is a type of visual disability that challenges standard thinking about visual impairment because improvement in vision for the student with CVI is not only possible, but is likely. Educators should plan interventions that will facilitate improvement in functional vision through systematic intervention strategies.

Attention to the Total Environment

The fifth principle is environment. The CVI characteristic of difficulty with visual complexity underscores the importance of attention

to the overall environment. In many cases a student's inconsistent responses are due to unintentional and unnoticed shifts in the environment, rather than changes in the student. A student who performs an object identification task against a nonpatterned black backdrop frequently cannot perform the same task in an unadapted, visually cluttered environment. (See color insert, Photo 13.) A student with CVI whose CVI Range score is 3–4 may be able to locate a red cup when it is placed on a single-color placemat, but may shift attention to the ceiling fan or lighted areas of the room when the same cup is presented on a plaid tablecloth. Unintentional, unrecognized changes in home, classroom, or outdoors may account for student behaviors that may be misunderstood as signs of disinterest. Ways to address the effects of the environment are discussed in the following section.

ENVIRONMENTAL CONSIDERATIONS

Most students with CVI are greatly influenced by their environment, and the more they are affected by CVI-related characteristics, the more they need environmental interventions or adaptations. When designing interventions to use with students with CVI, it is important to make sure that the environment supports the student's ability to pay attention to visual stimuli.

Students with CVI require adaptations to their learning environments in one of three ways that roughly correspond to the three phases of CVI progression. Level I environmental adaptations are those that are necessary for students who function in the CVI Range of approximately 0 to 3½. These students are affected most by CVI and are generally able to be visually attentive only when there are no visual distractors, and when other sensory inputs are carefully controlled. Students who require significant adaptation to their environment are generally able to be visually attentive only under these strict conditions. Students who require these environmental adaptations are in the phase of building visual behavior. In order to use vision in a more stable, consistent way, significant support from the environment is required. This degree of control in a classroom or in a home setting can be difficult to maintain. Use of trifold occluders, slant boards, visually quiet spaces within a classroom, or creative scheduling can facilitate a Level I environment. (See color insert, Photo 14.)

Level II environments are those in which a moderate degree of adaptation has been made. Students with CVI who require Level II environments are generally students who score 4 to 7½ on the CVI Range. These students typically can remain visually attentive even when low-level or familiar auditory inputs compete with visual demands. They continue to require environmental adaptations; however, the adaptations are far less restrictive because students can successfully suppress small amounts of background visual information. (See color insert, Photo 15a.) For example, the student who may have at one time required an environment in which a single object was presented against a black, 24-inch, trifold background may now, in Phase II, be able to locate the same object presented against a black towel. In Level II environments, near surfaces must still remain free of visual clutter. For example, in such an environment a student may be positioned to sort yellow and red spoons placed against a black background and can do so while other student activities are occurring within the classroom.

A Level III environment is an unadapted classroom or home environment. (See color insert, Photo 15b.) Students who can tolerate typical environments are generally students who function from approximately 7½ to 10 on the CVI Range. These students have resolved a number of the characteristics of CVI, and may be having some remaining difficulties with distance viewing, high levels of complexity, and visual-motor performance. Although some degree of CVI continues to act on the student, he or she now has enough functional vision that specialized adaptations are not required for the student to be visually attentive. Simple adaptations may continue to be put in place to heighten contrast and to reduce great amounts of complexity, especially in books or other two-dimensional materials. For example, a student may need to use a card with a cut-out window to isolate the target symbols or images, or they may need to be highlighted with a marker to help draw visual attention to them.

IFSP/IEP PLANNING WORKSHEET

The IFSP or IEP team may find the IFSP/IEP Intervention Planning Worksheet helpful as a template to integrate ways to address a student's CVI-related needs into his or her daily routines (see Figure 6.4). This is a critical step in effective program planning. The Intervention Planning Worksheet is used to incorporate the information gathered in assessment into the activities and routine of the student's day. The first section of the worksheet summarizes the CVI behavioral characteristics that remain unresolved and need to be addressed. The CVI Planning Table lists daily activities and routines that can be adapted to encourage use of vision. Rather than scheduling "CVI-time," the Intervention Planning Worksheet provides opportunities for CVI adaptations to be considered as part of the activities occurring throughout the day.

For example, Roberto, the student portrayed in the sample Intervention Planning Worksheet in Figure 6.4, scored 5–6 on the CVI Range and needs intervention focusing on all the CVI-related characteristics. The CVI

IFSP/IEP INTERVENTION PLANNING WORKSHEET

This worksheet may be useful for IEP planning and for creating a "template" of CVI considerations that can be applied to the child/student's daily routines.

Child/student's name: _Roberto Sanchez_   Date: ___12/07___

IFSP/IEP planning members: _parent, occupational therapist, classroom teacher, physical therapist, teacher of visually impaired students, orientation & mobility specialist_

CVI Range score: _____5-6_____   CVI Phase: _____II_____

Resolved CVI characteristics (check):
___color preference
___need for movement
___visual latency
___visual field preferences
___difficulties with visual complexity
    ___object
    ___array
    ___sensory
___light-gazing and nonpurposeful gaze
___difficulty with distance viewing
___difficulty with visual novelty
___absence of visually guided reach

Unresolved CVI characteristics (check):
_x_ color preference
_x_ need for movement
_x_ visual latency
_x_ visual field preferences
_x_ difficulties with visual complexity
    _x_ object
    _x_ array
    _x_ sensory
_x_ light-gazing and nonpurposeful gaze
_x_ difficulty with distance viewing
_x_ difficulty with visual novelty
_x_ absence of visually guided reach

(continued)

CVI Planning Table

Daily schedule/time and activity	CVI characteristics	CVI adaptations for this activity
9:00 AM, getting off van, travel to classroom	Distance viewing, movement, complexity of array, light-gazing	• Yellow or red Mylar highlighting of landmarks • Select route to class; reduced complexity • Environmental light as cues
9:30, Morning Circle	Color, complexity, novelty, latency, visual fields	• Present materials against black felt board • Begin with familiar object • Highlight with yellow or red • Allow ample wait time for response • Present materials in accordance with best peripheral and best central vision
10:15 AM, fine-motor skills with occupational therapist or classroom personnel	Color (red), movement, complexity of object/array/sensory environment, visual fields	• Present materials against a black, 8-inch, trifold board • No more than two to three total colors presented • Verbal directions or prompt before and after attempts, not during viewing • Present materials in accordance with best peripheral and best central vision
11 AM, pre-reading	Complexity, color, novelty	• Begin with familiar words, symbols • Highlight salient features with yellow • Present on black slant board
1:00 PM, Gross-motor activities with physical therapist, O&M specialist, or classroom staff	Movement, distance viewing, color, light-gazing, complexity of sensory environment, visual fields	• Select yellow and/or red equipment (balls, Theraband, etc.) • Incorporate use of lighted and/or moving targets for distance activities • Some physical therapy activities may be too multisensory for use of vision in simultaneous tasks • Position for best peripheral visual fields

(continued)

Daily schedule/time and activity	CVI characteristics	CVI adaptations for this activity
1:45 PM, hygiene and self-help routines	Complexity, color, novelty, visual fields	• Present soap, toothbrush, hairbrush against black towel on counter • Select materials for hygiene and self-help that are single-color (yellow or red) • Use familiar items • Present in accordance with best peripheral and best central vision
2:00 PM, Language activities	Novelty, color, complexity of object and array	• Select objects or simple two-dimensional materials for low complexity; one to two colors or items • Begin with familiar materials or objects • Highlight novel features with yellow • Present on black slant board
2:45 PM, prepare for and dismissal	Color, complexity, distance viewing, light-gazing, visual fields	• Use yellow Mylar to label coat hook and other environmental features of dismissal routine • Place materials to be packed in backpack in front of black 8-inch trifold board • Select route to van with reduced complexity • Use environmental light as cues

Activities not considered compatible for CVI interventions:

Example:
Classroom birthday parties are primarily social events planned by student's parents and therefore not easily adapted for this student's CVI needs.

1. Lunch time in Cafeteria
2. Classroom celebrations or parties
3. Music class
4.
5.

Planning Table section of the worksheet suggests that as soon as the student gets off the bus at school and walks to his classroom, adaptations such as highlighting landmarks with yellow or red Mylar (for example, a yellow Mylar star attached to the entrance door, to the water fountain near the student's home corridor, and near the opening of the student classroom) and selecting a route that does not offer too much visual complexity can address a number of characteristics. CVI adaptations can also be integrated into the class's daily morning circle activity. The teacher may begin the circle with an object familiar to the student, highlight the objects shown to the student with yellow or red, present them against a black felt board and in accordance with the student's with best peripheral and best central vision, and then allow ample time for the student to respond.

TIPS FOR PROVIDING INTERVENTIONS

The following sections provide basic suggestions for constructing interventions that are appropriate to each phase as part of a student's naturally occurring routines. In addition, sometimes students will make progress in visual skills and then seem to hit a plateau. It is not unusual for students to have difficulty in Phase I, when they first start using vision, or in Phase III, when they are refining their visual skills. Plateaus tend to be less likely in Phase II. Suggestions are also included for helping students continue to make progress when they seem to have hit a snag.

Providing Interventions for Phase I

Students in Phase I (those scoring between Levels 0 to 3 on the CVI Range) typically function with inconsistent attention to visual targets. They require support from the environment to eliminate competition from their other senses and the need to deal with auditory, tactile, or olfactory stimuli, as well as visual demands. These students generally require:

- Single-color objects
- Objects of preferred color
- Objects that are shiny or reflective or produce movement (see Sidebar 6.1)
- Objects presented against a simple background
- Objects that are familiar

In designing interventions, incorporate the activities into the child's daily routines as much as is feasible; for example, during mealtimes, leisure-time activities, bathing and grooming routines, fine-motor skills practice, gross-motor skills practice, and orientation and mobility (O&M) routines.

If a child has no known favorite colors or objects, a first set of preferred objects can be created for the child. First, assign a color by looking for logical choices from the child's own learning or living environment. Then assign a set of three to five objects that make sense for the student, such as

- a Slinky
- a pinwheel made of reflective material
- a windsock
- an Elmo doll
- a mobile made out of silverware

It is important to provide ample opportunity for repeated exposure and practice with the selected objects under appropriate conditions.

In trying out interventions during Phase I, some pitfalls include the following:

- Avoid the therapy model; think of the interventions as an overlay on the

SIDEBAR 6.1   *Reflective and/or Moving Materials for Interventions*

Materials with reflective properties can be useful in stimulating peripheral vision and therefore the child's desire to direct his or her visual attention toward the moving or reflective target. The following materials may be useful in motivating a student to look (see also color insert, Photo 2):

- Any single-color Mylar pompom that matches the child's preferred color. Gold sometimes works for students who prefer the color yellow.

- Mylar balloons with few or no added pictures or patterns. Patterns should be restricted to the child's favorite color and should have no more then one to two colors. Balloons that are tied to a floor weight also provide an opportunity for the child to reach for or bat at the object.

- Shakers or rattles that create little or no sound are useful. Sound in these objects may be acceptable if the instructional goal is for the child to look and reach, rather than to continuously regard the object in hand. Dollar stores and other bargain stores are filled with these items.

- Reflective "cuffs"—rings of reflective material—can be slipped onto the handles of utensils to encourage a child to visually attend to a utensil such as a spoon or fork during mealtime. Again, the color or pattern of the material should be matched to the child's favorite color.

- Other materials that are not reflective but have movement properties include colored pompoms, windsocks, lava lamps (cone-shaped, transparent lights containing a colored gel or fluid that moves slowly through the cone), aquariums, and specially selected videos.

child's daily life, not as activities in themselves
- Avoid using flashlights as a stand-alone intervention
- Avoid presenting materials that cannot be linked to new, functional activities
- Avoid changing materials without observing or reassessing the student

If a student does not seem to be visually attentive after basic interventions are attempted, or if the student seems to have reached a plateau at a certain point in Phase I, the factors that might be preventing a response need to be analyzed. First, evaluate issues pertaining to visual latency and visual field preferences. Has the child been given enough time to respond? Are the objects being presented in the appropriate portion of the child's visual field?

Next, analyze the environment for distractions or interference. Are people talking? Are lights interfering? Is there too much pattern or color on the target? Is there too much visual information or clutter in the background?

Also be aware of the student's position. Is he or she physically insecure or spending too long in one position? Is most of the student's energy diverted to maintaining position rather than engaging with the world?

Finally, watch for signs of stress or fatigue, such as

- hiccupping
- yawning
- gaze avoidance, light-gazing
- keeping eyes closed or frequent periods of sleeping
- facial grimacing

- hand or finger tension
- reflexive laughing/high-pitched vocalization

If after attending to all these factors, the student still is not responding, consider the following guidelines:

- Be sure the student has multiple opportunities to use vision throughout the day.
- Redesign the environment to further reduce stimuli.
- Try setting up favorite or preferred color objects for longer periods of time.
- Don't hover—let the student have more time without adults in direct, constant contact.

Providing Interventions for Phase II

Students in Phase II (those who score from about 4 to 7 on the CVI Range) are now able to use vision in functional ways. They now have enough consistent visual behavior to look at objects, reach for a desired object, or use their gaze to indicate a want or need. Students in Phase II can visually attend to objects of more than one color, can notice objects at distances as great as 4 to 5 feet away, can maintain visual attention while there are low levels of background noise, and have very little latency.

Interventions for Phase II students generally require attention to these considerations:

- Use the student's preferred color plus one, or later two, or more colors. Color preference generally resolves by the end of this phase.
- Be aware that latency will continue to be present but decreased throughout Phase II. Be aware of the potential for increased latency after seizures, when the child is

fatigued, or when the child is over-stimulated.

- Complexity will need to be controlled, but as the student moves through Phase II, more patterns on three-dimensional objects will be tolerated, and by the end of Phase II, the student will be able to use simple two-dimensional images. (Two-dimensional materials are discussed in greater detail under Providing Interventions for Phase III.)
- Light-gazing usually resolves by the end of Phase II. The use of a lightbox to motivate attention and to enhance two-dimensional materials may still be necessary.
- Shiny or reflective material used in Phase I can now be applied to objects in Phase II. Use shiny Mylar strips to help direct attention to any object used in functional routines; for example, to wrap or enhance cups, toothbrushes, or switches for switch-operated objects.
- Visually guided reach can be promoted by placing objects on black or plain backgrounds. (See color insert, Photo 16.)
- New objects can be selected, based on the traits of the familiar or favorite ones. For example, if the student has an Elmo doll as the original preferred object, new objects should be simple, red objects.

Providing Interventions for Phase III

Students in Phase III (those who score from about 7½ to 10 on the CVI Range) use vision in performing most tasks. They demonstrate visual curiosity by spontaneously examining a setting or environment. (See color insert, Photo 17.) Students generally have more normal and more functional visual fields, even if field preferences are not fully resolved. Visually guided reach is emerging. They still tend to have difficulties with complexity in two-dimensional materials, such as images or symbols on paper and with distance vision beyond 10 to 15 feet. Highly complex environments still affect their visual performance.

Thus, interventions for Phase III students generally require attention to these considerations:

- Reduce information when it is presented in two dimensions, in a book or on paper, for example (see Sidebar 6.2)
  - Use occluders or window cards to block out excess detail on a page of images or symbols
  - Highlight or outline critical features in symbols or pictures (such as the relationship of the lines and circles in the letters *d* and *p*) using color (see color insert, Photos 18 and 19)
- Provide assistance for dealing with complexity and visual field considerations in highly novel or overstimulating environments. This may be done by
  - Familiarizing the student with the environment
  - Highlighting landmarks as necessary and pairing them with natural landmarks; for example, placing a red triangle or other symbol on, not near, a drinking fountain. Later, the red highlighting fades away and the water fountain itself becomes the natural landmark
  - Providing assistance in moving safely through an environment from an adult or peer when necessary
  - Considering the use of a cane, possibly with a weighted tip, which helps the student remain anchored to the environment in the presence of a high degree of complexity

(For additional information relating to O&M considerations, see the section later in this chapter.)

- Address difficulties with distance viewing by
  - Asking the student to locate specific details, landmarks, or cues in the environment that are highlighted or adapted with color cues
  - Traveling to both known and new locations and comparing salient environmental features
  - Using maps, including tactile or high-contrast color maps, such as those made with Chang Kits (available from the American Printing House for the Blind; see the Resources section), to teach students to actively seek out information that helps them to be oriented, travel safely, and anticipate the features of a route
  - Increasing the distance to specified targets

Instruction in Phase III generally has two big themes: teaching sorting skills, with reference to the concepts of alike and different, and disembedding salient features from a background. Sorting skills are taught at this point in a student's visual development in order to create a framework in which the student can understand how things can be alike or different based on important visual features. (See color insert, Photo 20.) This understanding supports the ability to analyze novel information and to analyze visual complexity. It is helpful to incorporate comparative language into interactions and instruction to reinforce the student's awareness of like and different features. For example, when a student approaches the school bus, the instructor can describe the ways that the school bus is similar to and different from the family car. Or, when

SIDEBAR 6.2   *Introducing Two-Dimensional Materials*

The suggestions presented here provide methods for including two-dimensional materials in the learning routines of students who have CVI. It is important to remember that two-dimensional materials are generally used with students who score above 6 on the CVI Range. Moving from three-dimensional objects, such as Slinkies, pom-poms, and balls, to pictures, which are two-dimensional, requires careful planning, so that students will be challenged at, but not beyond, their assessed level of CVI. The suggestions that follow provide a framework for this progression. They primarily address issues related to the CVI characteristic of difficulty with complexity, but they are also helpful when dealing with other characteristics, including color preference and difficulty with visual novelty.

- Simple, colored, translucent pictures, such as the Familiar Object Pictures (available from the American Printing House for the Blind; see the Resources section), presented on a lightbox can teach picture discrimination, picture recognition, and picture identification.
- Symbols used for communication or to help students anticipate daily routines can be adapted to make them more easily viewed by children with CVI, by selecting them for such features as preferred colors, familiar items, low levels of complexity, movement, and so forth
- Simple picture books can be created with only one picture per double page. Images should be selected based on color preference, familiarity of subject, and simplicity.
- Books that have pictures based on a theme, for example, "foods I eat," "things I wear," or "toys I like," can be created or selected from books that are

commercially available. Only outline drawings should be used initially—avoid pictures with internal detail as well as photographs until the student is well into Phase III (7½ to 10 on the Range).
- Commercially available books that are very simple can be selected for use with a child, based on color preference and the child's interest.
- When photographs are presented, begin with faces, and only later present pictures of familiar people against neutral or plain backgrounds.
- Additional photo books can be designed around particular themes of interest, for example, photos of balls or of animals.
- Keep in mind that recognition of oneself in photographs generally occurs around the same time that an individual is able to recognize him- or herself in a mirror image (generally, after scoring 7 to 8 on the CVI Range).

a student is sorting groups of green blocks and green balls, the instructor can describe how they are alike in some ways, but not alike in other ways.

Skills related to disembedding salient features—that is, discriminating features from a background or surrounding environment—are

also emphasized at this point in order to help students create meaning and broaden visual and cognitive schemes. The better able students are to generalize information (for example, not all round objects are balls), the better they understand their world. Learning to differentiate a feature or object from a background or surrounding element supports the development of the ability to differentiate details and make fine visual discriminations, allowing the student to use his or her vision effectively in dealing with visually complex objects and environments.

One possible sequence for teaching students to recognize salient features, using Clifford the Big Red Dog, a prominent red character in children's picture books, is the following (see color insert, Photo 21a-d):

1. Find Clifford the Big Red Dog using a stuffed animal or other three-dimensional likeness
2. Find Clifford in a pop-up book
3. Find Clifford in a teacher-made book with a less complex background
4. Find Baby Clifford, a smaller version of Clifford
5. Find an action-specific Clifford (for example, "find Clifford wagging his tail")
6. Match Clifford cards that vary in a specific detail (for example, "Find all the Cliffords that are wagging their tails")
7. Continue with finding smaller Cliffords amid more background details

When working with students in Phase III, as with all students, it is important to be sensitive to the student's reactions and the possible influences acting on the student. A child's functional vision may be affected by such factors as stress, over-stimulation, fatigue, too much novelty, poor health, hunger, or seizures.

When CVI Resolves

As students progress through Phase III, eventually they will reach a plateau where they no longer continue to achieve improvements. Very few students actually resolve all CVI characteristics completely to the point where they no longer require specialized instruction for CVI. It is more likely that students will stabilize in Phase III at about 8 or 9 on the CVI Range and will continue to require support from a teacher of visually impaired students and an O&M specialist. When it becomes apparent that the student's CVI characteristics are no longer continuing to resolve further, the adaptations and interventions that have helped the student should be maintained as supports for the student's continued use of vision. As noted in Chapter 5, when most of the CVI characteristics have resolved, except for those that might be caused by an ocular condition (those marked "O" on the CVI Resolution Chart), it is likely that the CVI has essentially resolved and that the visual difficulty that remains can be explained by the ocular condition. At this point, the intervention approach should focus on methods and materials used with students with ocular visual impairments, rather than CVI. The educator might then consider doing a standard functional vision assessment to help in designing additional interventions to address the results of the ocular impairment.

SAMPLE ACTIVITIES

As has been noted throughout this book, intervention activities need to be tailored to address the affects that CVI has had on the student's specific visual behaviors and to be appropriate for the level at which he or she is affected by each CVI characteristic. In this section, a number of examples of activities and adaptations are presented to give teachers and family members ideas for activities that may be adapted for an individual student or child.

Table 6.1 presents hypothetical activities or guidelines for activities for a 5-year-old child in different phases of CVI. Activities or adaptations are integrated into routines and activities

TABLE 6.1   Sample Activities for the CVI Phases for a 5-Year-Old Student

CVI Characteristic	Phase I	Phase II	Phase III
Color preference (yellow preferred)	Yellow pompom suspended near wheelchair	Yellow switch to activate music toy	Yellow highlighting of new symbols for communication device
Need for movement	Yellow pompom suspended near wheelchair	Yellow switch covered with yellow/gold Mylar material	Moving toward a water fountain highlighted with gold Mylar from a distance of 15 feet away
Visual latency	Waiting at least 20 seconds for localization on yellow pompom	Waiting at least 20 seconds for eye-to-object contact on new objects or if the student is tired, overstimulated, or hasn't been attending visually for an extended period of time	Waiting 5 to 10 seconds when highly novel materials are used or when the student is in a highly complex setting
Visual field preferences	Yellow pompom presented in upper-right peripheral visual field	Yellow switch or other yellow or gold Mylar materials presented in right or left peripheral fields; student may need to turn head to examine details using eye-to-object contact	No field preference; no intervention needed
Difficulties with visual complexity	Yellow pompom presented against a black trifold board No sound or touch during attempts to look	Yellow or yellow and one additional color objects, activated by switch, placed on a black felt-covered slant board Visual attention maintained on yellow and black objects, even when music or voice present	Black communication symbols on white paper, highlighted or outlined with yellow highlighter
Light-gazing and nonpurposeful gaze	Yellow-filled lava-type lamp presented	Yellow Slinky toy presented on lightbox for manipulation, exploration	Light not required for visual attention; no intervention needed

(continued)

TABLE 6.1   *Sample Activities for the CVI Phases for a 5-Year-Old Student (continued)*

CVI Characteristic	Phase I	Phase II	Phase III
Difficulty with distance viewing	Yellow, moving, lighted materials presented within 18 inches	Identifies and/or moves wheelchair toward gold Mylar highlighted environmental landmarks within 5 to 10 feet	Identifies and/or moves wheelchair toward environmental landmarks within 20 feet
Difficulty with visual novelty	Visually attends (looks toward) yellow pom-pom, yellow lava-type lamp, yellow Big Bird toy, and yellow Slinky toy	Yellow or gold Mylar applied to objects that are simple and have movement properties for all fine-motor or self-help activities: yellow Mylar on toothbrush, yellow cup for drinking, yellow spoon or fork, gold Mylar highlighting on landmarks, and so on	New objects no longer need to resemble known or preferred objects
Absence of visually guided reach	Looks and occasionally explores objects tactilely, but no visually guided reach or swat. Turns head away while attempting to touch or swat at Slinky toy or other familiar objects	Looks, looks away, and then reaches for yellow or gold Mylar familiar objects. Occasionally uses visually guided reach for most familiar objects, but only if against a plain background	Visually guided reach is used unless the background is visually highly complex. Occasionally reaches but misses when attempting to grasp a game piece on a multipattern, multicolor game board

of the day. Some activities may address more than one CVI characteristic.

Lightboxes are commonly used as intervention tools with children who are visually impaired, for a number of reasons, such as the increased contrast they provide. For students with CVI who exhibit light-gazing behavior, the lightbox serves as a motivator for visual attention. Sidebar 6.3 lists a number of intervention activities using a lightbox that address a variety of CVI-related characteristics.

In addition, the appendix at the end of this chapter provides a number of suggestions about working with students with CVI, grouped according to CVI phase and characteristic. These suggestions were provided by the members of a team who are field-testing the CVI Range in a multistate project (see "My Introduction to CVI"). The comments refer to actual children in the project, although their names have been changed, to underscore the importance of matching an intervention to the specific needs of a specific child.

Lightbox Activities with Ziplock Freezer Bags

Ziplock freezer bags can be used on the lightbox to enhance looking behavior and to encourage progress in addressing the absence of visually guided reach. Consider double-bagging to avoid leakage. Use the lightbox only with battery power to avoid an unsafe electrical situation.

Activities	CVI Characteristics Addressed
Fill the bag with clear hair gel, then add several drops of food coloring. The color gets mixed as the child presses on the bag. The color, light, and movement properties will attract the child's visual attention. Begin with a single color only. (See color insert Photo 22.)	Color preference Difficulties with visual complexity Light-gazing and nonpurposeful gaze Need for movement
Fill the bag with warm water and release transparent, colored beads into the water. Touching the bag will cause movement of the beads without auditory competition. Again, color, light, and movement properties should attract the child's visual attention. Even the slightest touch will create movement, facilitating independent interaction	Color preference Difficulties with visual complexity Light-gazing and nonpurposeful gaze Need for movement
Fill the bag with water or gel and add bright single-color shapes (later, use two-color shapes) cut from acetate sheets. Shape punches from craft stores also work well to produce shapes from acetate.	Color preference Difficulties with visual complexity Light-gazing and nonpurposeful gaze Need for movement
Search at dollar stores for colored transparent objects that can be used in the ziplock bags. Select objects that have rounded edges. Bingo chips and small plastic balls work well.	Color preference Difficulties with visual complexity Light-gazing and nonpurposeful gaze Need for movement

Additional Lightbox Activities

Transparent containers used with transparent, colored objects can be used on the lightbox for visually guided reach, placing,	Color preference Difficulties with visual complexity Light-gazing and nonpurposeful gaze

(continued)

and sorting activities. For sorting, cover the lid of the container with black paper, leaving only the shape opening uncovered. The light from the lightbox will shine through the opening, creating a high-contrast target for placement of the shape.	Difficulty with visual novelty Absence of visually guided reach
A black grid and color pegs (available from APH) can or facilitate visually guided reach, placement, and sorting matching activities. Remember to consider visual field function when presenting the activity and to match the color to the child's color preference. (See color insert Photo 23.)	Color preference Difficulties with visual complexity Light-gazing and nonpurposeful gaze Difficulty with visual novelty Absence of visually guided reach
APH Familiar Object Pictures are very helpful for recognition of two-dimensional information. These colored translucent pairs of pictures depict 15 common household objects that are very simple in form and color.	Difficulties with visual complexity light-gazing and nonpurposeful gaze
Plexiglass Spinner and Patterns (available from APH) can be placed on the lightbox. This toy is easily activated by touch and does not have potentially distracting auditory input. Color may be added to the spinners to make them more appropriate for students with CVI.	Color preference Difficulties with visual complexity Light-gazing and nonpurposeful gaze Need for movement
Beginning puzzles can be made from black foam board and translucent color shapes (available from APH). Start with single-shape puzzles and favorite-color shapes.	Color preference Difficulties with visual complexity Light-gazing and nonpurposeful gaze Difficulty with visual novelty
Include other translucent, single-color, nonauditory objects for lightbox play, such as a Slinky	Color preference Difficulties with visual complexity Light-gazing and nonpurposeful gaze Difficulty with visual novelty Need for movement

Note: Many of the lightbox activities can be done with commercially available and teacher-made materials. Other activities are suggested that use products available from the American Printing House for the Blind (APH; see the Resources section).

CONSIDERATIONS FOR ORIENTATION AND MOBILITY

All children who have a visual impairment, including those with CVI, need to be evaluated for their requirements for orientation and mobilty instruction by a certified O&M specialist. This principle holds true whether the child is able to ambulate independently or is learning to operate a power wheelchair. However, as with other aspects of the behavior of students with CVI, their behavior when moving around is open to misinterpretation, as illustrated in the following case study.

> *Charles is an 8-year-old student who spends half of his school day in a typical third-grade class and half in a special education class. Charles has CVI associated with a rare syndrome. He is ambulatory but moves throughout the school using a random, inefficient pattern; he prefers to touch the arm or back of another student rather than walk independently. Charles is especially tentative on staircases and on occasion, he has stumbled and has even fallen down several steps. In the classroom Charles tends to have trouble staying seated. He avoids seat-work and is frequently moving away from his desk to other areas in the classroom. Charles appears to be fascinated by the decorations suspended from the ceiling. The school psychologist has talked to Charles' parents about possible attention deficit disorder (ADD).*

This scenario represents one example of how the behavior of students with CVI may be misinterpreted. The difficulties Charles displays with moving independently may be a result of the CVI-related characteristics of difficulty with complexity in the environment, visual field preferences, and difficulty with distance viewing. His apparent inattentiveness in the classroom may be attributable to difficulty

he may be experiencing with complexity, a tendency toward light-gazing, or an attraction to movement. Until Charles is carefully evaluated, it is impossible to know whether his behavior is being influenced by the presence of CVI or whether he has attention-related problems for some other reason. But, no matter what the cause, Charles is not moving efficiently and may not be safe in his school environment.

The CVI Range can be used by O&M specialists to determine the extent to which CVI-related characteristics are affecting a student. Results of the assessment can then be plotted on a CVI Resolution Chart that specifically focuses on considerations for O&M.

The CVI Orientation and Mobility Resolution Chart (see Figure 6.5) is constructed in accordance with the same principles as the CVI Resolution Chart. The chart integrates information about CVI-related characteristics, the degree of effect of the characteristics, the CVI phase, and the level of environmental adaptations in a single document. Unlike the CVI Range Across– and Within–CVI Characteristics assessment forms, which are used to evaluate the presence of CVI, this form is used to track and monitor progress and to support daily program planning. The O&M Resolution Chart uses information obtained from the CVI Range, but specifically interpreted for use by an O&M instructor: implications of the presence of CVI for safe and independent travel are the focus of the form.

Marking the O&M Resolution Chart involves the same procedures used with the CVI Resolution Chart:

- Mark an X through boxes that represent resolved visual behaviors
- Highlight boxes that represent current visual behaviors
- Mark an O inside boxes describing visual behaviors that may never resolve because of co-existing ocular conditions

FIGURE 6.5 *CVI O&M Resolution Chart*

CVI ORIENTATION AND MOBILITY RESOLUTION CHART

Use the following chart to help develop areas of needs for development of IEP goals and objectives.

CVI Characteristics	**Phase I:** Building Visual Behavior Level I Environmental Considerations		**Phase II:** Integrating Vision with Function Level II Environmental Considerations		**Phase III:** Resolution of CVI Characteristics Level III Environmental Considerations	
	Range 1–2 (0)	**Range 3–4 (.25)**	**Range 5–6 (.50)**	**Range 7–8 (.75)**	**Range 9–10 (1)**	
Color preference	Single-color environmental features may be attended to in near space	Strong single-color preference persists	Objects or environmental features that have two to three colors may now be attended to within 4 to 6 feet	More colors and high-contrast areas may elicit visual attention	Safe travel is not dependent on color cues	
Need for movement	Targets viewed have movement and/or reflective properties. May be attentive to ceiling fans	Movement in the environment may distract from primary target	Movement may be needed to establish attention on target/destination	Movement is not required for attention within 3 to 4 feet; may be necessary beyond	Movement is not necessary for near or distant visual attention	
Visual latency	Prolonged periods of visual latency	Latency slightly decreases after periods of consistent viewing	Latency present only when student is tired, stressed, or overstimulated	Latency is rarely present	Latency resolved	

(continued)

FIGURE 6.5 *CVI O&M Resolution Chart (continued)*

	Phase I: Building Visual Behavior Level I Environmental Considerations	Phase II: Integrating Vision with Function Level II Environmental Considerations			Phase III: Resolution of CVI Characteristics Level III Environmental Considerations
CVI Characteristics	**Range 1–2 (0)**	**Range 3–4 (.25)**	**Range 5–6 (.50)**	**Range 7–8 (.75)**	**Range 9–10 (1)**
Visual field preferences	Distinct field preferences; may use one eye for peripheral vision, the other eye for central vision	May be able to use both right and left peripheral fields but will continue to show strong preference for original peripheral field	Visual field preferences persist	Increasing use of right and left fields for near and distance activities	Visual fields unrestricted
Difficulties with visual complexity	Visually attends only in strictly controlled environments—those without sensory distractions. Engages in rote, assisted travel	Visually attends to or fixates on simple targets at near (within 3 feet), with environment controlled for sensory distractors	May be able to tolerate low levels of familiar background noise while maintaining visual attention on familiar targets. Engages in rote or route travel with adapted visual cues	Competing auditory stimuli tolerated during periods of viewing. May travel familiar routes using naturally occurring, simple landmarks or cues	Only the most complex environments affect independent travel. Environmental or traffic signs may now be useful for independent travel
Light-gazing and nonpurposeful gaze	Is overly attentive to lights. Room light may have to be reduced	Is less attracted to lights; can be redirected to other targets	Light is no longer a source of distraction		

Difficulty with distance viewing	Visually attends in near space only	Occasionally attends visually to familiar, moving, or large targets in simple or familiar settings, up to 3 to 4 feet	Visual attention extends beyond near space, up to 4 to 6 feet Complexity in the environment may reduce this distance	Visual attention extends to 10 feet with targets that produce movement Color cues, movement, and size of target may be factors in visual attention	Visual attention extends beyond 20 feet Demonstrates memory of routes, cues, or landmarks and may now be able to travel independently
Atypical visual reflexes	No blink in response to touch and/or visual threat	Blinks in response to touch, but response may be latent	Blink response to touch is consistently present Blink to visual threat is intermittently present	Blink response to visual threat is consistently present May now anticipate approaching obstacles	
Difficulty with visual novelty	Responds only to familiar objects	May visually attend to objects or environmental features if they share characteristics with the familiar objects	Visually attends to landmarks or cues that are highlighted with familiar color or pattern	Selection of objects or environmental or route cues remembered after several sessions of familiarization	Selection of objects, environments not restricted or specially adapted
Absence of visually guided reach	Reach, touch, and look occur as separate functions	Occasional visually guided reach, possibly with a single, preferred object	Visually guided reach is used with familiar materials, simple configurations, and "favorite" color	Look and reach occur in sequence, but not always together	Look and reach occur as a single action

Key:

- Draw an X through boxes that represent resolved visual behaviors
- Use highlighter to outline boxes describing current visual functioning
- Draw an O in boxes describing visual skills that may never resolve because of coexisting ocular conditions

In planning O&M instruction for students who have CVI, as with any other interventions, a number of guiding principles should be followed. (See color insert Photo 24a-c.) The environmental adaptations and specialized instruction should be designed in consideration of the identified CVI characteristics demonstrated by the student. In addition, the intervention is not a stand-alone intervention; it is an approach or overlay used in conjunction with best practices in O&M instruction. That is, the CVI interventions should be adaptations to activities designed to teach orientation in space or safe, efficient travel. For example, if a map is being used to facilitate orientation skills, the instructor should consider adapting the map to include the student's preferred color and lower levels of visual complexity.

CVI adaptations need to be paired with naturally occurring landmarks or cues. For example, if a student who is learning to visually identify his or her own classroom while traveling in the hallway displays the CVI characteristics of color preference (yellow), a need for movement to stimulate visual attention, and difficulty with complexity, the O&M instructor may place a yellow, reflective target on the water fountain next to the entrance to the classroom. The water fountain is a permanent landmark that will continue to exist in the same location even after the CVI adaptation is no longer necessary. If the same yellow indicator were to be placed on the wall, it might be far more difficult for the student to learn the distinct environmental feature that will help him or her identify the specific destination independently. (See color insert Photo 25.)

Even when many of the characteristics associated with CVI have become resolved, a student may not be able to travel safely in unfamiliar, highly novel, or complex environments. The characteristics of difficulty with distance viewing, visual field preferences, and difficulties with complexity generally continue to have an effect on the individual into Phase III. At this point, the student may be independent in a variety of activities that require vision and it is likely that the remaining effects of CVI will be subtle and not easily recognized. The O&M instructor has a responsibility to continue to provide instruction and to educate others regarding the student's abilities and needs as long as the student requires O&M instruction or until the CVI completely resolves.

Regardless of the level of additional disabilities, children with CVI have the same right to services from a certified O&M specialist as their counterparts with ocular visual impairments. Independence must be a goal for all visually impaired students. The model for service delivery must, of course, include a great degree of consultation with the child's primary caregivers and instructors, but the O&M goals and objectives need to be determined by an educational team that includes an O&M instructor.

Charles has been receiving O&M instruction for two years, since his parents disagreed with the school psychologist's impression about the presence of ADD. The O&M specialist assessed Charles and implemented a program to help him learn familiar indoor routes and to begin using simple maps to orient himself to unfamiliar areas in the school. Color adaptations helped Charles learn to look for important features of his indoor school environment, and now he moves through the hallways without the shiny yellow prompts. In his classroom, Charles is seated with his back to primary sources of light and he uses a slant board to help block out some of the visual information in the background. Charles continues to need adult assistance when the class goes on field trips, but as he becomes more skilled with his cane he seems to be willing to try to walk independently more often.

PLANNING FOR KATHY

As an example of program planning, this section presents the program that was developed for Kathy, the student whose assessment was presented in Chapter 5. Kathy still had all of the behavioral characteristics of CVI to be resolved. In completing Kathy's IFSP/IEP Intervention Planning Worksheet (see Figure 6.6), Kathy's mother, classroom teacher, teacher of students with visual impairments, occupational therapist, physical therapist, and O&M specialist identify eight times of the day in which CVI adaptations can be applied to the instruction of the day. The IFSP/IEP Intervention Planning Worksheet also helps the team identify activities

---

FIGURE 6.6 *Kathy's IFSP/IEP Intervention Planning Worksheet*

IFSP/IEP INTERVENTION PLANNING WORKSHEET

This worksheet may be useful for IEP planning and for creating a "template" of CVI considerations that can be applied to the child/student's daily routines.

Child/student's name: _____Kathy Wong_____ Date: _____12/12/05_____

IFSP/IEP planning members: _parent, occupational therapist, classroom teacher, physical therapist, teacher of visually impaired students, orientation & mobility specialist_

CVI Range score: _____5-6_____ CVI Phase: _____II_____

Resolved CVI characteristics (check):
___color preference
___need for movement
___visual latency
___visual field preferences
___difficulties with visual complexity
     ___object
     ___array
     ___sensory
___light-gazing and nonpurposeful gaze
___difficulty with distance viewing
___difficulty with visual novelty
___absence of visually guided reach

Unresolved CVI characteristics (check):
_X_color preference
_X_need for movement
_X_visual latency
_X_visual field preferences

(continued)

FIGURE 6.6   *Kathy's IFSP/IEP Intervention Planning Worksheet (continued)*

    _x_ difficulties with visual complexity
        _x_ object
        _x_ array
        _x_ sensory
   _x_ light-gazing and nonpurposeful gaze
   _x_ difficulty with distance viewing
   _x_ difficulty with visual novelty
   _x_ absence of visually guided reach

CVI Planning Table

Daily schedule/time and activity	CVI characteristics	CVI adaptations for this activity
9:00 AM: getting off van, travel to classroom	Distance viewing, movement, complexity of array, light-gazing, distance viewing	Yellow or red Mylar highlighting of landmarks Select route to class, reduced complexity Environmental light as cues
9:30: Morning Circle	Color, complexity, novelty, visual fields, latency	Present materials against black felt board Begin with familiar object Highlight with yellow or red Allow ample wait time for response Present materials in accordance with best peripheral vision and best central vision
10:15 AM: fine-motor activities with occupational therapist or classroom personnel	Color, movement, complexity of object/array/sensory environment, visual fields	Present materials against black trifold board No more than two to three colors presented on materials

(continued)

FIGURE 6.6   *Kathy's IFSP/IEP Intervention Planning Worksheet (continued)*

Daily schedule/time and activity	CVI characteristics	CVI adaptations for this activity
		Give verbal direction or prompts before and after looking, not during viewing Present materials in accordance with best peripheral and central vision
11 AM: pre-reading	Complexity, color, novelty	Begin with familiar words, symbols Highlight salient features with red or yellow Present on black slant board
1:00 PM: gross-motor activities with physical therapist, O&M specialist, or classroom staff	Need for movement, distance viewing, color, light-gazing, complexity of sensory environment, visual fields	Select yellow and/or red equipment (balls, Theraband, etc.) Incorporate use of lighted and/or moving targets for distance activities Some physical therapy activities may be too multisensory for use of vision Position for best peripheral and central visual fields
1:45 PM: hygiene and self-help routines	Complexity, color, novelty, visual fields	Present soap, toothbrush, and hairbrush against black towel on counter Select materials for hygiene and self-help that are single-color, yellow or red Use familiar items Present in accordance with best visual fields
2:00 PM: language activities	Novelty, color, complexity of object and array	Select objects or simple two-dimensional materials for low complexity; one to two colors or images Begin with familiar materials or objects Highlight novel features with yellow or red Present on black slant board

(continued)

FIGURE 6.6   *Kathy's IFSP/IEP Intervention Planning Worksheet (continued)*

Daily schedule/time and activity	CVI characteristics	CVI adaptations for this activity
2:45 PM: prepare for dismissal	Color, complexity, distance viewing, light-gazing, visual fields	Use yellow or red Mylar to label coat hook and other environmental features of dismissal routine and route Place materials to be packed in backpack in front of black 8-inch trifold board Select route to van with reduced complexity Use environmental light as cues along route

<u>Activities not considered compatible for CVI interventions:</u>

Example:

Classroom birthday parties are primarily social events planned by student's parents and therefore not easily adapted for this student's CVI needs.

1. Lunch time in cafeteria
2. Classroom celebrations or parties
3. Music class
4.
5.

that may not be compatible with CVI-related interventions. In Kathy's case the educational team determined that lunchtime in the cafeteria, classroom parties, and music class were not appropriate situations for addressing Kathy's CVI-related needs, because these activities had primary goals that were social or language based and not conducive to CVI adaptations. This does not preclude the team including CVI interventions in some or all of these activities at some time in the future.

CONCLUSION

Through the use of the CVI Range, CVI Resolution Chart, narrative reports, and the IEP/IFSP Intervention Planning Worksheet, teachers can help ensure that interventions are appropriate and effective for their students. Interventions that address a student's characteristics at an inaccurate level—that are targeted either too low or too high in terms of the student's visual skills—place the student's potential for progress at risk. In either case, the student will not make progress.

Through careful attention to the impact that CVI may be having on their students, and by basing their assessments and interventions on this understanding, teachers can help these children and their families to cope with what may at first seem like a mysterious and insurmountable challenge. Like all students who are visually impaired, students with CVI need to have their unique needs addressed and respected, with the probable result that they will be helped to reach their maximum potential.

As the effect of CVI on a child diminishes, he or she has an increased chance of experiencing successful growth, learning, and development; productive and independent school and leisure activities; and a satisfying family and social life. Through attention to the needs of the child, the observations of the family, and the sometimes pervasive impact of CVI, professionals can contribute in a far-reaching way to their students' well being. As understanding of the complexity, causes, effects, and implications of CVI increases through continued research and professional debate, it is to be hoped that the arsenal of tools at the disposal of educators continues to grow as well.

Diane Kelly and Sandra Newcomb

This set of recommendations was created as a "bank" of ideas for use in the CVI Multistate Mentorship Project, a collaborative project of Maryland, Delaware, Vermont, and West Virginia, whose purpose is to train mentors in each state to provide assessment and intervention services to children with CVI, their families, and their service providers. The mentors in this project were trained by Dr. Christine Roman-Lantzy.

The suggestions offered here are provided as examples of the types of interventions that teachers and other professionals need to consider when working with children with CVI. They were taken from actual assessment reports of children with CVI and represent ideas for working with children whose needs are varied, even within the same phase or in regard to the same CVI behavioral characteristic. This selection of recommendations is not exhaustive, but rather is a starting point, offering professionals ideas to consider after a child is assessed and his or her unique needs are identified. A variety of suggestions have been provided to avoid appearing to offer a standard solution for working with children with CVI and to emphasize that each child's individual needs must be considered. Likewise, first names have been left in these suggestions as a reminder that these are not generic recommendations but were developed for specific children in specific settings; however, the names have been changed to protect the identities of the children.

In some instances, the suggestions may not seem to vary much from Phase I to Phase II or even in Phase III, but the student's behavior may still be changing and there may be subtle differences in implementing the suggestions. For example, with regard to visual latency, the adaptation may still be to wait for the student to respond, but in Phase II, the latency period may be shorter or may occur less frequently. Difficulty with visual complexity may still require simple objects or adapted environments in Phase II, but the objects or environments will be less restrictive, slightly more complex, and less controlled for auditory or visual distractions.

Diane Kelly and Sandra Newcomb work for Connections Beyond Sight and Sound, the Maryland statewide deafblind project, and are members of the Planning Committee for the state of Maryland in the Multistate CVI Mentorship Project.

	Phase I: Building Consistent Visual Behavior	Phase II: Integrating Vision and Function	Phase III: Resolving CVI Characteristics and Developing Visual Curiosity
General recommenda-tions	Because it is difficult for Lekisha to use her vision, be sure to plan times in her school day when she can practice her vision without other demands being made of her. For each position in which Min spends time, place something (from her collection of "vision" toys) for her to look at. For example, when she is in her chair put a shiny Mylar balloon beside and close to her, for her to look at. When she is on the floor propped up on pillows, place the rope lights on her play gym frame and position it to either side to give her practice looking. By placing objects where she spends her time, you give her opportunities for repeated practice throughout the day. Provide Rashaun with multiple opportunities to practice looking. When he is sitting in his wheelchair or in other supported positions, place or suspend a favorite object nearby for him to look at.	Within each routine—eating, bath time, playing with toys, physical therapy, and so on—integrate vision into the activity by using familiar objects. Have Jennifer look at and then use the object. For example, use a brightly colored spoon for feeding. Pause and make sure she looks at the spoon before she takes a bite. Within each routine, integrate vision by using Carlos' favorite color object. Have him look and then touch the object, look and then use the object, look and then help him roll over to get the object. The overall goals for Judy are to use her vision in all routines, to use her vision to learn about her environment, and to use her eyes and hands together. Remember, if you present a toy and Boyd is not looking at it, go back to a more familiar toy to get him to look. If he is looking, you are doing	Consistently present objects in routine activities to develop visual memory. Objects can then be used meaningfully in developing communication skills. Give a visual cue paired with an auditory or tactile cue prior to any action by an adult. We want William to learn to anticipate what is happening next. On the CVI Range Pilar scored in the 7 to 8 range. Pilar is developing visual curiosity. She is interested in people, activities, and objects around her. She is able to visually attend to and learn from what is going on around her and she is beginning to look at two-dimensional objects (pictures). Lauren's visual behaviors are often confusing because she does look sometimes and sometimes not. Just because Lauren has looked at a particular object in the past does not mean she will automatically look at it when it is presented again. Routine,

(continued)

APPENDIX 6.A   Sample Recommendations and Interventions for CVI (continued)

	Phase I: Building Consistent Visual Behavior	Phase II: Integrating Vision and Function	Phase III: Resolving CVI Characteristics and Developing Visual Curiosity
	Kaylee is beginning to use her vision, but needs to be given opportunities to do so in quiet, controlled settings. She needs to consistently look at toys. She needs to expand the number of objects she looks at, and she needs to begin to use her eyes and hands together.	the right things. If he is not, simplify (easier toy to look at, easier position, favorite color, etc.) or look to see if something else is wrong (tired, hungry, unfamiliar person, etc.). Adam needs repeated practice using his vision every day. Use his favorite toys for practice. Show him the toys and have him reach and hold them. Then give him a few minutes to manipulate the toy and opportunities to look at what he is doing. Repeat this throughout his day. Be sure that wherever Artie is, there is a toy or object that he likes to look at. Place something that he likes to look at beside him in his bed. Place his favorite toys beside him on the floor when he is playing.	touch, familiarity, and interest help to initiate visual attention. Be sure to note whether Leah is attending and using strategies to initiate visual attention if she is not looking. The main visual goal for Leah is for her to spontaneously use her vision in all routine activities.
Color preference	Jamie needs red objects to look at consistently. Red and shiny objects, or red with lights are good choices for Jamie. Provide repeated practice	Use toys with only one or two bright colors. Jon looks at a variety of colors, but prefers toys with only one or two colors.	Use color as a way to direct Jake's attention. In the same way that his teacher made a comment about the color of the bunny's pants in his

with several toys so they become familiar. This will help Jamie use his vision consistently.

Use objects that are gold or yellow for Latoya to look at. Shiny gold is her favorite color and she will look at that more consistently than other colors.

Make a box of "vision" toys for Ming that include red or gold shiny paper, red or gold shiny windsock, red or gold shiny balloon, rope lights, etc. Give Ming repeated opportunities to practice looking at those objects.

Use single-colored objects for Raymond, without competing auditory input. Begin with his favorite toys. When introducing new toys, select those that share characteristics with his preferred, familiar toys: green, reflective, simple. It may be helpful to gather an initial set of "things Raymond likes to look at" to be used frequently by all service providers working with the child.

Use Ed's favorite colors—gold, yellow, or red for the objects needed in routine activities. For example, use a yellow spoon and have him look at it before he opens his mouth. Use a yellow cup for his formula.

Use Benito's favorite color. Benito looks at several colors, but prefers blue. Use blue toys and objects to encourage Benito to look.

Introduce new colors with movement qualities. For example, Billy also looked at red and gold. Try also shiny red or gold objects. (Note: This also addresses novelty and movement)

---

storybook, give Jake color information to help him focus his attention.

Add color as necessary to give Quentin information. For example, point out and teach Quentin bright-colored landmarks around the school to orient him to where he is. Add color to line pictures to help him interpret black-and-white pictures.

When using color as an "anchor" for Sean, use colors that he is most familiar with, for example, red, yellow, blue, and green.

Jacob looks at brightly colored toys. Use toys with only two to three primary colors (red, yellow, green, blue). A toy with many colors has too much detail that may be hard for Jacob to see.

Sophie does not have a favorite color, but color can be used to help her know where to focus her attention. Just as her cubby is outlined in bright red, highlight other critical areas to get her visual attention.

(continued)

APPENDIX 6.A   Sample Recommendations and Interventions for CVI (continued)

	Phase I: Building Consistent Visual Behavior	Phase II: Integrating Vision and Function	Phase III: Resolving CVI Characteristics and Developing Visual Curiosity
	When initiating visual activities, Taylor should be given items that are of the color red. Her quickest responses were to red reflective materials. Objects that she uses on a daily basis such as cups, spoons, toothbrushes, combs, etc. should be red, be outlined in red, or be wrapped in a red cloth/paper.		Arnie does not have a favorite color, but color and shiny materials can be used to help him know where to focus his attention. Shiny materials can be added to his switches. Pictures can be mounted on shiny materials.
Need for movement	Move objects slightly to get Hunter to look. Use shiny toys that simulate movement (reflective material has a movement quality as light reflects off it).

Movement, or shiny or reflective materials, help initiate looking for Jimmy. Use shiny materials and move the object slightly to get him to look. Use materials that move naturally, such as a windsock or a balloon.

Movement or shiny/reflective properties seem to help Carlos. Use shiny red objects for practice. Examples | Use shiny materials (that have movement properties) on switches to encourage Christy to look before activating.

Hold toys in front and slightly to either side of Cara. Move them slightly to get her attention. | Movement helps Peter attend at a distance. When trying to get him to attend at a distance, move the object. For example, for Peter to look at the flag in his first-grade class during the Pledge of Allegiance, wave the flag for him.

Movement helps get Joshua's attention. If you show him a toy and he is not looking at it, move it slightly to get his attention.

Shiny toys are easy for Tim to look at. Use toys with shiny metallic colors. Shiny paper or material can be added to toys to get his attention and |

	are a red metallic pompom, shiny Mylar balloon, red sequins, or a shiny red garland. You might move the object slightly to encourage him to look. Be sure to wait for him to look. Use metallic gold for Latoya because it has a movement quality. For other gold or yellow objects, present them in her left visual field, move them slightly, and wait for her to look.		encourage him to look. For example, make a picture book and use bright shiny pictures or shapes to get him to look at the book. Movement helps get Jessica's visual attention. She moves her head to get visual movement input. Use shiny materials to help her direct her visual attention. Highlight switches, pictures, etc., with shiny paper to get her attention. If you want Nick to shift his gaze between two objects in order to make a choice, be sure he shifts his gaze between them. If he does not, move each one alternately so that he looks at each one.
Visual latency	Latency is a delay in looking at something when it is presented to the child. Chris exhibited latency in all visual tasks, but less in his preferred field (left) and with his favorite objects (red and shiny). When objects were silver or presented to the right, it took Chris longer to look, but given enough time he did turn and look. Provide ample wait time for Chris.	Be sure to factor in latency in all Ellie's activities. Present an object and wait for her to look. You might move the object slightly to encourage her to look. Often it takes Carrie a long time to look at something presented to her. Allow for this latency by pacing slowly and waiting when giving her visual input.	Give Caleb time to look. When a toy is presented or when you approach him and speak to him, wait for him to look.

(continued)

	Phase I: Building Consistent Visual Behavior	Phase II: Integrating Vision and Function	Phase III: Resolving CVI Characteristics and Developing Visual Curiosity
	When presenting Teisha with a visual task, allow time for the looking process to occur. Offer the object, ask her to look, and wait quietly for the action to occur. Present toys and wait. Give Devin time to organize and look. Do not talk or provide auditory input when you are asking Devin to use his vision. Keep the object in the same visual field long enough for him to see it. Wait, wait, wait! . . . Maria has a very long latency period. When a toy is placed to either side, it takes her a very long time to become aware of it and turn to look.	If Billy doesn't look, wait and give him time. Slightly move the toy to get his attention. Looking is not automatic for Benito. Be sure in each routine activity to present the object and WAIT, WAIT, WAIT for Benito to look before he interacts with the object or before you use the object in the routine. For example, at bath time, show Benito a blue wash cloth (or sponge, or toy) and have him look before you wash him with the cloth. Integrating vision into all activities will give him repeated practice using his vision each day. Practice will help him improve his vision skills.	
Visual field preferences	Present toys to Kyle to the left and to center. Once he is consistently looking in those fields, we can try to the right. Remember to present objects in Latoya's left visual field.	Present toys to the right, left, and center. Present highly motivating toys on the right, because this is more difficult for Melanie. Present more complicated toys (multicolored) and faces on her left,	Present toys for Harry in the center and to the right. Gradually teach him to scan over to the left to compensate for vision loss on the left. Michael does not have a field preference, but sometimes does not

	Present objects to either side, but not to the middle. Cynthia looks at things in her left and right fields, but not in the center. When presenting choices to Charlie, you may need to present each one individually in his left field at first. Then present them close together in the left field. Present objects at midline. If Sammy does not respond to the object at midline, provide slight movement to the object and verbally ask her to look. Allow ample time for her to respond.	which is her preferred and "easier" place to look. Allow more time when toys are presented on the right.	notice things in his lower field if he is in a challenging position (e.g., in a stander). When he is in his stander, use toys that are his favorite, very visually motivating toys. Position materials on a slant board to accommodate for Lateef's lower field preference, while encouraging him to maintain his head in an "up" position.
Difficulties with visual complexity	Delonte is not able to do anything else when he is looking. This means he may not be able to use his vision in activities such as physical therapy or circle time when he is stimulated by many things. He needs times during the day to practice looking, when he is not being required to do other things. Keep visual input simple for Chang by using a plain, preferably black background. Use a black cloth over his tray when he is in his chair. Use a tri-fold black poster board to block	*Note: The objects or environments that children in Phase II can handle are less restrictive, slightly more complex, and less controlled for auditory or visual distractions.* Keep visual input simple by using a plain, preferably black background. Use a black cloth over her tray when Tori is in her chair or sitting on the floor Keep input simple. Erica has a hard time looking and listening to a toy. She will listen to a musical toy, but not look at the same time. It's OK	*Note: Complexity is often the most difficult characteristic of CVI to resolve and tends to linger in students even as they approach resolution of their visual difficulties.* If Danny is not looking at a toy or person, try to simplify the task. There are many ways that a task can be too complex, including: too many toys out at one time; too many toys in front of him; toys with lights, sounds, and movement; performing difficult motor tasks while looking (e.g., jumping); and new environments with lots of people, objects, and sounds.

(continued)

APPENDIX 6.A   Sample Recommendations and Interventions for CVI (continued)

	Phase I: Building Consistent Visual Behavior	Phase II: Integrating Vision and Function	Phase III: Resolving CVI Characteristics and Developing Visual Curiosity
	out visual clutter in front of Chang when he is on the floor.	to use such toys sometimes, but be aware that during that activity, she may not use her vision. Be sure to give other toys that she will look at as well as play with, such as the Slinky.	Use Kyle's verbal skills to get him to look. Looking is not always an immediate response, but if Kyle is directed to look with verbal cues, e.g., "Look" or with other information, e.g., "The ball is red," then he is better able to use his vision.
	Katie uses her vision best in positions where she is supported, such as on her back on the floor, or in adaptive seating. She may not be able to use her vision when she is being challenged to work on her motor skills, such as during PT. Work with her physical therapist to find the best positioning for her to use her vision.	Use Jornaya's favorite objects, such as the Slinky, when working on difficult motor skills.	William looks better at familiar colors and objects. When teaching difficult or new concepts such as shape, use colors that are his favorite. When William is engaged in a difficult task, such as a motor task, make the task visually easier. In general, if the task is difficult, make the visual component easier. If the task is easier, the visual demands can be more difficult.
	Stephanie cannot look and touch at the same time. Show her an object before she interacts with it. Have her look at something like the yellow Slinky or gold beads before touching them.	Reduce complexity of sensory input by presenting objects without sound, e.g., have her look at a toy or switch before she touches it and hears the sounds/voices. Use a solid-color blanket, black or white, when working on the floor and presenting toys on the floor for Tyrelle to look at.	Reduce complexity by using the light box. Objects on a light box really stand out!
	Melika has a hard time looking and listening. To work on vision, use toys that do not make noise. When a toy plays music, she will listen and not look. Choose specific times for Celeste to actively focus on visual tasks. Create	Extremely challenging positions, such as propped on his tummy, are the most difficult positions for Matt to use his eyes. Use his favorite objects, such as his gold pompom, when working on difficult motor skills.	Understand that in very complex environments such as the cafeteria or hallway, Patrick will have a harder time using his vision.

a space where she is free from outside noise and distractions. Turn off overhead lights, provide a plain background, and reduce background noise. Create a space in the classroom that is clutter-free. Remember to take into account any patterns surrounding Celeste such as adult clothing, objects and pictures hanging on nearby walls, etc. Metallic red objects are her favorite and may be needed as the initial warm-up activity.

Use single-colored objects, without competing auditory input when the goal is vision. Many of Elijah's favorite toys are sound-producing, which are fine for learning cause and effect and independent play. However, they will be less effective for Elijah visually. When introducing toys or objects to Elijah, select those that share characteristics with his preferred, familiar toys: red/yellow, shiny, high-contrast, simple. Present objects on a contrasting background.

Matthew is orienting toward faces. When you talk to him and he turns,

Even though Cam can use his vision to look at multicolored toys or to find a toy in a complicated array of toys, keeping the toys simple or the array simple, with a plain background, helps Cam focus his attention.

Reduce complexity of sensory input. Kelly may not be able to look at a face and listen to you talk at the same time. Speak to her and then be quiet and wait for her to look.

Reduce complexity by limiting background music, conversations, etc., during times Sonia needs to attend to an activity.

Use Jordan's favorite objects, such as the Slinky or shiny paper, when working on difficult motor skills. If the motor demands are high, make vision task easier. If the vision task is difficult, provide her with the most supported position, e.g., in her adapted seat.

Reduce complexity of toys by limiting use of toys that are "multisensory" and have lights, music, and lots of different colors

Reduce the impact of complexity in visual tasks by presenting only one toy at a time on a plain background. Be aware of what is in the background, including what you are wearing, what is behind the object or teacher on the wall or on the toy shelf, what objects are in front of him, etc. A very "busy" background makes it hard for Tommy to pick out what we want him to look at.

Reduce complexity by having Kenny in a very supported position when you want him to look, or especially look and reach. If he has to work on motor skills and try to look at the same time, it may be too hard for Kenny.

Joseph is ready to look at a mirror. Watch for complexity in what is being reflected in the mirror.

Explain what is going to happen next, to prepare Felipe to look.

Nathan can look at two-dimensional objects, i.e., pictures. Use pictures that are simple with a plain background. When showing books to Nathan, simplify the presentation

(continued)

APPENDIX 6.A   Sample Recommendations and Interventions for CVI (continued)

	Phase I: Building Consistent Visual Behavior	Phase II: Integrating Vision and Function	Phase III: Resolving CVI Characteristics and Developing Visual Curiosity
	pause and be quiet to give him time to look at your face without listening to your voice. With a face and voice, he will probably prefer to listen and not look, so we want to build in time for him to look at a face without competing auditory input. If you present an object that you know Elizabeth can look at and she does not look, try reducing the complexity. Notice whether she is well positioned. Is the background plain? Is there too much sound in the environment?	and patterns. Brendan may enjoy activating musical toys and that is a great cause-effect activity, but he probably cannot look and listen. Use these toys to teach cause and effect and know that you may need to use other toys for looking. As Brendan's vision improves, he may be able to look and listen together. When a task has a high motor demand, i.e., supported sitting, propping on forearm, use Byron's favorite objects to look at. When he is in a more supported position, i.e., in his chair or on his back, the vision task can be more difficult. For example, when you want him to look at a new toy, keep him fully supported. When you want him to work on his motor skills, use his shiny blue pinwheel or another favorite toy. Encourage Demonte to look at your face. You may have to speak to get his attention, then be quiet and	by using a piece of black cardboard with a cutout window to highlight specific portions of text or problems and block out extraneous information. Place a plain background behind the sink to help Kim attend to the shiny faucet and limit her looking at the lines of the wall behind the sink. Avoid visual clutter. Use a plain background at snack, at table work, at circle, etc., to help Darci sort out what she is supposed to look at. Think of visual clutter as trying to play "Where's Waldo?" When he is on a page by himself, he's easy to find and look at. When he is in the typical "Where's Waldo" book, you have to look for a long time to isolate him from his background. If Ann-Marie is not looking, have her touch the materials to help her look. Limit hand-over-hand prompting. When an adult moves Alana's hands,

she does not look at what she is doing.

Sam is making the transition to looking at pictures. To transition from three-dimensional to two-dimensional objects, begin by pairing photographs of the object with the actual object. This should be a photo of the exact thing he is looking at. Use photos of his favorite toys and people. Gradually fade the object and see if he understands that the picture represents the object.

During instruction with Shoshanna, you might want to try using an FM system to block out some of the background noise and reduce some of the environmental complexity.

Play a game of "I Spy" with Roberto, giving him a specific feature/color to help him "find" the target item.

At home Jessica is ready to look at pictures. Use simple picture books with only one or two pictures on a page with a plain background. If pictures are more complex, give her color cues.

wait for him to look. He has a hard time looking and listening at the same time.

Reduce complexity by only having one toy available at a time. Too many toys out at the same time are difficult for Alexi.

(continued)

APPENDIX 6.A   Sample Recommendations and Interventions for CVI *(continued)*

	Phase I: Building Consistent Visual Behavior	Phase II: Integrating Vision and Function	Phase III: Resolving CVI Characteristics and Developing Visual Curiosity
			Reduce the amount of information on a written page to reduce visual clutter. You can do this by enlarging the print, using a magnifier, or using pages with less information printed on them.
			Watch for visual clutter in the background of printed material. Mark does best with a plain, solid-color background.
			Keep Frankie's working space (school work) simple and free from lots of visual distractions, e.g., posters on the wall or extra papers on the desk. These educational materials can be on another wall where they do not compete with what Frankie is currently working on.
			Because extensive reading is difficult for Will, provide him with alternative ways to read long books or complicated passages. Some ideas are books on tape or computer screen reading programs. There are also pens that scan material and

store it into a file that can be transferred to a computer. On the computer, material can be enlarged or screen reader programs can read the passage out loud.

Continue to work directly on reading skills and having Phillip read as much as he can tolerate. Continue to teach organizational skills, such as how to scan a page to solve a problem. He does beautifully with systematically looking at a page or picture from left to right and top to bottom.

Many strategies are already being used by Tamara's team to reduce complexity in her work sheets: fewer words on a page, color coding or outlining words to help her attend, and adding color outlines to pictures to help her know what to attend to. On complex worksheets or book pages, Tamara needs assistance to know what she needs to look at. Strategies such as color outlining help her disembed the object she needs to see from its background. Continue to use these strategies in Tamara's school work.

(continued)

APPENDIX 6.A   *Sample Recommendations and Interventions for CVI (continued)*

	Phase I: Building Consistent Visual Behavior	Phase II: Integrating Vision and Function	Phase III: Resolving CVI Characteristics and Developing Visual Curiosity
			Use verbal strategies to assist Margaret in using her vision. Explain what she is looking for. With verbal explanations, Margaret can use her cognitive skills to assist her in using her vision skills. For example, Sally in *The Cat in the Hat* always has a red bow in her hair. Use that feature to help Margaret look for Sally in each picture.
			Teach Cathy to attend to faces and facial expressions. If Cathy is taught what to look for, she may learn to read facial expressions better.
			Look at pictures of familiar faces. Discuss salient features, such as expressions, emotions, etc., helping Keva to sort out the relevant information.
			Talk about the salient features of letters, such as, "The circle is on the right, with a long tail on the 'p'; it is on the left with a tall stick on the 'd.'"

Light-gazing and nonpurposeful gaze	Keep something available, such as a Mylar balloon, Elmo toy, or a wind sock that can be placed in front of or beside Stevie when he is in his chair. The chair, because of the position Stevie has to be in, encourages light-gazing. We want to give Stevie another visual target when he is in his chair. The movement of the balloon or windsock will attract his attention. The more he looks at an object and the less he light-gazes, the better. Position Melina so that she is not facing the window. We want her to look at an object, not gaze nonpurposefully at the window. Use light as a motivator for José to look, preferably colored light blue or light green. You can use the lightbox as a stage to illuminate objects, or use light from behind, shining it on the object for José to look. Use light as a way to initiate looking behavior. Present familiar objects on a lightbox or use a flash light to illuminate the object. Looking at the light itself should not be used as an activity. Light should be used to support the activity.	In an environment with reduced complexity, e.g., the room adjacent to the classroom, use a lightbox with materials for Marisa to manipulate to determine if light helps her improve the use of her eyes and hands together. Position Danny with the light source behind him so that light is shining on the toys and is not a distraction. Position Jillian so that she is not facing distracting light sources such as windows. Use a lightbox to help Kellan know where to direct his visual attention. Use the light box to help him learn to attend to detail and develop visual discrimination skills. Use light to get Brent to attend, e.g., his lighted spinning toy. Try activities on a lightbox. Be sure Patrick is positioned so that the light source is from beside or behind him. Do not face Patrick towards the light source.	*Note: Light-gazing is generally resolved by Phase III.*

(continued)

APPENDIX 6.A   Sample Recommendations and Interventions for CVI (continued)

	Phase I: Building Consistent Visual Behavior	Phase II: Integrating Vision and Function	Phase III: Resolving CVI Characteristics and Developing Visual Curiosity
	Continue to reduce light-gazing by positioning Andre away from lights and turning off overhead lights.		
Difficulty with distance vision	Present all objects close to Lilly (12 to 18 inches). Brenden is only looking at things that are very close to him (12 to 18 inches). Place objects nearby for him to view. When presenting objects to Ashley, keep them within her arms' reach. This will ensure placement for distance viewing and allow opportunity for tactile exploration at her discretion.	Continue to present objects close to Fely, e.g., 1 to 2 feet away. Gradually move highly motivating objects further away to practice distance viewing. Nora needs objects and people close to her to be able to look at them.	Tristan is curious if he hears a sound or if he notices something moving. Use his curiosity to encourage him to attend at a distance. Preview environments to point out important features. Once Denny is familiar with an environment, he remembers what is there and does very well. Provide Marty with verbal information about what he is seeing. Use his language skills to help him interpret visual information or to prepare him for what he is looking for. Use bright, colorful, naturally occurring landmarks in the hallway to help Brittany know where she is and where she is going. By explaining what to look for in a complex

			environment, you simplify the visual task for her. For example, teach Brittany to look for those items in her environment, such as a large picture painted on a particular place in the hall or a large plant that is always present. Annie's classroom team has placed materials close to Annie. When her classmates were working at the board, Annie had the same materials in front of her on her desk. For any information provided at a distance, such as on the board, continue to provide Annie with a copy she can look at up close. Douglas looks best at near distance, but is beginning to attend several feet away. With favorite toys, begin to present them further away to see if he will look. Then bring them close to have him interact with the object.
Difficulty with visual novelty	Introduce novel toys or objects that are similar in color and properties to the toys Bryce consistently looks at, i.e., red. Limit the number of new objects to one or two and have him practice with them until you get consistent viewing before introducing other objects.	Introduce novel toys or objects that are similar in color and properties to the toys she consistently looks at. If you present a new toy and Patty is not looking at it, go back to a more familiar toy to get her to look and then try the new one. Present novel	Foster looks better at familiar colors and objects. When teaching difficult or new concepts such as shape, use colors that are his favorite. Give Thad mostly familiar and favorite toys. Limit novelty. If too

(continued)

	Phase I: Building Consistent Visual Behavior	Phase II: Integrating Vision and Function	Phase III: Resolving CVI Characteristics and Developing Visual Curiosity
	If you present a new toy and Jamal is not looking at it, go back to a more familiar toy that you know he can look at. The goal is to provide practice to build consistent visual behavior. Practice at his current level is the most important intervention at this time. He will let us know when he is ready to move forward.	objects that are part of routine activities. Repeated use will make the object familiar and help her look at it.	much is novel, Thad may not be able to look or interested in looking. Present novel toys that are similar to what he already looks at.
		Introduce novel toys or objects that are similar in color and properties (shiny) to the toys Ramon consistently looks at.	With novel materials, allow Brooke to touch and hold them to help her learn about them and visually attend.
	Find a few things in the class that Noah will look at consistently and use those items repeatedly. Introduce only novel objects that are similar to those objects.	Familiar is easier to look at. Taylor will not get bored if you use the same objects. She prefers her favorite and familiar toys. Introduce novel toys or objects that are similar in color and properties to the toys she consistently looks at.	Use the same or similar materials in classroom activities. Familiarity helps Kamiah visually attend. Repeated use of materials helps her become familiar with them.
	Continue to present familiar objects to Kelsey. When initiating looking behaviors, use objects that she sees on a daily basis and that also meet her color and complexity requirements. Kelsey will indicate her readiness for new objects when she begins to independently look at items found daily in her environment.	Limit novelty. Find the things that Malik likes to look at and give him practice with those objects. His brain is learning to use vision information and things that are familiar are easier for him to look at. He will not get bored. Use the same objects in each routine activity. For example, use the same blue spoon each time you feed him.	Peter is making the transition to looking at pictures. To transition from three-dimensional to two-dimensional objects, begin by pairing photographs of the object with the actual object. This should be a photo of the exact thing he is looking at. Use photos of his favorite toys and people. Gradually fade the object and see if he understands that the picture represents the object.

Absence of visually guided reach			
	Allow Jennifer the opportunity to find the object visually, turn her head or eyes away, and then reach out and touch it. Refrain from talking to her during this action. The look, look away, look again pattern may take place several times before Jennifer physically reaches out for the object. Place objects where Rasheed can look and bat at them. Suspend toys over him when he is on the floor. Use a gold Mylar balloon attached to his wrist. As he moves his arm, he will see the balloon move and watch it. These activities will help him learn to use his vision and hands together.	Becky has a difficult time looking and using her hands at the same time. Be sure to have her look at a toy *before* she reaches. Even if she doesn't look while she is playing with the toy, she will have seen it before she interacts with it. Take note of toys that she can look at and reach, such as the Slinky. Give her practice with those toys to develop visual motor skills. Give Shawna opportunities to look at a toy before she touches it. Allow for latency and use movement to encourage her to look before touching a toy. Continue to use a small playroom (modeled after Lily Nielsen's Little Room) for him to practice looking and batting, to learn to use his eyes and hands together. Zachary attempted to move his arm when he saw his pinwheel. Help him begin to use his eyes and hands together by placing or suspending objects where his movements will cause the toy to move also. The movement will encourage him to look. At first he will accidentally make the toy move, but with practice he will realize that his	When Vince is doing something with his hands, be sure he looks at the object first. When an adult is helping Jackson use his hands, be sure he is using his eyes also. Bobby is reaching for and batting at favorite toys. Because of Bobby's motor problems, it is hard for him to use his eyes and hands together. He understands when he sees something he wants that he can try to get it with his hands. Be sure he is in a well-supported position. Place toys so that he can touch them and also see what he is touching. Attach a Mylar balloon to his wrist so that he can practice moving his arm and seeing the balloon move as a result. To assist with visual-motor tasks such as writing, highlight lines to help Spencer know where to write. Spencer is not dependent on color for looking, but color helps him sort out what is important to look at. With all of the black lines on a page, highlighting the ones he is to write on helps him narrow his focus and know where he needs to write. Because writing is difficult for him, have Roy dictate his stories or even

(continued)

Phase I: Building Consistent Visual Behavior	Phase II: Integrating Vision and Function	Phase III: Resolving CVI Characteristics and Developing Visual Curiosity
	movements are causing the toy to move and will be able to move intentionally. Try also a Mylar balloon (shiny blue, red, or gold) attached to his wrist so that it is 12 to 18 inches away. As he moves his arm, he will see the balloon move and watch it.	some of his assignments. He can dictate to tape, or he can use a speech recognition program that types what he says on the computer.

Jake is ready to look at simple actions and begin to imitate the action. This may be difficult due to his motor delays. Begin with simple actions such as shaking, patting, or clapping. Begin by copying his actions and see if he continues. Later, you can initiate the familiar action and see if he imitates you.

Have Corey practice looking and reaching with smaller objects, such as finger foods.

Use visual motor skills to reinforce cause and effect. Garrett will reach and activate a toy he is interested in, so present toys that have a movement quality, such as shiny items, to encourage Garrett.

Consistently have Ernesto look before asking him to interact with a toy or object.

Sometimes it may help Christopher to initiate reaching by touching his hand with the object. Avoid hand-over-hand. Have him reach independently. |

References

Als, H. (1999). Reading the premature infant. In E. Goldson (Ed.), *Nurturing the premature infant* (pp. 3–85). New York: Oxford University Press.

Arditi, A., & Zihl, J. (2000). Functional aspects of neural visual disorders of the eye and brain. In *The Lighthouse handbook of visual impairment and rehabilitation* (pp. 263–286). New York: Lighthouse International.

Atkinson, J. (1984). Human visual development over the first six months of life. A review and a hypothesis. *Human Neurobiology, 3,* 61–74.

Atkinson, J. (1993). The Cambridge assessment and screening of vision in high-risk infants and young children. In N. Anastasiow & S. Harel (Eds.), *At-risk infants* (pp. 33–46). Baltimore, MD: Paul H. Brookes.

Banks, M. S., & Dannemiller, J. L. (1987). Infant visual psychophysics. In G. Robins & J. Davis (Eds.), *Handbook of infant perception* (pp. 115–184). New York: Academic Press.

Batshaw, M., & Perret, Y. (1992). *Children with disabilities: A medical primer.* Baltimore: Paul H. Brookes.

Brodsky, M. C. (1996). The apparently blind infant. In M. C. Brodsky, R. S. Baker, & L. M. Hamed (Eds.), *Pediatric Neuro-opthalmology* (pp. 11–41). New York: Springer Publications.

Brodsky, M., Fray, K. J., & Glasier, C. M. (2002). Perinatal cortical and subcortical loss. American Academy of Opthalmology, 109, 85–95.

Bruer, J. (2001). A critical and sensitive period primer. In D. Bailey, J. Bruer, F. Symons, & J. Lichtman (Eds.), *Critical thinking about critical periods* (pp. 3–26). Baltimore, MD: Paul H. Brookes.

Castano, G., Lyons, C., Jan, J., & Connolly, M. (2000). Cortical visual impairment in children with infantile spasms. *Journal of AAPOS* [American Association for Pediatric Ophthalmology and Strabismus], *4,* 175–178.

Casteels, I., Demaerel, P., Spileers, W., Lagae, L., Missotten, L., & Casaer, P. (1997). Cortical visual impairment following perinatal hypoxia: Clinicoradiologic correlation using magnetic resonance imaging. *Journal of Pediatric Ophthalmology and Strabismus, 34*(5), 297–305.

Dennison, E. M. (2003). *Eye conditions in infants and young children that result in visual impairment and syndromes and other conditions that may accompany visual disorder.* Logan, Utah: SKI-HI Institute.

Dennison, E. M., & Lueck, A. H. (Eds.). (2006). *Proceedings of the Summit on Cerebral/Cortical Visual Impairment: Educational, Family, and Medical Perspectives, April 30, 2005.* New York: AFB Press.

DeReuck, J. (1984). Cerebral angioarchitecture and perinatal brain lesions in premature and full term infants. *Acta Neurol. Scand., 70,* 391–395.

DeReuck, J., Chattha, A. S., & Richardson, E. P. (1972). Pathogenesis and evolution of periventricular leukomalacia in infancy. *Archives of Neurology, 27,* 229–236.

de Vries, L., Dubowitz, L., Dubowitz, V., & Pennock, J. (1990). *Brain disorders in the newborn.* London: Wolfe Medical Publications Ltd.

Dutton, G. N. (2001). Cerebral visual impairment in children. *Semin Neonatal,* (6): 477–485.

Dutton, G. N. (2003). Cognitive vision, its disorders and differential diagnosis in adults and children: Knowing where and what things are. *Eye, 17,* 289–304.

Dutton, G. N. (2006). Cerebral visual impairment: Working within and around the limitations of vision. In E. Dennison & A. H. Lueck (Eds.), *Proceedings of the Summit on Cerebral/Cortical Visual Impairment: Educational, Family, and Medical Perspectives, April 30, 2005.* New York: AFB Press.

Farel, P. B., & Hooper, C. R. (1995). Biological limits to behavioral recovery following injury to the central nervous system: Implications for early intervention. *Infants and Young Children, 8,* 1–7.

Farley, M. M., Harvey, R. C., & Stull, T. (1993). A population-based assessment of invasive disease due to group B streptococcus in nonpregnant adults. *New England Journal of Medicine, 328;* 1807–1811.

Good, W. (2001). Development of a quantitative method to measure vision in children with chronic cortical visual impairment. *Transactions of the American Opthalmologic Society, 99,* 253–269.

Good, W. (2004). Cortical visual impairment: Overview and historical perspective. Unpublished manuscript presented at the Conference on Low Vision and Blindness in Infants and Children with Special Emphasis on Cortical Visual Impairment, June 3–June 5, 2004, Pittsburgh, PA.

Good, W., Brodsky, M., Angtuaco, T., Ferriero, D., Stephens, D., & Khakoo, Y. (1996). Cortical visual impairment caused by twin pregnancy. *American Journal of Opthalmology, 122,* 709–716.

Good, W., Jan, J., Burden, S., Skoczenski, A., & Candy, R. (2001). Recent advances in cortical visual impairment. *Developmental Medicine and Child Neurology, 43,* 56–60.

Groenendaal, F., & van Hof-van Duin, J. (1992). Visual deficits and improvements in children after perinatal hypopxia. *Journal of Visual Impairment & Blindness, 86,* 215–218.

Groenveld, M., Jan, J., & Leader, P. (1990). Observations on the habilitation of children with cortical visual impairment. *Journal of Visual Impairment & Blindness, 82,* 11–15.

Groopman, J. (2004). *The anatomy of hope.* New York: Random House.

Heath, P. T., Yusoff, N. K., & Baker, C. J. (2003). Neonatal meningitis. *Archives of Disease in Childhood* (Fetal and Neonate Edition). *88:* 173.

Hertz, L., Hansson, E., & Ronnback, L. (2001). Signaling and gene expression in the neuron-glia unit during brain function and dysfunction: Holger Hyden in memoriam. *Neurochemistry International, 39,* 227–252.

Hoyt, C. (2002, July 9), Visual function in the brain damaged child. Doyne Lecture, Oxford, England.

Hubel, D. H. (1995). *Eye, brain, and vision.* Scientific American Library Series No. 22 (New York: Scientific American Library).

Hubel, D. H., & Wiesel, T. N. (1970). The period of susceptibility to the physiological effects of unilateral eye closure in kittens. *Journal of Physiology, 206,* 419–436.

Huo, R., Burden, S., Hoyt, C., & Good, W. (1999). Chronic cortical visual impairment in children: Aetiology, prognosis, and associated neurological deficits. *British Journal of Opthalmology, 83,* 670–675.

Jan, J. E., Farrell, K., Wong, P. K., & McCormick, A. Q. (1986). Eye and head movements of visually impaired children. *Developmental Medicine and Child Neurology, 28,* 285–293.

Jan, J. E., & Groenveld, M. (1993). Visual behaviors and adaptations associated with cortical and ocular impairment in children. *Journal of Visual Impairment & Blindness, 87,* 101–105.

Jan, J. E., Groenveld, M., & Sykanda, A. M. (1990). Light gazing by visually impaired children. *Developmental Medicine and Child Neurology, 32,* 755–759.

Jan, J. E., Groenveld, M., Sykanda, A. M., & Hoyt, C. (1987). Behavioral characteristics of children with permanent cortical visual impairment. *Developmental Medicine and Child Neurology, 29,* 571–576.

Jan, J. E., Sykanda, A. M., & Groenveld, M. (1990). Habilitation and rehabilitation of visually impaired and blind children. *Pediatrician, 17,* 202–207.

Jan, J. E., & Wong, P. E. K. H. (1991). The child with cortical visual impairment. *Seminars in Opthalmology, 6,* 194–200.

Johnson-Kuhn, J. (1995). The Blind Babies Foundation: Registry of early childhood visual impairment in central and northern California. In Bernas-Pierce, J. (Ed.), *Hoyt-Akeson Selected*

Readings in Pediatric Ophthalmology. San Francisco: Blind Babies Foundation.

Lantzy, A., & Roman, C. (2002-2007). Pediatric VIEW Data Bank (unpublished data). Western Pennsylvania Hospital, Pittsburgh, PA.

Lichtman, J. (2001). Developmental neurobiology overview. In D. Bailey, J. Bruer, F. Symons, & J. Lichtman (Eds.), *Critical thinking about critical periods* (pp. 27-42) Baltimore, MD: Paul H. Brookes.

Ment, L., Duncan, C. C., & Ehrenkranz, R. A. (1987). Intraventricular hemorrhage of the pre-term neonate. *Seminars in Perinatology, 11,* 132-141.

Ment, L., Scott, D., & Ehrenkranz, R. A. (1985). Neurodevelopmental assessment of very low weight neonates: Effect of germinal, matrix, and intraventricular hemorrhage. *Pediatric Neurology, 1,* 164-168.

Morse, M. T. (1990). Cortical visual impairment in young children with multiple disabilities. *Journal of Visual Impairment & Blindness, 84,* 200-203.

Morse, M. T. (2006). Another view of cortical visual impairment: Issues related to facial recognition. In E. M. Dennison & A. H. Lueck (Eds.), *Proceedings of the Summit on Cerebral/Cortical Visual Impairment: Educational, Family, and Medical Perspectives, April 30, 2005,* pp. 131-135. New York: AFB Press.

Nickel, R. (1992). Disorders of brain development. *Infants and Young Children, 5,* 1-11.

Norcia, A. M., & Tyler, C. (1985). Spatial frequency sweep VEP: Visual acuity during the first year of life. *Vision Research, 25,* 1399-1408.

Norcia, A. M., Tyler, C. W., & Hamer, R. D. (1990). Development of contrast sensitivity in the human infant. *Vision Research, 30*(10), 1475-1486.

Orel-Bixler, D. A. (1989). Subjective and Visual Evoked Potential measures of acuity in normal and amblyopic adults and children. Unpublished doctoral dissertation. University of California at Berkeley.

Papile, L. A., Burstein, R., & Koffler, H. (1978). Incidence and evolution of subependymal and intraventricular hemorrhage: A study of infants with birth weights less than 1,500 gm. *Journal of Pediatrics, 92,* 529.

Pennefather, P., & Tin, W. (2000). Ocular abnormalities associated with cerebral palsy after pre-term birth. *Eye, 14,* 78-81.

Perlman, J. M. (2001). Intraventricular hemorrhage and periventricular leukomalacia. In R. Polin, M. Yoder, & F. Burg (Eds.), *Workbook in practical neonatology*. Philadelphia: W.B. Saunders.

Pike, M., Holmstrom, G., deVries, L. S., Pennock, J. M., Drew, K. J., Sonksen, P. M., & Dubowitz, L. M. S. (1994). Patterns of visual impairment associated with lesions of the preterm infant brain. *Developmental Medicine & Child Neurology* 36: 849-862.

Polin, R., Yoder, M., & Burg, F. (2001). *Workbook in practical neonatology*. Philadelphia: W.B. Saunders.

Restak, R. (2003). *The new brain: How the modern age is rewiring your brain*. Emmaus, PA: Rodale Publishing.

Rivkin, M. J. (1997). Hypoxic-ischemic brain injury in the term newborn. In A. J. duPlessis (Ed.), *Clinics in perinatology* (pp. 607-625). Philadelphia: W.B. Saunders.

Roland, E. H., & Hill, A. (1997). Intraventricular hemorrhage and posthemorrhagic hydrocephalus. In A. J. duPlessis (Ed.), *Clinics in perinatology* (pp. 589-605). Philadelphia: W.B. Saunders.

Roman, C. (1996). Validation of an interview instrument to identify behaviors characteristic of cortical visual impairment in infants. Unpublished doctoral dissertation, Ann Arbor: University of Michigan.

Scher, M. A. (2001). Neonatal seizures. In R. Polin, M. Yoder, & F. Burg (Eds.), *Workbook in practical neonatology* (pp. 339-369). Philadelphia: W.B. Saunders.

Schwartz, J. M., & Begley, S. (2002). *The mind and the brain*. New York: HarperCollins.

Shankaran, S., Bauer, C. R., & Bain, R. (1996). Pernatal and perinatal risk factors for neonatal intracranial hemorrhage. *Archives of Pediatric and Adolecent Medicine, 150,* 491-497.

Skoczenski, A., & Good, W. (2004). Vernier acuity is selectively affected in infants in children with cortical visual impairment. *Developmental Medicine & Child Neurology, 46,* 526-532.

Steinkuller, P. G., Du, L., Gilbert, C., Foster, A., Collins, M. L., & Coats, D. K. 1999. Childhood blindness. *Journal of AAPOS* [American Association for Pediatric Ophthalmology and Strabismus], 26–32.

Teplin, S. W. (1995). Visual impairment in infants and young children. *Infants and Young Children, 8*, 18–51.

Thompson, L. A., Fagan, J. F., & Fulker, D. W. (1991). Longitudinal prediction of specific cognitive abilities from infant novelty preference. *Child Development, 62*(3), 530–538.

Tychsen, L. (2001). Critical periods for development of visual acuity, depth perception, and eye tracking. In D. Bailey, J. Bruer, F. Symons, & J. Lichtman (Eds.), *Critical thinking about critical periods* (pp. 66–80). Baltimore, MD: Paul H. Brookes.

Vaucher, Y. E. (1988). Understanding intraventricular hemorrhage and white matter injury in premature infants. *Infants and Young Children, 1*, 31–45.

Volpe, J. J. (1987). *Neurology of the newborn.* Philadelphia: W.B. Saunders.

Volpe, J. J. (1997). Brain injury in the premature infant. In A. J. duPlessis (Ed.), *Clinics in perinatology* (pp. 567–587). Philadelphia: W.B. Saunders.

Ward, M. E. (1996). Anatomy and physiology of the eye, In A. L. Corn & A. J. Koenig (Eds.), *Foundations of low vision: Clinical and functional perspectives* (pp. 69–85). New York: AFB Press.

Weiss, A., Kelly, J., & Phillips, J. (2001). The infant who is visually unresponsive on a cortical basis. *American Academy of Opthalmology, 108*, 2076–2087.

Whiting, S., Jan, J., Wong, P., Flodmark, O., Farrell, K., & McCormick, A. (1985). Permanent cortical visual impairment in children. *Developmental Medicine and Child Neurology, 27*, 730–738.

Williamson, W. D., & Demmler, G. J., (1992). Congenital infections: Clinical outcome and educational implications. *Infants and Young Children, 4*, 1–10.

Zupan, V., Gonzalez, P., Lacaze-Masmonteil, T., Boithias, C., d'Allest, A. M., Dehan, M., & Gabilan, J. C. (1996). Periventricular leukomalacia: Risk factors revisited. *Developmental Medicine and Child Neurology, 38*, 1061–1067.

Resources

As with everything else in today's rapidly changing information landscape, sources of information about cortical visual impairment/cerebral visual impairment (CVI) continue to evolve. The following sections list organizations and web sites that provide information about CVI; sources of assessment and intervention materials; and publications available in a variety of formats.

ORGANIZATIONS AND WEB SITES

ADVISOR Coordinating Center
Children's Hospital Boston
Department of Ophthalmology
Fegan Building, 4th Floor
300 Longwood Ave
Boston MA, 02115
(617) 735-5746
Fax: (617) 730-0392
E-mail: advisor@childrens.harvard.edu
www.e-advisor.us/contact.html

Maintains an online resource for parents, educators, and physicians about the development of children with visual impairments.

American Printing House for the Blind/CVI
1839 Frankfort Avenue
P.O. Box 6085
Louisville, KY 40206-0085
(502) 895-2405; (800) 223-1839 (U.S. and Canada)

Fax: (502) 899-2274
E-mail: info@aph.org
www.aph.org/cvi/index.html

Maintains an online compilation of articles and various materials on cortical visual impairment for vision professionals and families created by CVI Synergy, a group of researchers, educators, and physicians who work with children diagnosed with CVI.

DB-LINK
Teaching Research Institute
345 North Monmouth Avenue
Monmouth, OR 97361
(800) 438-9376; TTY: (800) 854-7013
Fax: (503) 838-8150
E-mail: dblink@tr.wou.edu
dblink.org/lib/topics/cvi-bib.htm

Offers information on cortical visual impairment, full text publications, articles, Internet resources, and the DB-LINK collection on its web site.

Lea Test
Apollonkatu 6 A 4
00100 Helsinki
Finland
Fax: (358 9) 420 8968
E-mail: lea.hyvarinen@lea-test.fi
www.lea-test.fi/index.html

Offers information about low vision, early intervention, and vision assessment.

Texas School for the Blind and Visually Impaired
1100 W. 45th Street
Austin, TX 78756
(512) 454-8631; (800) 872-5273; TDD: (512) 206-9451
Fax: (512) 206-9450
www.tsbvi.edu/Education/index.htm

Features several articles on cortical visual impairment on its web site.

SOURCES OF ASSESSMENT AND INTERVENTION MATERIALS

American Printing House for the Blind/CVI
1839 Frankfort Avenue
P.O. Box 6085
Louisville, KY 40206-0085
(502) 895-2405; (800) 223-1839 (U.S. and Canada)
Fax: (502) 899-2274
E-mail: info@aph.org
www.aph.org/cvi/index.html

Offers a range of assessment and intervention products, such as ISAVE: Individualized Systematic Assessment of Visual Efficiency and the Sensory Stimulation Kit.

HOPE Inc.
1856 North 1200 East
North Logan, UT 84341
(435) 245-2888
E-mail: hope@hopepubl.com
www.hopepubl.com/index.cfm

Distributes materials from the SKI-HI Institute, as well as from other sources, for children with special needs, their families, and the service providers who work with them. Many of the materials are for use in family-centered early intervention programs including materials for children who are deaf and hard of hearing, visually impaired, deaf-blind, multiply disabled, sensory impaired, and for children with any special needs.

Lea Test
Apollonkatu 6 A 4
00100 Helsinki
Finland
Fax: (358 9) 420 8968
E-mail: lea.hyvarinen@lea-test.fi
www.lea-test.fi/index.html

Offers vision assessment tests developed by Dr. Lea Hyvärinen.

SKI-HI Institute
Communicative Disorders and Deaf Education
Utah State University
6500 Old Main Hill
Logan, UT 84322-6500
(435) 797-5600; TTY: (435) 797-5584
Fax: (435) 797-5580
E-mail: skihi@cc.usu.edu
www.skihi.org

Developed the VIISA (Vision Impaired Inservice in America) Project to provide in-service training to early intervention and early childhood personnel serving young children, ages birth to 5, with blindness and visual impairments. The VIISA Project works with other groups across the country to bring new resources and learning opportunities on cerebral/cortical visual impairment to the field. Also distributes the VIISA and INSITE Training Package on CVI.

Vision Associates
2109 US Hwy 90 West, #170–312
Lake City, FL 32055
(407) 352-1200
Fax: (386) 752-7839
E-mail: kathleen@visionkits.com
www.visionkits.com/index.html
Retailer of vision assessment kits.

ONLINE COURSES

Association for Education and Rehabilitation of the Blind and Visually Impaired (AER)
1703 N. Beauregard Street, Suite 440
Alexandria, VA 22311
(877) 492-2708
(703) 671-4500
Fax: (703) 671-6391
www.aerbvi.org

AER's Division 7, Low Vision Rehabilitation, offers "Prematurity, ROP, and Cortical Visual Impairment," and "CVI—Damage to the Brain: Common Cause of Visual Impairment in Children," online continuing education courses.

Vision Associates
2109 US Hwy 90 West #170–312
Lake City, FL 32055
(407) 352-1200
Fax: (386) 752-7839
E-mail: kathleen@visionkits.com
www.visionkits.com/index.html

Offers "CVI—Damage to the Brain—A Common Cause of Visual Impairment to Children," an online course by Dr. Gordon Dutton.

PUBLICATIONS*

Books

Bruce, V. & Humphreys, G. (Eds.). (1994). *Object and face recognition: A special issue of visual cognition.* London: Psychology Press.

Dennison, E. M., & Lueck, A. (2006). *Proceedings of the summit on cerebral/cortical visual impairment: Educational, family, and medical perspectives, April 30, 2005.* New York: AFB Press.

Farah, M. (1995). *Visual agnosia: Disorders of object recognition and what they tell us about normal vision.* Boston: MIT Press, Bradford Books.

Love, C. Y. (1994). *The effect of specific vision enhancement on the functional vision of children with cortical visual impairment.* Unpublished doctoral dissertation, University of Texas at Austin.

Lueck, A. H. (Ed.). (2004). *Functional vision: A practitioner's guide to evaluation and intervention.* New York: AFB Press.

Padula, W. (1996). *Neuro-optometric rehabilitation.* Santa Ana, CA: Optometric Extension Program Foundation, Inc.

Roman, C. (1996). *Validation of an interview to identify behaviors characteristic of cortical visual impairments in infants.* Unpublished doctoral dissertation, University of Michigan at Ann Arbor.

Articles

Overview and General

Afshari, M. A., Afshari, N. A., & Fulton, A. B. (2001). Cortical visual impairment in infants and children. *International Ophthalmology Clinics, 41*(1), 159–169.

Alexander, P. (2001). Cortical visual impairment. *Focus, 18,* 5–16.

Anthony, T. (n.d.). *Cortical visual impairment: An overview of current knowledge.* Retrieved April 16, 2007, from www.tsbvi.edu/Education/cvioverview.htm.

Jaffe, M. S. (1999). Support group for adults with cortical visual impairment: An innovative model. *Journal of Visual Impairment & Blindness, 93*(11), 728–732.

*This listing was adapted from Michelle Wilson, "Selected Bibliography," in E. Dennison and A. H. Lueck (Eds.), *Proceedings of the Summit on Cerebral/Cortical Visual Impairment: Educational, Family, and Medical Perspectives* (New York: AFB Press, 2006), pp. 332–342. The bibliography was originally compiled by the members of FOVI (Focus on Visual Impairments) for the CVI Summit held in San Francisco, CA on April 30, 2005.

Mississippi Deaf-Blind Services. (2001). Cortical visual impairment: What it is? *Focus Flyer* (2), 1–9.

Nielsen, L. (1994, April). Cortical visual impairment: Causes and manifestations. *VIP Newsletter, 10*(1), 1–4.

Assessment

Blind Babies Foundation. (1997). *Pediatric visual diagnosis fact sheet: Cortical visual impairment.* Retrieved March 31, 2007, from www.blindbabies.org/factsheet_cvi.htm.

Characteristics of cortical visual impairment checklist. (n.d.). Austin: Texas School for the Blind and Visually Impaired. Retrieved April 11, 2007, from www.tsbvi.edu/Education/corticalassess.html.

Dutton, G. N., Day, R. E., & McCulloch, D. L. (1999). Who is a visually impaired child? A model is needed to address this question for children with cerebral visual impairment. *Developmental Medicine and Child Neurology, 41*(3), 211–213.

Good, W. V. (2001). Development of a quantitative method to measure vision in children with chronic cortical visual impairment. *Transactions of the American Ophthalmology Society, 99,* 253–269.

Harrell, L. (1992). Cortical visual impairment—A challenging diagnosis. In *Children's Vision Concerns: Looks beyond the eyes* (pp. 51–54). Placerville, CA: L. Harrell Productions.

Houliston, M. J., Taguri, A. H., Dutton, G. N., Hajivassiliou, C., Young, D. G., & Dutton, G. N. (1999). Evidence of cognitive visual problems in children with hydrocephalus: A structured clinical history-taking strategy. *Developmental Medicine and Child Neurology, 41*(5), 298–306.

Hyvärinen, L. (2003). Assessment of CVI. Presentation at San Francisco State University, November 15, 2003. Retrieved from www.lea-test.fi, May 4, 2007.

Hyvärinen, L. (n.d.). *Transdisciplinary assessment of vision.* Retrieved from www.lea-test.fi/en/assessme/trans/3.html on March 13, 2007.

Hyvärinen, L. (2004). *Understanding the behaviours of children with CVI.* Retrieved April 20, 2007 from www.aph.org/cvi/articles/hyvarinen_1.html.

Jan, J., Groenveld, M., Sykanda, A. M., & Hoyt, C. (1987). Behavioral characteristics of children with permanent cortical visual impairment. *Developmental Medicine and Child Neurology, 29*(5), 571–576.

Lauger, K. (2003). Can CVI co-exist with other ocular impairments in CHARGE? A parent's perspective. *CHARGE Accounts, 13*(2), 2–4.

LaVenture, S. (1995, Spring). Cortical visual impairment. *Awareness,* 6–8.

Ross, L. M., Heron, G., Mackie, R., McWilliam, R., & Dutton, G. N. (2000). Reduced accommodative function in dyskinetic cerebral palsy: A novel management strategy. *Developmental Medicine and Child Neurology, 41*(10), 701–703.

Rudanko, S. L., Fellman, V., & Laatikainen, L. (2003). Visual impairment in children born prematurely from 1972 through 1989. *Ophthalmology, 110*(8), 1639–1645.

Brain Damage and CVI

Baker-Nobles, L. (Summer 1996). Cortical visual impairment. *Ski-Hi Institute News Exchange, 1*(3), 1–4.

California Deaf-Blind Services. (January 1998). *Neurological visual impairment* (Fact sheet). Retrieved March 31, 2007, from www.sfsu.edu/~cadbs/Eng022.html.

Cioni, G., Bertuccelli, B., Boldrinni, A., Canapicchi, R., Fazzi, B., & Guzzetta, A. (2000). Correlation between visual function, neurodevelopmental outcome, and magnetic resonance imaging findings in infants with periventricular leucomalacia. *Archives of Disease in Childhood: Fetal and Neonatal Edition, 82,* 134–140.

Dale, N., & Sonkson, P. (2002). Developmental outcome, including setback, in young children with severe visual impairment. *Developmental Medicine and Child Neurology, 44*(9), 613–622.

Downie, A. L. S., Jacobson, L. S., Frisk, V., & Ushycky, I. (2003). Periventricular brain injury, visual motion processing, and reading and spelling abilities in children who were extremely low birth weight. *Journal of the International Neuropsychological Society, 9,* 440–449.

Dutton, G. N. (2003). Cognitive vision, its disorders and differential diagnosis in adults and children: Knowing where and what things are. *Eye, 17,* 289–304.

Dutton, G. N., Ballantyne, J., Boyd, G., Bradman, M., Day, R., McCullough, D., Macki, R., Phillips, S., & Saunders, K. (1996). Cortical visual dysfunction in children: A clinical study. *Eye, 10,* 302–309.

Dutton, G. N., & Jacobson, L. K. (2001). Cerebral visual impairment in children. *Seminars in Neonatalology, 6*(6), 477–485.

Dutton, G. N., McKillop, E. C., & Saidkasimova S. (2006). Visual problems as a result of brain damage in children. *British Journal of Ophthalmology, 90*(8), 932–933.

Dutton, G. N., Saaed, A., Fahad, B., Fraser, R., McDaid, G., McDade, J., Mackintosh, A., Rane, T., & Spowart, K. (2004). Association of binocular lower visual field impairment, impaired simultaneous perception, disordered visually guided motion and inaccurate saccades in children with cerebral visual dysfunction—a retrospective observational study. *Eye, 18,* 27–34.

Gillen, J. A., & Dutton, G. N. (2003). Balint's syndrome in a 10-year-old male. *Developmental Medicine and Child Neurology, 45*(5), 349–352.

Good, W. V., Jan, J. E., Burden, S. K., Skoczenski, A., & Candy, R. (2001). Recent advances in cortical visual impairment. *Developmental Medicine and Child Neurology, 43*(1), 56–60.

Good, W. V., Jan, J. E., DeSa, L., Barkovich, A. J., Groenveld, M., & Hoyt, C. S. (1994). Cortical visual impairment in children. *Survey of Ophthalmology, 38*(4), 351–364.

Groenveld, M. (n.d.). *Children with cortical visual impairment.* Retrieved March 31, 2007, from www.aph.org/cvi/articles/groenveld_1.html.

Groenveld, M. (1993). Visual behaviors and adaptations associated with cortical visual impairment. *Journal of Visual Impairment & Blindness, 87*(3), 101–105.

Groenveld, M., Jan, J. E., & Leader, P. (1990). Observations on the habilitation of children with cortical visual impairment. *Journal of Visual Impairment & Blindness, 84*(1), 11–15.

Gronqvist, S., Flodmark, O., Tornqvist, K., Edlund, G., & Hellstrom, A. (2001). Association between visual impairment and functional and morphological cerebral abnormalities in full-term children. *Acta Ophthalmolgica Scandinavia, 79*(2), 140–146.

Hoyt, C. S. (2003). Visual function in the brain-damaged child. *Eye, 7*(3), 369–384.

Hoyt, C. S., Jastrzebski, G., & Marg, E. (1983). Delayed visual maturation in infancy. *British Journal of Ophthalmology, 67*(2), 127–130.

Huo, R., Burden, S. K., Hoyt, C. S., & Good, W. V. (1999). Chronic cortical visual impairment in children: Aetiology, prognosis, and associated neurological deficits. *British Journal of Ophthalmology, 83,* 670–755.

Jacobson, L. K., & Dutton, G. N. (2000). Periventricular leukomalacia: An important cause of visual and ocular motility dysfunction in children. *Survey of Ophthalmology, 45,* 1–13.

Jacobson, L., Ek, U., Fernell, E., Flodmark, O., & Broberger, U. (1996). Visual impairment in preterm children with periventricular leukomalacia—visual, cognitive, and neuropaediatric characteristics related to cerebral imaging. *Developmental Medicine and Child Neurology, 38*(8), 724–735.

Jacobson, L., Ygge, J., & Flodmark, O. (1998). Nystagmus in periventricular leukomalacia. *British Journal of Ophthalmology, 82,* 1026–1032.

Jan, J. E., Groenveld, M., & Anderson, D. P. (1993). Photophobia and cortical visual impairment. *Developmental Medicine and Child Neurology, 35*(6), 473–477.

Jan, J. E., & Freeman, R. D. (1998). Who is a visually impaired child? *Developmental Medicine and Child Neurology, 40*(1), 65–67.

LaVenture, S. (1995, Fall). Cortical visual impairment: Anatomy of the brain and how it relates to vision. *Awareness,* 6–8.

Matthews, C. G., & Das, A. (1996). Dense vitreous hemorrhages predict poor visual and neurological prognosis in infants with shaken baby syndrome. *Journal of Pediatric Ophthalmology and Strabismus, 33*(4), 260–265.

McCulloch, D. L., & Taylor, M. J. (1992). Cortical blindness in children: Utility of flash VEPs. *Pediatric Neurology, 8*(2), 156.

Mercuri, E., Atkinson, J., Braddock, O., Anker, S., Cowan, F., Rutherford, M., Pennoc, J., & Dubowitz, L. (1997). Visual function in full-term infants with hyposix-ischaemic encephaolopathy. *Neuropediatrics, 28*(3), 155–161.

Powell, S. (1996). Neural-based visual stimulation with infants with cortical impairment. *Journal of Visual Impairment & Blindness, 90*(5), 445–448.

Roland, E. H., Jan, J. E., Hill, A., & Wong, P. K. (1986). Cortical visual impairment following birth asphyxia. *Pediatric Neurology, 2*(3), 133–137.

Takeshita, B. (1996, March). *Neurological visual impairment.* Paper presented at the annual conference of the California Transcribers and Educators of the Visually Handicapped.

Ungerleider, L. G., & Haxby, J. V. (1994). 'What' and 'where' in the human brain. *Current Opinion in Neurobiology, 4*(2), 157–165.

Van den Hout, B. M., de Vries, L., Meiners, L. C., Stiers, P., van der Schouw, Y. T., Jennekens-Schinkel, A., Wittebol-Post, D., van der Linde, D., Vandenbussche. E., & van Nieuwenhuizen, O. (2004). Visual perceptual impairment in children at 5 years of age with perinatal haemorrhagic or ischaemic brain damage in relation to cerebral magnetic resonance imaging. *Brain and Development, 26*(4), 251–261.

Whiting, S., Jaer, J. E., Wong, P. K., Flodmark, O., Farrell, K., & McCormick, A. Q. (1985). Permanent cortical visual impairment in children. *Developmental Medicine and Child Neurology, 27*(6), 730–739.

Classification and Terminology

Frebel, H. (2006). CVI?! How to define and what terminology to use: Cerebral, cortical or cognitive visual impairment *British Journal of Visual Impairment 24*(3), 117–120. Retrieved April 30, 2007 from http://jvi.sagepub.com/cgi/reprint/24/3/117.pdf.

Jan, J. E., Good, W. V., & Hoyt, C. S. (n.d.). An international classification of neurological visual disorders in children. Retrieved April 15, 2007, from aph.org/cvi/articles/jan_1.html.

Maclean, H. (n.d.). *CVI—An ophthalmologist's perspective.* Retrieved April 16, 2007, from www.svrc.vic.edu.au/111_Maclean.doc.

Education

Broughton, A. (1998, July/August). Cortical visual impairment. *VIPS News,* 5–7.

Demchak, M., Rickard, C., & Elquist, M. (2002, December). An overview of cortical visual impairment. *Nevada Dual Sensory Impairment Project Newsletter, 13*(2), 1–4. Retrieved April 16, 2007, from www.unr.edu/educ/ndsip/newsletters/dec2002.pdf.

Demchak, M., Rickard, C., & Elquist, M. (2002). *Tips for home or school: Cortical visual impairment.* Reno, NV: Nevada Dual Sensory Impairment Project 2002. Retrieved April 11, 2007, from www.unr.edu/educ/ndsip/tipsheets/cvi.pdf.

Déruaz A., Matter, M., Whatham, A. R., Goldschmidt, M., Duret, F., Issenhuth, M., & Safran, A. B. (2004). Can fixation instability improve text perception during eccentric fixation in patients with central scotomas? *British Journal of Ophthalmology, 88,* 461–463.

Déruaz, A., Whatham, A. R., Mermoud, C., & Safran, A. B. (2002). Reading with multiple preferred retinal loci: Implications for training a more efficient reading strategy. *Vision Research, 42*(7), 2947–2957.

Edelman, S., Lashbrook, P., Carey, A., Kelly, D., King, R. A., Roman-Lantzy, C., & Cloninger, C. (2006, Spring). Cortical visual impairment: Guidelines and educational considerations. *Deaf-Blind Perspectives, 3*(3). Retrieved April 16, 2007, from www.tr.wou.edu/tr/dbp/may2006. htm#cvi.

Ek, U., Fellenius, K., & Jacobson, L. (2003). Reading acquisition, cognitive and visual development, and self-esteem in four children with cerebral visual impairment. *Journal of Visual Impairment & Blindness, 97*(12), 741–754.

Erin, J. (n.d.). *Cortical visual impairment: An educator's perspective.* Retrieved April 10, 2007, from www.svrc.vic.edu.au/112_Erin.DOC.

Fellenius, K., Ek, U., & Jacobson, L. (2001). Reading strategies in children with cerebral visual impairment caused by periventricular leuko-malacia. *International Journal of Disability, Development and Education, 48*(3), 283–302.

Goehl, K., & Hambrecht, K. (2000/2001). Research to practice: Parents use a research technique to help their children with cortical visual impairments. *Deaf-Blind Perspectives, 8*(2), 7–8.

Levack, N. (1991). Programming for students who have severe cortical visual impairments. In *Low vision: A resource guide with adaptations for students with visual impairments* (pp. 16–17, 131). Austin, TX: Texas School for the Blind and Visually Impaired Press.

Lueck, A. H., Hart, J., & Dornbusch, H. (1999). The effects of training on a young child with CVI: An exploratory study. *Journal of Visual Impairment & Blindness, 93*(12), 778–793.

Morris, R. D., Fletcher, J. M., & Francis, D. J. (2002). Conceptual and psychometric issues in the neuropsycholgic assessment of children: Measurement of ability discrepancy and change. In F. Boller and J. Grafman (Eds.), *Handbook of Neuropsychology, 2nd Edition. S. Sigalowitz and I. Rapin (Eds.) Volume 8, Part I. Child Neuropsychology, Part I* (pp. 217–227). Amsterdam: Elsevier.

Morse, M. T. (1992). Augmenting assessment procedures for children who have severe and multiple handicaps in addition to sensory impairments. *Journal of Visual Impairment & Blindness, 86,* 73–77.

Morse, M. T. (2000). *Autistic spectrum disorder and CVI: Two worlds on parallel courses.* Paper presented at the International Conference of the Association for Education and Rehabilitation of the Blind and Visually Impaired, Denver, July 2000. Retrieved March 14, 2007 from www.tsbvi.edu/Education/vmi/autism.htm.

Morse, M. T. (1990). Cortical visual impairment in young children with multiple disabilities. *Journal of Visual Impairment & Blindness, 84,* 200–203.

Morse, M. T. (Spring, 1999). Cortical visual impairment: Some words of caution. *RE:view, 31,* 21–26.

Morse, M. T. (2002). Neurological issues: And the brain leads the way. In L. Alsop (Ed.), *Understanding deafblindness: Issues, perspectives, and strategies* (pp. 323–347). Logan, UT: SKI-HI Institute, Utah State University Press.

Morse, M. T. (Summer, 2001). Teaching children with cortical visual impairment. *Eye Contact, 30,* 10–12.

Morse, M. T. (Spring, 1991). Visual gaze behaviors: Considerations in working with visually impaired multiply handicapped children. *RE:view, 23*(1), 5–15.

Palmer, C. (2000). *Children with cortical vision impairment: Implications for education.* Paper presented at the Australia National Deafblindness Conference in April 2000. Retrieved April 10, 2007, from internex.net.au/~dba/palmer.doc.

Southwell, C. (1999, Autumn). Working with children who have cortical visual impairment. *The SLD Experience, #25,* 7–10.

Wright, S. (2000). The child with cortical visual impairment: Considerations for performing activities with the light box. Retrieved March 31, 2007, from www.aph.org/cvi/articles/wright_1.html.

Facial Recognition

Buxbaum, L. J., Glosser, G., & Branch Coslett, H. (1998). Impaired face and word recognition without object agnosia. *Neuropsychologia, 40*(8), 41–50.

Damasio, A. R., Damasio, H., and Van Hoesen, G. (1982). Prosopagnosia: Anatomic basis and behavioral mechanisms. *Neurology, 32,* 331–342.

De Renzi, E. (2000). Disorders of visual recognition. *Seminars in Neurology, 20*(4), 479–485.

De Renzi, E., & di Pellegrino, G. (1998). Prosopagnosia and alexia without object agnosia. *Cortex, 34*(3), 403–415.

Dixon, M. J., Bub, D. N., and Arguin, M. (1998). Semantic and visual determinants of face recognition in a prosopagnosi patient. *Journal of Cognitive Neuroscience, 10,* 362–376.

Eimer, M. (2000). Event-related brain potentials distinguish processing stages involved in face perception and recognition. *Clinical Neurophysiology, 111*(4), 694–705.

Gauthier, I., Behrmann, M., & Tarr, M. J. (1999). Can face recognition really be dissociated from object recognition? *Journal of Cognitive Neuroscience, 11,* 349–370.

Gauthier, I., & Nelson, C. A. (2001). The development of face expertise. *Current Opinion in Neurobiology, 11*(2), 219–224.

Jambaqué, I., Motron, L., Ponsot, G., & Chiron, C. (1998). Autism and visual agnosia in a child with right occipital lobectomy. *Journal of Neurology, Neurosurgery, and Psychiatry, 65,* 555–560.

Joseph, R. M., & Tanaka, J. (2003). Holistic and part-based face recognition in children with autism. *Journal of Child Psychology and Psychiatry, 44*(4), 529–542.

Klin, A., Sparrow, S. S., Bildt, A., Cicchetti, D. V., Cohen, D. J., & Volkmar, F. (1999). A normed study of face recognition in autism and related disorders. *Journal of Autism and Developmental Disorders, 29*(6), 499–508.

Schultz, R. T., Gauthier, I., Klin, A., Fulbright, R. K., Anderson, A. W., Volkmar, F., Skudlarski, P., Lacadie, C., Cohen, D. J., & Gore, J. C. (2000). Abnormal ventral temporal cortical activity during face discrimination among individuals with autism and Asperger syndrome. *Archives of General Psychiatry, 57*(4), 331–340.

Teunisse, J. P., & De Gelder, B. (1994). Do autistics have a generalized face processing deficit? *The International Journal of Neuroscience, 77*(1-2), 1–10.

Motion Perception

Blanke, O., Landis, T., Safran, A. B., & Seeck, M. (2002). Direction-specific motion blindness induced by focal stimulation of human extrastriate cortex. *European Journal of Neuroscience, 15*(12), 2043–2048.

Cohen-Maitre, S. A., & Haerich, P. (2005). Visual attention to movement and color in children with cortical visual impairment. *Journal of Visual Impairment & Blindness, 99*(7), 389–402.

Visual Perception

Boyle, N. J., Jones, D. H., Hamilton, R., Spowart, K. M., & Dutton, G. N. (2005). Blindsight in children: Does it exist and can it be used to help the child? Observations on a case series. *Developmental Medicine and Child Neurology, 47*(10), 699–702.

Burkhart, L. J. (2003). *Developing visual skills for children who face cortical visual impairments.* Paper presented at the Center on Disabilities Technology and Persons with Disabilities Conference 2003 at the California State University in Northridge. Retrieved April 11, 2007, from www.csun.edu/cod/conf/2003/proceedings/277.htm.

Celesia, G. G., & Brigell, M. G. (1999). Cortical blindness and visual processing. *Electroencephalography and Clinical Neurophysiology, Supplement 49,* 133–141.

Celesia, G. G., Bushnell, D., Cone Toleikis, S., & Brigell, M. G. (1991). Cortical blindness and residual vision: Is the "second" visual system in humans capable of more than rudimentary visual perception? *Neurology, 6,* 862–869.

Fazzi, E., Bova, S. M., Uggetti, C., Signorini, S. G., Bianchi, P. E., Maraucci, I., Zoppello, M., & Lanzi, G. (2004). Visual-perceptual impairment in children with periventricular leukomalacia. *Brain and Development, 26*(8), 506–512.

Goodale, M. A., & Westwood, D. A. (2004). An evolving view of duplex vision: Separate but interacting cortical pathways for perception and action. *Current Opinion in Neurobiology, 14*(2), 203–211.

Hard, A. L., Aring, E., & Hellstrom, A. (2004). Subnormal visual perception in school-aged ex-preterm patients in a paediatric eye clinic. *Eye, 18,* 628–634.

Harris, C. M., Kriss, A., Shawkat, F., Taylor, D., & Russell-Eggitt, I. (1996). Delayed visual maturation in infants: A disorder of figure-ground separation? *Brain Research Bulletin, 40*(5-6), 365–369.

Jan, J., Wong, P. K., Groenveld, M., Flodmark, O., & Hoyt, C. S. (1986). Travel vision: "Collicular visual system?" *Pediatric Neurology, 2,* 359–362.

Lim, M., Soul, J. S., Hansen, R. M., Mayer, D. L., Moskowitz, A., & Fulton, A. B. (2005). Development of visual acuity in children with cerebral visual impairment. *Archives of Ophthalmology, 123*(9), 1215–1220.

Livingstone, M. S., & Hubel, D. H. (1987). Psychophysical evidence for separate channels for the perception of form, color, movement, and depth. *Journal of Neuroscience, 7*(11), 3416–3468.

Stiers, P., de Cock, P., & Vandenbussche, E. (1999). Separating visual perception and non-verbal intelligence in children with early brain injury. *Brain and Development, 21*(6), 397–406.

Stiers, P., van den Hout, B. M., Haers, M., Vanderkelen, R., de Vries, L. S., van Nieuwenhuizen, O., & Vandenbussche, E. (2001). The variety of visual perceptual impairments in preschool children with perinatal brain damage. *Brain and Development, 23*(5), 333–348.

Videos and CD-ROMS

CVI perspectives. (2006). Louisville, KY: American Printing House for the Blind.

Hyvärinen, L. (2005). *CVI lecture series.* Logan, UT: SKY-HI Institute, HOPE Inc.

Visually Impaired Program, Sunny Hill Health Center (Producer). (1996). *Cortical visual impairment in young children.* (Available from Sunny Hill Health Centre for Children, 3644 Slocan St, Vancouver, BC V5M 3E8; and HOPE Inc.)

Essential Forms

THE CVI RANGE

Student/child's name:_____ Age:_____

Evaluator(s):_____ Evaluation Date: _____

This assessment protocol is intended for multiple evaluations over a period of time. Suggested scoring (no less than three times per school year):

  a. Initial assessment (red)
  b. Second assessment (blue)
  c. Third assessment (green)
  Further assessments will require a new form.

Totals:	Evaluation #1 (red)	Evaluation #2 (blue)	Evaluation #3 (green)
1. Range for Rating I			
2. Total for Rating II			
3. Combine both ratings to get overall CVI Range			

0   1   2   3   4   5   6   7   8   9   10

No functional vision

Typical or near-typical visual functioning (continued)

The CVI Range: Across–CVI Characteristics Assessment Method

Rating I

Rate the following statements as related to the student/child's visual behaviors by marking the appropriate column to indicate the methods used to support the scores:

O = information obtained through observation of the child/student
I = information obtained through interview regarding the child/student
D = information obtained through direct contact with the child/student

In the remaining columns, indicate the assessed degree of the CVI characteristic:

- **R**   The statement represents a resolved visual behavior
- **+**   Describes current functioning of student/child
- **+/−** Partially describes student/child
- **−**   Does not apply to student/child

CVI Range 1–2: Student functions with minimal visual response

O	I	D	R	+	+/−	−	
							May localize, but no appropriate fixations on objects or faces
							Consistently attentive to lights or perhaps ceiling fans
							Prolonged periods of latency in visual tasks
							Responds only in strictly controlled environments
							Objects viewed are a single color
							Objects viewed have movement and/or shiny or reflective properties
							Visually attends in near space only
							No blink in response to touch or visual threat
							No regard of the human face

(continued)

CVI Range 3–4: Student functions with more consistent visual response

O	I	D	R	+	+/–	–	
							Visually fixates when the environment is controlled
							Less attracted to lights; can be redirected
							Latency slightly decreases after periods of consistent viewing
							May look at novel objects if they share characteristics of familiar objects
							Blinks in response to touch and/or visual threat, but the responses may be latent and/or inconsistent
							Has a "favorite" color
							Shows strong visual field preferences
							May notice moving objects at 2 to 3 feet
							Look and touch completed as separate events

CVI Range 5–6: Student uses vision for functional tasks

O	I	D	R	+	+/–	–	
							Objects viewed may have two to three colors
							Light is no longer a distractor
							Latency present only when the student is tired, stressed, or overstimulated
							Movement continues to be an important factor for visual attention
							Student tolerates low levels of background noise
							Blink response to touch is consistently present
							Blink response to visual threat is intermittently present
							Visual attention now extends beyond near space, up to 4 to 6 feet
							May regard familiar faces when voice does not compete

(continued)

CVI Range 7–8: Student demonstrates visual curiosity

O	I	D	R	+	+/–	–	
							Selection of toys or objects is less restricted; requires one to two sessions of "warm up"
							Competing auditory stimuli tolerated during periods of viewing; the student may now maintain visual attention on objects that produce music
							Blink response to visual threat consistently present
							Latency rarely present
							Visual attention extends to 10 feet with targets that produce movement
							Movement not required for attention at near distance
							Smiles at/regards familiar and new faces
							May enjoy regarding self in mirror
							Most high-contrast colors and/or familiar patterns regarded
							Simple books, picture cards, or symbols regarded

(continued)

CVI Range 9–10: Student spontaneously uses vision for most functional activities

O	I	D	R	+	+/–	–	
							Selection of toys or objects not restricted
							Only the most complex environments affect visual response
							Latency resolved
							No color or pattern preferences
							Visual attention extends beyond 20 feet
							Views books or other two-dimensional materials, simple images
							Uses vision to imitate actions
							Demonstrates memory of visual events
							Displays typical visual-social responses
							Visual fields unrestricted
							Look and reach completed as a single action
							Attends to two-dimensional images against complex backgrounds

The CVI Range: Within–CVI Characteristics Assessment Method

Rating II

Determine the level of CVI present or resolved in the 10 categories below and add to obtain total score. Rate the following CVI categories as related to the student/child's visual behaviors by circling the appropriate number (the CVI Resolution Chart may be useful as a scoring guide):

  0 Not resolved; usually or always a factor affecting visual functioning
.25 Resolving
 .5 Resolving; sometimes a factor affecting visual functioning
.75 Resolving
  1 Resolved; not a factor affecting visual functioning

		Not Resolved		Resolving		Resolved
1.	**Color preference**	0	.25	.5	.75	1
	Comments:					
2.	**Need for movement**	0	.25	.5	.75	1
	Comments:					
3.	**Visual latency**	0	.25	.5	.75	1
	Comments:					
4.	**Visual field preferences**	0	.25	.5	.75	1
	Comments:					
5.	**Difficulties with visual complexity**	0	.25	.5	.75	1
	Comments:					
6.	**Light-gazing and nonpurposeful gaze**	0	.25	.5	.75	1
	Comments:					
7.	**Difficulty with distance viewing**	0	.25	.5	.75	1
	Comments:					

(continued)

CVI Range (continued)

8.	Atypical visual reflexes	0	.25	.5	.75	1

Comments:

9.	Difficulty with visual novelty	0	.25	.5	.75	1

Comments:

10.	Absence of visually guided reach	0	.25	.5	.75	1

Comments:

CVI RANGE: PHASE III EXTENSION CHART

Approaching Literacy

This chart can be used as a guide to obtain more detailed information when a student scores 7–10 on the CVI Range, a phase in which he or she may be developing the visual skills for literacy activities. The CVI characteristics considered in this extension are difficulties with visual complexity, visualfield preferences, difficulty with distance viewing, and absence of visually guided reach. No separate score is derived from the Extension; it is used to help organize appropriate interventions. Thisextension may not be appropriate for Phase III students who have both CVI and co-existing ocularvisual impairment.

Date _____ Student's Name _____ Evaluator_____

Recognition of Salient Features with Increasing Levels of Complexity at Near							
O	I	D	R	+	+/–	–	Statement
							Visually discriminates between same and different objects ("Show me one like . . .")
							Visually recognizes same and different objects ("Show me the _____"). Recognition can be based on object name, color name, or shape
							Visually identifies object, color, or shape in three dimensions ("What is this?")
							Visually discriminates between same and different symbols in two dimensions, such as photographs
							Visually recognizes symbols in two dimensions, such as photographs
							Visually identifies symbols of two dimensions, such as photographs
							Visually discriminates "same" three-dimensional object (1 inch or smaller) from a field of 10 or fewer objects
							Visually discriminates "same" three-dimensional object (1 inch or smaller) from a field of 11 or more objects
							Visually recognizes a named object (1 inch or smaller) from a field of 10 or fewer objects
							Visually recognizes a named object (1 inch or smaller) from a field of 11 or more objects

(continued)

							Visually identifies objects (1 inch or smaller) from a field of 10 or fewer objects
							Visually identifies objects (1 inch or smaller) from a field of 11 or more objects
							Visually discriminates "same" two-dimensional picture or symbol from a field of 10 or fewer images
							Visually recognizes a named two-dimensional picture or symbol from a field of 11 or more images
							Visually identifies pictures or symbols from a field of 10 or fewer images
							Visually identifies pictures or symbols from a field of 11 or more images
							Visually discriminates hidden or embedded pictures or symbols when provided an identical prompt
							Visually recognizes hidden or embedded pictures or symbols when provided a verbal prompt ("Find the ____")
							Visually identifies hidden or embedded pictures or symbols without visual or verbal prompt ("Can you find the hidden pictures/symbols?")
							Visually discriminates, recognizes, and identifies faces in three dimensions
							Visually discriminates, recognizes, and identifies two-dimensional images of faces
							Visually discriminates, recognizes, and identifies their name, sight words, or communication symbols
							Visually recognizes, identifies, and functionally uses words or symbols presented in a group of two to five symbols
							Visually recognizes, identifies, and functionally uses words or symbols presented in a phrase or group of six or more symbols

(continued)

							Recognition of Salient Features with Increasing Levels of Complexity at a Distance (O&M)
							Visually recognizes or identifies three-dimensional landmarks in familiar indoor settings at distances up to 20 feet
							Visually recognizes or identifies three-dimensional landmarks in familiar indoor settings at distances beyond 20 feet
							Visually recognizes or identifies two-dimensional signs, symbols, or pictures in familiar indoor settings at distances up to 20 feet
							Visually recognizes or identifies two-dimensional signs, symbols, or pictures in familiar indoor settings at distances beyond 20 feet
							Visually recognizes or identifies three-dimensional landmarks in familiar outdoor settings at distances up to 20 feet
							Visually recognizes or identifies three-dimensional landmarks in familiar outdoor settings beyond 20 feet
							Visually recognizes or identifies three-dimensional landmarks in unfamiliar indoor settings up to 20 feet
							Visually recognizes or identifies three-dimensional landmarks in unfamiliar indoor settings beyond 20 feet
							Visually recognizes or identifies three-dimensional landmarks in unfamiliar indoor settings beyond 20 feet with low levels of sensory complexity
							Visually recognizes or identifies three-dimensional landmarks in unfamiliar indoor settings beyond 20 feet with high levels of sensory complexity
							Visually recognizes or identifies three-dimensional landmarks in outdoor settings beyond 20 feet with low levels of sensory complexity

(continued)

							Visually recognizes or identifies three-dimensional landmarks in outdoor settings beyond 20 feet with high levels of sensory complexity
							Visually locates three-dimensional moving or reflective objects presented in upper, lower, right, and left peripheral visual fields
							Visually locates three-dimensional stable objects presented in upper, lower, right, and left peripheral visual fields
							Visually locates two-dimensional moving or reflective materials presented in upper, lower, right, and left peripheral visual fields
							Visually locates two-dimensional stable materials presented in upper, lower, right, or left peripheral visual fields
							Moves through familiar indoor or outdoor settings without unintended contact with walls, doorways, or objects on the floor
							Moves through unfamiliar indoor or outdoor settings without unintended contact with walls, doorways, or objects on the floor
							If appropriate, ascends and descends stairways safely and without assistance

Visually Guided Reach with Increasing Levels of Complexity

							Visually guided reach occurs when a 1-inch target is presented on a visually noncomplex background
							Visually guided reach occurs when a 1-inch target is presented on a moderately patterned or cluttered background
							Visually guided reach occurs when a 1-inch target is presented on a nonadapted, highly patterned, or cluttered background

CVI RANGE ASSESSMENT REVIEW

This worksheet can be used as a quick review for evaluators who wish to double-check the completeness of the CVI Range.

Interview and Observation Check-Off

The following chart can be used to check off whether the presence of a medical cause for CVI has been determined as well as whether all the information has been obtained from the interview and observation portions of the assessment. (Not all characteristics are represented, only those determined by interview or observation.) For the CVI behavioral characteristics, the chart can be used as follows:

Yes: information from interview and observation suggests the possibility of the presence of this characteristic

No: information from interview and observation does not suggest the presence of this characteristic

Pending: information from interview and observation is incomplete

Recheck: information gathered from interview and observation is conflicting, more information needed

	Yes	No	Pending	Recheck
Medical cause				
Interview and observation				
Color preference				
Need for movement				
Visual latency				
Visual field preferences				
Difficulties with visual complexity				
Light-gazing and nonpurposeful gaze				
Difficulty with distance				
Atypical visual reflexes				
Difficulty with visual novelty				
Absence of visually guided reach				

(continued)

Direct Assessment Guide

The following Direct Assessment guideline questions can be reviewed by the evaluator as a quick self-check of key information that must be gathered prior to the completion of the CVI Range. These questions represent behaviors frequently demonstrated by students in Phases I to III. Answers to the guiding questions may also provide useful information for report preparation.

Phase I: Building Visual Behavior

Did I check . . . ?

- Are viewed objects primarily one color?
- Are the objects similar to one another in degree of complexity?
- Is the child/student able to look toward parent or my face?
- Can the child/student simultaneously look and process other sensory information?
- Is a black or nonpatterned background required?
- Is there persistent latency?
- Is movement or shiny or reflective material required?
- Is light a significant motivator, and is it also interfering with visual attention?
- Do materials always have to be presented within 18 inches?

Phase II: Integrating Vision with Function

Did I check . . . ?

- Is the preferred color still important?
- Can the student look at two- or three-color items?
- Is movement or shiny or reflective material less critical?
- Is latency decreasing?
- Is light-gazing decreasing or resolved?
- Is look and reach occasionally completed as a single action?
- Is the child/student able to look toward or into faces?
- Is the child/student able to look while voices or music occur?
- Is the child/student able to locate an object in the presence of several additional objects?
- Does the child/student have a repertoire of objects that resemble one another?
- Does distance viewing now extend as far as 10 feet?

(continued)

Phase III: Resolution of CVI Characteristics

Did I check . . . ?

- Can objects be presented against increasingly complex backgrounds?
- Are novel objects preferred over familiar objects?
- Is light-gazing almost never or never present?
- Is visually guided reach seen more frequently, or is it related to motor rather than visual issues?
- Can the child/student now use vision even in the presence of voices or music?
- Do highly complex environments (such as malls, assemblies, or parties) continue to affect visual performance?
- Is distance viewing now extended up to or beyond 20 feet?
- Are simple two-dimensional images discriminated, recognized, or identified?
- Are small objects placed on patterned backgrounds located?
- Are small, single-color images found in two-dimensional backgrounds?
- Is the child/student able to locate salient features in two-dimensional materials or in the environment?
- Is the child/student able to differentiate faces?

CVI RESOLUTION CHART

Date _____   Student's Name _____   Evaluator _____

Use the following chart to help develop areas of needs for development of IEP goals and objectives.

CVI Characteristics	Phase I: Building Visual Behavior Level I Environmental Considerations		Phase II: Integrating Vision with Function Level II Environmental Considerations		Phase III: Resolution of CVI Characteristics Level III Environmental Considerations	
	Range 1–2 (0)	Range 3–4 (.25)	Range 5–6 (.50)	Range 7–8 (.75)	Range 9–10 (1)
Color preference	Objects viewed are generally a single color	Has "favorite" color	Objects may have two to three favored colors	More colors, familiar patterns regarded	No color or pattern preferences
Need for movement	Objects viewed generally have movement or reflective properties	More consistent localization, brief fixations on movement and reflective materials	Movement continues to be an important factor to initiate visual attention	Movement not required for attention at near	Typical responses to moving targets
Visual latency	Prolonged periods of visual latency	Latency slightly decreases after periods of consistent viewing	Latency present only when student is tired, stressed, or overstimulated	Latency rarely present	Latency resolved
Visual field preferences	Distinct field dependency	Shows visual field preferences	Field preferences decreasing with familiar inputs	May alternate use of right and left fields	Visual fields unrestricted

(continued)

CVI Resolution Chart (continued)

CVI Characteristics	Phase I: Building Visual Behavior		Phase II: Integrating Vision with Function		Phase III: Resolution of CVI Characteristics		
	Level I Environmental Considerations		Level II Environmental Considerations		Level III Environmental Considerations		
	Range 1–2 (0)	Range 3–4 (.25)	Range 5–6 (.50)	Range 7–8 (.75)	Range 9–10 (1)	
Difficulties with visual complexity	Responds only in strictly controlled environments Generally no regard of the human face	Visually fixates when environment is controlled	Student tolerates low levels of familiar background noise Regards familiar faces when voice does not compete	Competing auditory stimuli tolerated during periods of viewing; student may now maintain visual attention on musical toys Views simple books or symbols Smiles at/regards familiar and new faces	Only the most complex visual environments affect visual response Views books or other two-dimensional materials Typical visual/social responses	
Light-gazing and nonpurposeful gaze	May localize briefly, but no prolonged fixations on objects or faces. Overly attentive to lights or perhaps ceiling fans	Less attracted to lights; can be redirected to other targets	Light is no longer a distractor			

Difficulty with distance viewing	Visually attends in near space only	Occasional visual attention to familiar, moving, or large targets at 2 to 3 feet	Visual attention extends beyond near space, up to 4 to 6 feet	Visual attention extends to 10 feet with targets that produce movement	Visual attention extends beyond 20 feet Demonstrates memory of visual events
Atypical visual reflexes	No blink in response to touch and/or visual threat	Blinks in response to touch, but response may be latent	Blink response to touch consistently present Visual threat response intermittently present	Visual threat response consistently present (both reflexes near 90 percent resolved)	Visual reflexes always present; resolved
Difficulty with visual novelty	Only favorite or known objects elicit visual attention	May tolerate novel objects if the novel objects share characteristics of familiar objects	Use of "known" objects to initiate looking sequence	Selection of objects less restricted, one to two sessions of "warm up" time required	Selection of objects not restricted
Absence of visually guided reach	Look and touch occur as separate functions Look and touch occur with large and/or moving objects	Look and touch occur with smaller objects that are familiar, lighted, or reflective Look and touch are still separate	Visually guided reach used with familiar objects or "favorite" color	Look and touch occur in rapid sequence, but not always together	Look and touch occur together consistently

Key:

- Draw an X through boxes that represent resolved visual behaviors
- Use highlighter to outline boxes describing current visual functioning
- Draw an O in boxes describing visual skills that may never resolve because of coexisting ocular conditions

IFSP/IEP INTERVENTION PLANNING WORKSHEET

This worksheet may be useful for IEP planning and for creating a "template" of CVI considerations that can be applied to the child/student's daily routines.

Child/student's name: _____   Date: _____

IFSP/IEP planning members: _____

_____

CVI Range score: _____   CVI Phase: _____

Resolved CVI characteristics (check):

___color preference
___need for movement
___visual latency
___visual field preferences
___difficulties with visual complexity
    ___object
    ___array
    ___sensory
___light-gazing and nonpurposeful gaze
___difficulty with distance viewing
___difficulty with visual novelty
___absence of visually guided reach

Unresolved CVI characteristics (check):

___color preference
___need for movement
___visual latency
___visual field preferences
___difficulties with visual complexity
    ___object
    ___array
    ___sensory
___light-gazing and nonpurposeful gaze
___difficulty with distance viewing
___difficulty with visual novelty
___absence of visually guided reach

(continued)

CVI Planning Table

Daily schedule/time and activity	CVI characteristics	CVI adaptations for this activity

Activities not considered compatible for CVI interventions:

Example:

Classroom birthday parties are primarily social events planned by student's parents and therefore not easily adapted for this student's CVI needs.

1.

2.

3.

4.

5.

CVI ORIENTATION AND MOBILITY RESOLUTION CHART

Date _____

Student's Name _____

Evaluator _____

Use the following chart to help develop areas of needs for development of IEP goals and objectives.

CVI Characteristics	Phase I: Building Visual Behavior Level I Environmental Considerations		Phase II: Integrating Vision with Function Level II Environmental Considerations		Phase III: Resolution of CVI Characteristics Level III Environmental Considerations	
	Range 1–2 (0)	Range 3–4 (.25)	Range 5–6 (.50)	Range 7–8 (.75)	Range 9–10 (1)
Color preference	Single-color environmental features may be attended to in near space	Strong single-color preference persists	Objects or environmental features that have two to three colors may now be attended to within 4 to 6 feet	More colors and high-contrast areas may elicit visual attention	Safe travel is not dependent on color cues
Need for movement	Targets viewed have movement and/or reflective properties. May be attentive to ceiling fans	Movement in the environment may distract from primary target	Movement may be needed to establish attention on target/destination	Movement is not required for attention within 3 to 4 feet; may be necessary beyond	Movement is not necessary for near or distant visual attention
Visual latency	Prolonged periods of visual latency	Latency slightly decreases after periods of consistent viewing	Latency present only when student is tired, stressed, or overstimulated	Latency is rarely present	Latency resolved

Visual field preferences	Distinct field preferences; may use one eye for peripheral vision, the other eye for central vision	May be able to use both right and left peripheral fields but will continue to show strong preference for original peripheral field	Visual field preferences persist	Increasing use of right and left fields for near and distance activities	Visual fields unrestricted
Difficulties with visual complexity	Visually attends only in strictly controlled environments— those without sensory distractions Engages in rote, assisted travel	Visually attends to or fixates on simple targets at near (within 3 feet), with environment controlled for sensory distractors	May be able to tolerate low levels of familiar background noise while maintaining visual attention on familiar targets Engages in rote or route travel with adapted visual cues	Competing auditory stimuli tolerated during periods of viewing May travel familiar routes using naturally occurring, simple landmarks or cues	Only the most complex environments affect independent travel Environmental or traffic signs may now be useful for independent travel
Light-gazing and nonpurposeful gaze	Is overly attentive to lights Room light may have to be reduced	Is less attracted to lights; can be redirected to other targets	Light is no longer a source of distraction		
Difficulty with distance viewing	Visually attends in near space only	Occasionally attends visually to familiar, moving, or large targets in simple or familiar settings, up to 3 to 4 feet	Visual attention extends beyond near space, up to 4 to 6 feet Complexity in the environment may reduce this distance	Visual attention extends to 10 feet with targets that produce movement Color cues, movement, and size of target may be factors in visual attention	Visual attention extends beyond 20 feet Demonstrates memory of routes, cues, or landmarks and may now be able to travel independently

(continued)

CVI O&M Resolution Chart (continued)

CVI Characteristics	Phase I: Building Visual Behavior Level I Environmental Considerations		Phase II: Integrating Vision with Function Level II Environmental Considerations		Phase III: Resolution of CVI Characteristics Level III Environmental Considerations
	Range 1-2 (0)	Range 3-4 (.25)	Range 5-6 (.50)	Range 7-8 (.75)	Range 9-10 (1)
Atypical visual reflexes	No blink in response to touch and/or visual threat	Blinks in response to touch, but response may be latent	Blink response to touch is consistently present; Blink to visual threat is intermittently present	Blink response to visual threat is consistently present; May now anticipate approaching obstacles	
Difficulty with visual novelty	Responds only to familiar objects	May visually attend to objects or environmental features if they share characteristics with the familiar objects	Visually attends to landmarks or cues that are highlighted with familiar color or pattern	Selection of objects or environmental or route cues remembered after several sessions of familiarization	Selection of objects, environments not restricted or specially adapted
Absence of visually guided reach	Reach, touch, and look occur as separate functions	Occasional visually guided reach, possibly with a single, preferred object	Visually guided reach is used with familiar materials, simple configurations, and "favorite" color	Look and reach occur in sequence, but not always together	Look and reach occur as a single action

Key:

- Draw an X through boxes that represent resolved visual behaviors
- Use highlighter to outline boxes describing current visual functioning
- Draw an O in boxes describing visual skills that may never resolve because of coexisting ocular conditions

Index

Locators in italics refer to figures and sidebars

About the Author

Christine Roman-Lantzy, Ph.D., is the director of the Pediatric VIEW (Vision Information and Evaluation at West Penn Hospital) Program at Western Pennsylvania Hospital in Pittsburgh, and a private consultant for CVI Resources. A teacher of visually impaired students, certified orientation and mobility specialist, and infant developmentalist, Dr. Roman-Lantzy is also a CVI project leader for the American Printing House for the Blind. She is consultant to the Delaware, Maryland, Vermont, and West Virginia CVI Mentor Training Project and to the New England Deaf-Blind CVI Advisor Training Project, projects that aim to create a pool of professionals trained in working with students with cortical visual impairment (CVI) as well as to the Watson Institute in Sewickley, Pennsylvania.

Dr. Roman-Lantzy was previously the director and assistant professor in the Program in Visual Impairment at Marshall University Graduate College, South Charleston, West Virginia; research assistant professor at the University of Pittsburgh Special Education–Vision Studies Program; and Infant Developmentalist in the Neonatal Intensive Care Unit of Western Pennsylvania Hospital and the Children's Home of Pittsburgh. She has contributed journal articles and book chapters on orientation and mobility, children with multiple disabilities, and visual assessment for infants and has presented lectures and workshops on cortical visual impairment all over the United States and around the world.

Since first working with children who had CVI in the mid-1970s and then completing her doctoral dissertation on the subject in 1996, Dr. Roman-Lantzy has worked with over 1,000 children with CVI in a variety of settings, from which experience her approach to assessment and intervention has evolved.